The Whole Universe Book

Published by Omra Infinite.
All Photographs By Richard S. Omura except where otherwise
noted. All deep space photos by NASA.

ISBN: 978-0-615-95195-9

Other books by Richard S. Omura:
The Illustrated Journey to the Center of the Whole
The Seven Circles
The Tao of God
Katsugen – The Gentle Art of Well-Being
Alien Angels
The Self-Creating Consciousness

www.RichardOmura.com

OMRA INFINITE, LOS ANGELES

We are evolving.

From beings of quantity…

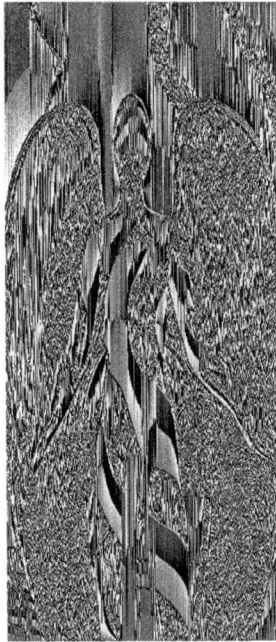

to beings of quality.

To those
who are skeptical
of their own skepticism...

Contents

6

Life As Art
II. Relationships with Others
The Golden Rule and the Golden Ratio
III. Relationship with Ourselves
The Big Picture of Our Lives
Happiness
Pain and Suffering
Fear

Free Will
Positive Thinking
Insecurity, Guilt, and Shame
Life and Death, Happiness and Despair
Mastery
  I. Mastery of Destiny
    1. Direction and Nature of Progression
    2. Movement Through Space and Time
    3. Upgrading From Lower Spiritual Influences
      To Higher Spiritual Influences
  II. Mastery of Self
    1. Organismal Drives And Attitudes
    2. Levels Of Self-Realization
      The Seven Cosmic Circles
    3. Reactions To Environment
      Returning Good For Evil
  III. Mastery of Environment
    1. Coordination
    2. Association
    3. Self-hood Organization

Spiritual Technology
Got Rituals?
Soul Work
    1. Connecting to the Source: Meditation
    2. Connecting to the Self: Prayer
    3. Connecting to Others: Service

Trading In Your Body
  Will They Take It?

Photos & Verse

Charts & Graphics

Preface

My words fly up, my thoughts remain below:
Words without thoughts never to heaven go.

\- Shakespeare

This is a book with a cosmic perspective. It is not solely rational, nor is it solely mystical. It is both and more. If you read this book with a scientific mind, you will only gain a partial understanding of it. If you read this book with a mystical mind, your understanding will also be incomplete. You must use both the analytical faculties sharpened by science AND insights gained from spiritual practices PLUS the wisdom gleaned from your day-to- day experiences coping with reality.

This book is also an exploration of perception and transformation, as individuals and as a collective. It is about becoming aware of who we are, how we are evolving, and what we are evolving into. You will find seeming contradictions and paradoxes here. You will be challenged, for I may have to break open the boundaries of your precious conceptions and extend them out into infinity, for everything I write here is true, and at the same time false. Is that possible? Some people really think they know what is impossible. When you think you know what is impossible, that is the closing of the mind – the end of true inquiry and discovery.

What I share with you is more than a patchwork of ideas and concepts. This is a presentation of new conceptual frameworks, new boxes, new envelopes that deal in larger scales and deeper understandings of the material and spiritual universe than the ones commonly accepted. Like finding undiscovered windows into unknown vistas or new angles of perception into familiar scenes, we must shift our view by shifting where we stand.

From the cosmic viewpoint, i.e., not geocentric but universe centric, true reality is elliptical—both material and spiritual. Being an elliptical document, this book must be both linear and circular, rational and mystical, scientific and spiritual, artistic and practical.

The point of the book is to see things from a bigger perspective. To see things from beyond the perception of most human beings, to see things from the outside, looking in, rather than from the inside, looking out. The universe out there is a mystery and we have our skepticism, but there is information that is purportedly from out there, information that is helpful and friendly, even spiritual. Why not, at least, listen?

Gently run this book through your mind and soul a few times. Read it casually, skipping the parts that do not speak to you. Put it down and come back to it. Play with the concepts. You will begin to absorb the patterns with your soul just by being exposed to it, with no effort apart from giving it a chance. When the patterns begin to fall into place, understanding will come, and you will start to see glimmers of a reality that had been hidden from you.

Information that comes from outside the box is often hard to understand because it comes from outside our experience. If we can understand this difficulty we can get around it by the use of metaphors. The following story of The Visitor is an illustration of this.

Prologue: The Visitor

A person from a modern industrialized country goes to a land called Urpa in a neglected part of the world that is still virtually in the stone age. The inhabitants, who are called Urps, live in a desert, with no streams, rivers or lakes, obtaining water only from the rain. They have no technology, no contact with the rest of the world and hunt and forage for a living, but they have simple tools and make bowls and cups out of clay. The Urps have only a rudimentary language which the visitor learns.

The natives are curious about the rest of the world and asks the visitor how he arrived. The newcomer tells them that part of the journey was across an ocean on a large ship, an ocean liner. This information is bewildering to the Urps. What is an ocean, they ask? What is an ocean liner? They have never seen a large body of water, not even a lake, and have never seen a boat or a ship. They have no concept of what the visitor is talking about.

The modern person is stumped. How can he tell them of these things when they have never experienced anything similar? After pondering this for a while he decides to use an analogy. He tells them, an ocean is like a very big bowl full of water. He takes a clay bowl and fills it with water. He says, just imagine this bowl if it was the size of the desert, and as this bowl is full of water, imagine the desert full of water. That would be the ocean. Then he puts a tiny leaf and floats it on the water in the bowl. This leaf is like an ocean liner, he says, except the liner is many times greater and holds thousands of people.

Up to that point, the Urps have a tiny inkling of what he is talking about, then he tells them that the ocean liner has movie theaters, pools, bowling alleys, dining rooms and a huge engine that propels the ship across the ocean. Since the natives have never been to a movie theater, swam in a pool, used a bowling alley, eaten in dining rooms or seen an engine, they are totally befuddled.

So the civilized person breaks down those concepts using further analogies; he likens a movie theater to a play that the natives perform during special occasions, the pool to a tiny drop of water that he places on the leaf floating in the bowl, a bowling alley to a place where the passengers play games such as the natives sometimes play, a dining room to a huge hut where hundreds of people gather to eat, an engine to the mill in which the natives grind their seeds.

In this way the modern visitor gives the Urps a very limited idea of the ocean and the ocean liner. What he describes is far from the reality but it is the closest the natives can come within their conceptual framework. Even among the Urps, there are differing levels of understanding. Those without much imagination only see the bowl and the leaf and cannot comprehend how thousands of people can fit on it, much less perform a play, play games, eat and grind seeds on it. Even those with greater imagination are able to imagine only a very huge earthen bowl filled with water upon which floats a very large leaf and on which is a smaller bowl of water, a shack in which to have skits, some room for playing games, a place to eat and mill for grinding seeds. It's nothing close to an ocean and a real transoceanic liner.

Without having experienced anything similar to an ocean, whether it's a lake or a large river, they are simply unable to imagine the depth and vastness of an ocean. Without knowledge of boats, they cannot comprehend a ship. It is simply beyond the range of their experiences. But what the visitor has done is to give the Urps the idea that there is much more to the world than their small corner of it. That there are people, machines, systems, ideas and natural wonders that they can experience by going beyond their horizons. The minds of the Urps have opened up to a new reality. When the time comes when the visitor departs, a few brave Urps want to go with him.

***

We are the Urps in our small corner of the universe. The Visitor comes in many forms and can be a thing or person. Unlike the story, he may not be easily identifiable as such. It is the avenue of knowledge and wisdom that streams out from the Creator and penetrates into our personal and collective souls. It can be a book, a person, a song, and/or a picture. The messages and stories are all around us, we only need to open our eyes, ears and our hearts, and use our imagination to see beyond the material. And if we can trace the path he took, we, too can go to those lands from where he came. When we do, we will find a universe filled with creatures way beyond our present comprehension.

Could this be true, or just a fantasy? Are we but isolated creatures in an otherwise thriving and populated universe, or are we alone in the vast expanse of the cosmos? Are we to work out the mysteries of life by ourselves or are there others out there, possibly a universal family of creatures – material and spiritual with whom we can associate? And…is it possible? Can we really live forever?

Introduction

When thinking "out of the box" becomes exceptional,
that means there are too many thoughts in boxes.

In order to perceive our own transformation, we must have a point of view inside and outside of ourselves, for the changes that we are undergoing is not just of the individual, but to the cells inside of us and to the planet and even to the universe. But because we are so close to the process and so intrinsically connected to its outworking, we are often only dimly aware of what is happening to us and around us. That is why we must sometimes put our viewpoint outside of ourselves, to see who and what we are from another person's point of view. And when they speak to us to tell us what they think, we can learn from it. If we can do that with the Earth and human beings as a whole, how interesting would that be? To see the cosmic point of view regarding the most important thing to know in life: the purpose of existence.

The Big Assumption

Copernicus theorized scientifically that the Earth revolves around the sun and not the other way around. Galileo gave us empirical proof. Previous to his conclusions, most people thought that the universe was geocentric, that the Earth was at the center of everything and that the universe revolved around us.

Astronomically, our views have changed, but socially, we are still geocentric. Because we have no scientific evidence of other living beings outside of our planet, we still consider ourselves at the center of the universe; socially, we are the sole inhabitants of space and time as we know it and there is nothing more. We base our activities and behavior according to this assumption.

Which is fine, if the assumption is correct.

However, let us go on the assumption that it is not correct.

The big assumption based on lack of scientific evidence otherwise is that we are alone. Living as we are in our corner of the universe, it appears that we, humans, are the only sentient beings in existence. Our scientific curiosity sends probes out to the distant planets in an effort to find life. Programs such as SETI, or the Search for Extra-Terrestrial Intelligences use the latest instruments and radio telescopes to search the sky for messages that may have arisen from other civilizations. Yet, we find nothing, no conclusive proof that there are any intelligent creatures out there with advanced technology. Our limited scientific explorations and endeavors have so far made us assume that we are alone. I was thrilled when SETI first started and am still hopeful that we will detect other civilizations in that way. But in the meantime, I decided to look into the assumption that was opposite to the one commonly held. That we are NOT alone.

The new assumption based on spiritual awareness and cosmic consciousness became: The universe is fully inhabited, organized, ordered and maintained. We are not alone. We are separated from the rest of the universe by our lack of spiritual growth. When we, as a planet, have attained self-mastery, that is, self-control as a single cohesive unit, the universe will be open to us. We are still embryonic. The world's consciousness must be born so that we can grow into an entity with a single mind and a coordinated body before we can be welcomed into the "adult" universe.

It logically follows that the outside universe is inhabited by highly intelligent, spiritual and moral beings, much more intelligent, spiritual and moral than us: spiritual adults.

We, ourselves, know from our past history that when an advanced civilization encounters a less advanced society, the lesser society suffers. No matter how beneficent the more advanced civilization is, just the influx of new ideas and new technologies, if too potent, destroys the motivation, self-respect and culture of the less developed society. And if a civilization with highly advanced technology gives some of that knowledge to a society that has not developed the necessary restraint and control, that society will destroy itself. It is like allowing a twelve year old to drive a powerful sports car.

It seems obvious that beings from a highly advanced and spiritual civilization will know that if they give us unearned technology that we will abuse it. We even know that ourselves. So why do we think that just because we open up our electronic ears to the universe, that these loving beings will whisper to us secrets that will be our undoing? Are they so irresponsible? When the assumptions change, so do everything else that follows.

It does not even require that big of an assumption. Take a step back and look at the Earth. There is no central head, which means a lack of direction. The body is disjointed, one part fighting another. It defecates and soils its immediate environment, wallows in its own filth and is a breeding ground for terrible diseases. If Earth was a person, would you want to associate with him? Which is a more reasonable assumption: That we are alone or that they don't want to associate with us just yet? Follow the right assumption and everything begins to fall into place.

It is quite evident that the rest of the universe out there do want to help us. They cannot just sit back and watch us torment and kill each other and degrade our environment. It is in their hearts and minds to do something to benefit our situation without inadvertently doing us harm. What they have been doing for a long time is to send us spiritual information which we can use to better ourselves so that we can raise our level of consciousness to match the acceptable levels of conduct in the rest of the universe. Before we are invited to the party, we must learn how to behave, you know, simple things, like keep from killing other people, clean up after yourself and be nice. Information on how we can evolve in that direction has been revelatory and were streamed to the minds of those who were capable of receiving such information, and some of it was written down and became scriptural. The true essences of the major revelations still last to this day, but a great deal of it became dogmatized doctrine.

Fortunately, our celestial brothers and sisters did not give up and are still constantly sending us new and updated information all the time – but due to the complexities of communication, these messages get garbled. In order to understand what they have been trying to teach us, we have to cut through all the human misconceptions, religious dogma and baggage, scientific biases, false assumptions and fear, the things that have kept us from understanding their messages, the things that have made it so difficult for people to evolve. I have been able to overcome much of the static and have compiled and interpreted this information by following the instructions embedded in the highest levels of science, philosophy and religion.

With this book, I make the case that we are not alone, that the universe is friendly, and that the answers to life's concerns are being given to us daily. And included are detailed instructions on how to find these answers. By looking at this view from this angle, everything will fall into place. The pieces of the puzzle will fit neatly together. There will be no loose ends. Everything functions smoothly like a healthy and thriving organism. A feeling of rightness ensues.

This state of harmony is based on logic, reason *and* faith, it is not just scientific nor is it solely spiritual, but both, and I express it here not as a linear, scientific document with dry data nor as a mystical, religious tract but as an artistic work that embodies the universe of living beings. That is why you will find not only scientific facts and religious truths in this book but also verse, photos, graphs and illustrations, because I feel that the best way to understand the soul of living systems is through artistic expression.

All in all, true universe reality is not merely a thing, it is a symphony, an opera, a sculpture, a song, a dance, a painting, a play, a cosmic drama…what part do you play?

Megamorph

One of the most important things that are being communicated to us is that we are evolving beings. We are not static. We change for the better. We are megamorphs.

The word comes from *mega*, meaning large, and *morph*, to be transformed, a shortening of metamorphose; I use it here to designate a being on the verge of a major metamorphic transformation.

Are you a megamorph?

Do you believe in life after death? Do you believe you have a soul? Do you believe that there is more to life than the material? Are you angered, saddened, and or concerned about the problems that abound in this world? Do you sometimes wonder if there is a better place in the universe? Are you becoming more aware of a higher self that often criticizes the animalistic aspects of yourself and want to manifest the best of you and not the least? Are you becoming more aware that you are aware?

Just thinking such thoughts as the above may mean that yes, you are a megamorph, for those thoughts are like the newly forming legs on a metamorphosing tadpole.

I look around and I see many who are in various stages of transformation. Many are bewildered, confused. They see themselves changing, metamorphosing, but are not really sure, not really aware of what's going on, and what they are changing into. They are like tadpoles transforming into another state of being. The ones who are losing their "tails" are curious and excited. The ones who already have rudimentary "legs" are anxious at the prospect of leaving the "pond" to emerge into a new reality. The methods and processes of transformation from human to spirit have been communicated to us in various forms, in ways that are not obvious, but they are there, in our religions, in our art, our philosophies, in our cultural traditions, and they are being partially confirmed by our sciences. It was my intent to put all this together comprehensibly in this book.

I had no consciousness before a certain time. I am not sure exactly when I began to have consciousness. My first memory is that of sitting in a baby swing. Since that is my earliest memory, maybe that is when I first became conscious, when I became aware of the reality of my surroundings.

As I grew physically and mentally, I learned more of the reality in which I lived: the people around me, that is, my family and friends, the manners and protocols of social behavior, basic skills of self-maintenance, etc. My education continued on to more academic subjects as I became old enough to go to school. I learned, not just from the classes at school but also from just living, things about our community, our government, our environment, ethics. It was indeed wonderful to see so much knowledge available to those who would want it.

However, there was an upper limit to where that knowledge extended. Regarding the space beyond our own planet, we had more and more scientific data coming in as our technology in astronomy advanced and larger and larger telescopes were made, but nothing as to if there were other intelligent beings out there. Was there a bigger community out there? Other societies? Governments? Are we alone? As far as we know, going by what science can tell us at this present time, it appears we are alone. Seemingly. That is the external world.

Within our minds, in our consciousness, there is another realm, the inner world. We are free to explore our inner world. In fact, we have total freedom here. We can think what we want, imagine what we want, do anything we like within the confines of our imaginative mind. However, one of the greatest mysteries is the nature of consciousness. What is consciousness? Who are you? What happens to consciousness after death? What happens to *you* after death of your mortal body? Is there life after death?

These big unanswered questions can be summed into one big all-encompassing question: Is there a plan and purpose to our lives and the universe? Is everything in existence just a chance event that happened randomly in the cosmic stew, or is there some kind of rhyme and reason to this unfolding drama that we call life? And what is the connection between the internal and external realities?

The age old questions. So what else is new? Am I going to rehash the same old concepts and philosophies that have been covered over the past millennia or three?

Definitely not!

The basis for the information in this book is based on a fractal perspective coordinated with the latest scientific discoveries, incredible information that is purportedly from off-world, and spiritual teachings from the oldest faith traditions to the newest. The rigidity of science and the intangibles of religion will be dissolved within the framework of this fractal perspective. This is not science, nor is it religion. It is an elliptical philosophy that uses fractal theory, spiritual insight, scientific discoveries and revelatory information from outside to see reality within the context of the micro and macro, matter and spirit, the part and the whole.

Fractal Properties In Nature

Fractals can be most simply defined as images that can be divided into parts, each of which is similar to the original object. Fractals are said to possess infinite detail, and some of them have a self-similar structure that occurs at different scales, or levels of magnification. In many cases, a fractal can be generated by a repeating pattern, in a typically recursive or iterative process. The term *fractal* was coined in 1975 by Benoît Mandelbrot, from the Latin *fractus* or "broken". Before Mandelbrot coined his term, the common name for such structures (the Koch snowflake, for example) was *monster curve*.

Fractals of many kinds were originally studied as mathematical objects. Fractal geometry is the branch of mathematics which studies the properties and behavior of fractals.

Because a true fractal possesses infinite granularity, no natural object can be a fractal. However, natural objects can display fractal-like properties across a limited range of scales.

"Approximate fractals are easily found in nature. These objects display complex structure over an extended, but finite, scale range. These naturally occurring fractals (like clouds, snowflakes, mountains, river networks, and systems of blood vessels) have both lower and upper cut-offs, but they are separated by several orders of magnitude. Trees and ferns are fractal in nature and can be modeled on a computer using a recursive algorithm. This recursive nature is clear in these examples — a branch from a tree or a frond from a fern is a miniature replica of the whole: not identical, but similar in nature." *Hunting the Hidden Dimension* Nova PBS WPMB-Maryland. 10/28/2008

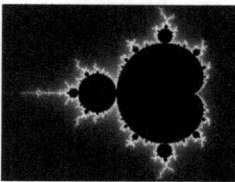

Computer Generated Fractal
Created By Wolfgang Beyer

Lightning
Photo by Nelumadau

Galaxy
By ESA/NASA

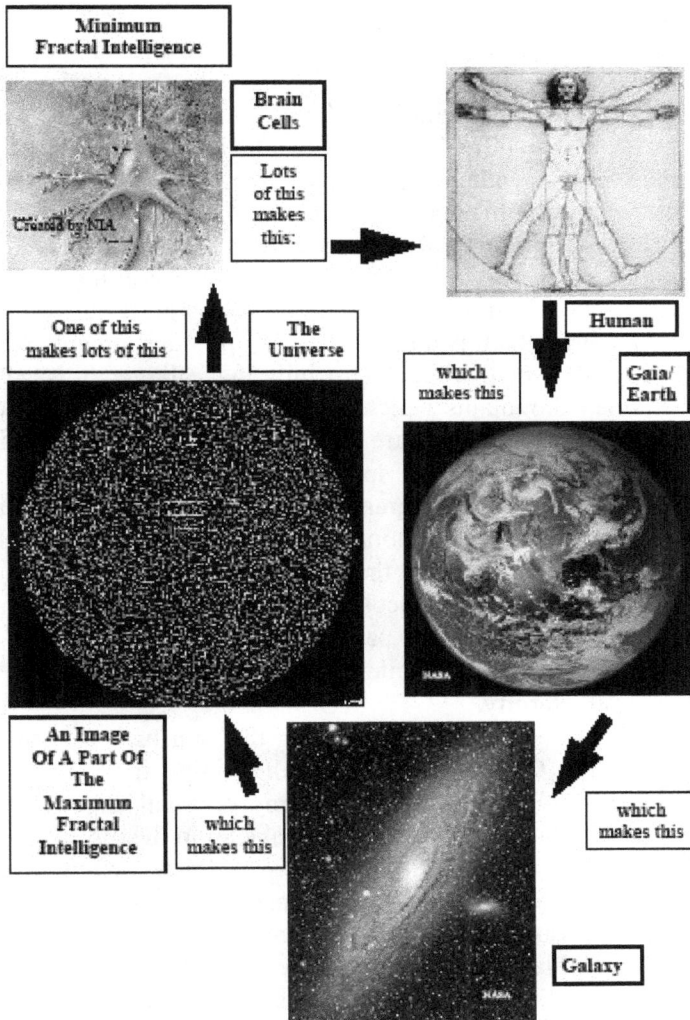

The Fractal Pattern: Minimum to Maximum

Minimum Fractal Intelligence

Brain Cells

Lots of this makes this:

Created by NIA

Human

One of this makes lots of this

The Universe

which makes this

Gaia/ Earth

An Image Of A Part Of The Maximum Fractal Intelligence

which makes this

which makes this

Galaxy

Fractals and Holons

Looking at universe reality through patterns is an elliptic way of perception. It is logical and reasonable, yet, it requires a certain amount of faith, insight and imagination.

Fractals are patterns in the universe that are reflected from the smallest to the largest, the largest to the smallest. (See accompanying text and graphics.)

A **holon** (Greek: *holos*, "whole") is something that is simultaneously a whole and a part. the word was coined by Arthur Koestler in his book *The Ghost in the Machine.*

Holons are fractal units. Fractals can be evident without forming a unit. I see the fractal nature of reality in my life, and the older I get, the more I see it around me on all levels. A small mound of dirt, which is a holon, makes up larger mounds which together make small hills. These hills make larger hills which makes small mountains which then make up a large mountain. Those individual mounds are holonic units. The pattern of an atom with its tiny revolving spheres is reflected in the pattern of the solar system and on a grander scale in globular clusters and galaxies, which are all holonic units. The design of a leaf is reflected on a larger scale in the branch, and then in the tree.

The purpose of the cosmic adventure we call life can be examined by seeing the patterns of fractal reality in the immediate now. The holonic pattern in the now is also the pattern of all eternity.

I also see these fractals in the spiritual patterns of existence. The Christian concept of the trinity: the Father, Son and the Holy Ghost can be seen in my personal experience of gaining consciousness. When I first wake up in the morning I am pure existential awareness, without expression or action. This is the pattern of the Father. As I recognize my consciousness and express the awareness of my state to myself, saying to myself "I am awake", this is the pattern of the Son. When I act on this thought in my head and open my eyes, this is action, the pattern of the Holy Ghost. Existence, expression and action. As I see this pattern in the awakening of my consciousness, I see that that is the pattern of the beginning of all existence. It is only three by explanation, in actuality the three happen simultaneously and are as one. I am one, as God is one.

I can see fractals all around me even as I write this on my computer. This rectangle □ is a holon reflected on a bigger scale as a white rectangle representing the page, then as the edge of my software graphic interface, then as the inside edge of the monitor screen, the outside edge, then as the square wall behind the screen, then as a three dimensional extension to the whole room, then to the apartment unit, then to the building, to the lot, to the block, etc.

Fractal patterns also happen in behavior. In the book "Sperm Wars" by Robin Baker, he cites research data that only one percent of sperm is designed to penetrate the egg. The rest are killers and blockers that ward off sperm from competing male ejaculates so that its egg getters can achieve its goal. I see this competitive behavior reflected fractally in our society, as aggression to each other, in sports, on the roads and freeways and in our militaristic adventures.

The living cell extends its fractal patterns to the human organism, of which it is a part. Human beings are a part of this planet, Earth, which is an extension of the fractal pattern of the cell on a large scale. As the cell and the human being is a living organism, it is fractally logical that Earth, too, is a living organism, which hypothesis has been proposed by research scientist Dr. James Lovelock in 1960. The name Gaia was also attached to the planet by Dr. Lovelock.

By looking further into larger and large holonic scales, we can even hypothesize on a Supreme Being, the maximum pattern of consciousness in the universe, without impinging on the mystical aspects of religion or the constrains of science.

If one were to have a broken box, with only fragments left, such as a corner piece, one could extrapolate what it might have been by taking the available evidence and fitting it in with the fractal patterns you can see in smaller and larger scales, giving you an idea that it was probably a box.

As we look around us with more and more awareness and mindfulness, we will see this fractal reality everywhere. It explains our motivations, our behavior, and who we are and can become, in the total framework of discernible reality. And when we can see this reality for what it truly is, we can have power over it, and we can keep from being manipulated by the dictates of material circumstances.

If this Introduction is the only part that you read in the entire book, then I would like to, at least, leave you with a fractal concept which you may find interesting, which may also encourage you to read the rest of this book.

For this, take a look at the memory cell in our brains and its fractal pattern.

There are long-term memory cells and short-term memory cells. Without getting too technical, we can understand from our own personal experiences that short term memory is what we use for information that is temporary, say the phone number of a restaurant. We may see it or hear it and remember it long enough to dial it, but then is forgotten rather quickly in most cases. Then there are memories that we keep longer, say, the name of a person we just met. But we will not retain the memory unless we see the person frequently. Then there are long-term memories; the memories that we keep all our lives. The details regarding our family, their likes, dislikes, our values, meaningful experiences, important data, etc. Long-term memories are kept because they have long term value to the organism, the individual. The more value the memory has, the better chance that it will be kept for a longer time. We can see this plainly through our experiences; importance and repetition. Just repetition will not do. We may see something everyday, say, the order of the books on our bookshelf, but if we don't put much importance to it, we will probably not recall the exact order if asked to do so. But if something is important enough, for instance a beautiful face, just a single glance will imprint its image in our memory. For most things, the two combined; repetition and importance (or value) seems to make the longest lasting memory.

Looking from a much larger fractal perspective, we, human beings, are very much like memory cells. One short definition of a memory cell by a neuroscientist is "a stored pattern of connections". Of course! The memory cell is defined by the connections and relationships it has with other cells! Without these connections, the memory cell has no memory. And when you come down to it, that is what we, humans, are also. We are "a stored pattern of connections" to other people, things and events. That is what defines us. Without other people and things, we are nothing.

In the book *The Brain That Changes Itself* by Norman Doidge, M.D., there is interesting information about psychiatrist and researcher Eric Kandel and molecular biologist James Schwartz's work in understanding how long-term memories are formed in snails. They found out that for short-term memory to become long-term memory in snails, a protein kinase A moved from the body of the neuron to its nucleus which turns on a gene that alters the structure of the nerve endings so that more connections are made between neurons. He writes: "The same process occurs in humans. When we learn, we alter which genes in our neurons are "expressed" or turned on."

The genes have two functions, one that replicates and produces copies and one that transcribes, which is influenced by our thoughts and behavior. This means that with the genetic change, it can be replicated and the information transferred even when the original cell dies. The material shell goes away but the information it contained is kept and becomes part of the whole human organism for the long term.

Now, take a look at our holonic relationship to the maximum fractal intelligence of the universe, known by some as God. Fractally, it works the same way in the total scheme of things. By becoming of value to the totality of the universal consciousness (God), those who are "short-term memory cells" can become "long-term memory cells" and continue to exist in the reality of the universal organism. Because these "memory cells" are of value to God, they will be kept eternally, (or at least for a very long time.)

That is the fractal explanation of how we can attain eternal life. Once you see it in this light, it becomes rather obvious, with no need for scientific evidence or scriptural authority. This is what the many religions have been trying to tell us for so long. But by looking at reality from a fractal viewpoint, we can see the true picture by transcending the fuzziness of religion and the strict requirements of science.

Most of us are well aware of the holonic units which are our cells, our selves, and the planet. Some of us have an awareness and a direct personal relationship with God, the maximum holonic unit. Very few are aware of the holonic intelligences that exist in the levels between Gaia, the planetary holonic being and God, the universal holonic being. There is information available that fills this gap and we will get to that in just a bit.

We know that there is communication between the person and the cells in our body. When the cells feel heat, or pain, or any sensation, that information is communicated to the brain cells and to the unified whole: body, mind and soul. Conversely, when the person desires to think or act in some way; to exercise, play music, read, eat, etc., the command is communicated to the cells and enables the body to behave accordingly. It has been shown that even just our thoughts affect our cells in some way.

However, this exchange of information is not limited to the individual and the cells in the body. This communication process extends all the way to the maximum holonic entity – the Creator/Supreme Being…and back, in a universal cycle.

With our present day knowledge, it is easy to see the physical connections between the person and his cells, and even the connections between the person and the planet. But there is no material evidence of any links between us and the Creator. Even the spiritual evidence of such a connection is unprovable and is dependent solely on faith. The incredible news is that this large unfilled gap in our awareness of what lies between us and the maximum holonic intelligence is now being filled, not by science or religion, but by revelatory information from larger holonic entities that inhabit this huge space.

One of the sources of this information is *The Urantia Book*. It designates these larger holonic units of the universe in increments from local systems on up to local universes, superuniverses and to the grand universe – this last grouping comprising all of Creation. This information comes from entities that purport to be part of the superuniverse holonic intelligence.

The teachings of many of our religions are handed down from the large and various holonic intelligences that exist in the intervening levels between the planet and the grand universe, but they all originate from the First Source and Center – the maximum holonic entity – the Universal Parent – God, the spirit personality of the material universe; the Infinite Mind, the Primal Consciousness, the Love Intelligence of the Cosmos. The consciousness and spirit of this being are non-material. The material universe is but the physical body of this being. And according to celestial sources, "this material and living organism is penetrated by intelligence circuits, even as the human body is traversed by a network of neural sensation paths."

This work, *The Whole Universe Book*, is about the information that has come through this network of intelligence circuits, and how it has been stepped down by necessity. This graduated stepping down of information from the maximum holonic entity to us is necessary because we, humans, do not have the prerequisite frames of reference that can enable us to fully understand the ideas and concepts that come from such a high source. The story of the Visitor in the Preface of this book is an illustration of this limitation.

The problem with information from such a lofty origin is that it is often overly simplified and made too illogical and mystical, or inversely, completely disregarded because it doesn't fulfill the requirement of material evidence demanded by science. This problem is resolved in this book by the use of elliptical philosophy, wherein we consider that true reality is neither solely spiritual nor material, but both, and in light of this awareness, I present this book, not as a religious tract nor a scientific document, but as an artistic expression using the insights of both disciplines to portray a universal reality that can be understood by the whole personhood unifying body, mind and soul.

Oh, and one more thing. I think it is important that we do not take ourselves too seriously, that we embody a feeling of lightness, humor and a sense of adventure and, most of all, fun!

And so, in exploring this fractal reality, I use the metaphor of the human being as an automobile, beginning with a description of our components, then some ideas about our destination, our range of movement and how we get there.

So are you ready to go? Well, get in and close the door. Put the key in.

Ignition!

Chapter One
Exploring Reality
With The Awesome Human Vehicle

Body and spirit are twins
God only knows which is which.

-Algernon Charles Swinburne

Reality starts from your own consciousness. If you are not conscious of reality, to you there is no reality. So let's start from you.

Who the heck *are* you?
Who the heck are *you*?
Who the heck are you?

Do you even know?

You know your name. You know your vital stats. You know your life. You know what you look like. You know what you like. What you love. What you hate.
But...
Who the heck are you?

Are you more than a bunch of memory cells tied together by strands of protein?
Are you more than a programmed bio-machine? Do you have volition?
Are you all material? If not, what are your other parts made of?

Are you what others tell you that you are?
Or what others tell you that you should be?
How much are you the product of circumstances?
How much control do you have to determine what kind of life you have?

Most likely, you have some control over your life, but not as much as you'd like. The human life vehicle is quite a complicated piece of equipment and it requires many years of practice and experience before we can begin to master it.

The human vehicle, with all its endowments unified and coordinated by the personhood matrix, is indeed awesome. Human cultures have thrived on this planet in the coldest places to the hottest, we have penetrated into the deepest parts of the ocean, have climbed the highest mountains, learned to fly and have even transcended our planet to step foot on the moon.

The most amazing thing about the human vehicle is that we can actually change a negative into a positive. We can return good for evil. We have the ability to countermand our physically hardwired responses to environmental forces. We have the ability to limit our personal gain for the benefit of others, such as in freely giving goods and services without thought of personal gain. We have free will to take the spiritual route over a purely mechanical one. We do not have to return tit for tat. We can "turn the other cheek". It is this ability that truly separates us from animals with their slavish obedience to their physical demands.

The vehicle used to accomplish all this, that we ride through in the ever changing vicissitudes of luck, energy manipulation, strength and brainpower does not consist of just the physical body; the human body is but the chassis which holds the patterns and systems of forces that transcend the material.

Personhood

From the omniscient view of the Creator spirit, we are soul, from the viewpoint of the material, we are body, from the logic of the intellect, we are mind. From the total perspective, we are all of the above, a package consisting of body, mind and soul held together by the Personhood matrix. This thread of personhood holds us together, so that we can be identified as a unified human vehicle.

I now use the word personhood instead of the word personality as personality is too often used to mean character traits or surface behavior patterns and most people can't seem to get beyond that definition. Personhood goes much beyond that. Personhood makes a being different from an animal, a machine, or a plant. But personhood is not just an attribute of humans, as God is often referred to as a person and has personhood. A purported extra-terrestrial being can be a person. A being with a free will has personhood, anything less is a machine. An automaton. Personhood is an unchanging essence that is the basis of the person's makeup. Personhood is changeless. The body changes as we evolve spiritually. The mind and soul and even our spirit changes. Personhood is the one unchanging factor in our life vehicle. Through spiritual evolution, a person may change drastically in a million years, but that person would be recognizable by the flavor of the unchanging personhood.

This concept of a never changing aspect of ourselves is important because our relationships with others is built upon knowing who they are. If there is nothing constant about a person, we cannot have a deep, lasting relationship with that person. It is difficult, if not impossible, to have the same relationship with a person that we had affection for and loved years ago, if that person is no longer the person that we knew. The human is a complex creature and we are constantly changing.

The body changes. A ten year old looks little like a thirty year old. Even at twenty-five and forty-five, the person could have changed drastically in weight, health, and other things that affect the body. For instance, if one were to fall in love just with someone's physical characteristics in their twenties, the love may no longer be there after the person's material beauty had faded in the fifties.

The mind changes also. Idealism may be replaced with pragmatism or vice versa. A warrior mentality could be replaced with a sage mentality. An agnostic or atheist could become religious. The mind's position on reality could flip-flop more than once depending on life's circumstances.

Even the soul changes and evolves. A young person often grows up to become wiser. The soul learns and evolves over time and from experiences. A soul that you knew in his teens might be totally different from the same soul in his forties and fifties.

It is thought by some that the spirit within does not change nor evolve, but in certain ways it does. The divine spark within us adapts to the changes in our body, mind and soul in order to guide us better. It evolves by becoming more accommodating to us, as we become more accommodating to it. This divine spark, this still, small voice within us is a conduit, a connection to the eternal Creator. The Creator does not change, but as we evolve, our connection to it/he/she does. We develop a clearer and faster connection, a wider conduit, a better tuned amplifier so to speak, linking us with the Creator and Source of All. So in this sense the spirit does change.

With all these changes going on, what remains constant? How can we maintain our own identity if practically everything that is in our makeup changes?

Personhood is the seat of our identity. Personhood is the one thing that does not change. There are some analogies that can be used to better describe this concept. One is that of a thread or a string within a jeweled necklace. The jewels may change and more could be added but the thread remains the same. The jewels are like the body, mind, soul and spirit. They change and evolve but the thread, the Personhood remains constant.

Another analogy is that of soup. Chicken soup can be made in a variety of ways and the ingredients may be different in each rendition, but it remains a soup with chicken broth as the base. Whatever additional material is put into it, the essence of the soup remains unchanged; it is still chicken soup and recognizable as such.

The Personhood of mortal man is neither body, mind, nor spirit; neither is it the soul, but a matrix that unifies them all. Personhood is the one changeless reality in an otherwise ever-changing creature experience; and it unifies all other associated factors of individuality. The Personhood is the unique package which the Universal Creator makes of the living energies of matter, mind, and spirit, and which survives with the survival of the soul. Personhood is the matrix, which holds together the unified self.

Mind, Soul and Spirit

There is some confusion in the world about the distinctions between mind, soul and spirit. As we need to be clear on these terms, mind will mean the electro-chemically based consciousness of the intellect. Soul will refer to the consciousness based on our self-awareness of the spirit, and the spirit to the spark of divinity within us, which guides us to perfection. The difference between the electro-chemical intellectual consciousness and spiritual soul consciousness is that while the intellect may be aware of itself and it's surroundings, the soul is aware that it is aware (that it is aware). The soul is a product of intellectual consciousness guided by the leadings of the spirit. Another way of looking at it is to say that spirit is the essence of the Creator, while soul is the essence of our human self.

This is a very important distinction. Until you can truly differentiate within yourself the concepts of your soul and your spirit, not just on paper and in your intellectual comprehension of the words, but truly have a grasp of the reality of your soul and the reality of your spirit within yourself, these concepts will merely be formless mental constructs that will have little meaning and value. However, reading this book will greatly help you in getting a better idea of your soul and spirit, and upon doing this, your mind will flex and expand and a deeper understanding of the nature of spiritual reality within yourself will ensue. Having these concepts down on paper help the mind to have something to refer to in order to think and re-think the ideas involved. These thoughts are on one level simple and elegant, but on other levels are very intricate, inter-related and multi-dimensional, so that having a written source as such, with diagrams and graphs, help as visual aids to the mind in grasping intangible realities.

Mind - The mind is the mechanism of the human organism that thinks, perceives, and feels. It is the total superconscious, conscious, subconscious and unconscious experience, including the information that is transmitted and received by the mind circuits to and from the universal mind but it is not your identity.

Your mind is the arena of decision-making. Your mind is yours and you have free will to do as you see fit. You can choose to follow the divine leadings or you can choose to reject or ignore it. Every time you make a decision to follow the guidance of the divine spark, it is done in the arena of your mind. In your mind, you create a small portion of your new self, your soul of eternal survival. It is extremely important to your spiritual progression that you make the right moral decisions in the arena of your mind. However, it does not necessarily require the highest intelligence to make the right moral choices. There are many with limited intellect that can and have made the good choice over the bad. Spiritual discernment is sometimes more a matter of love and humility rather than intelligence, although intelligence is highly desirable.

Soul - The soul is the essence of your humanity. Your soul is created and grows in quantity and quality as you make the right moral choices. Once your soul is of sufficient quality and quantity, your mind may delegate authority to it, based on its experience, to call the shots. That is why a moral decision that has been previously made by your mind and has been stored in your soul will be accessed to make any such future decisions. The more you evolve as a human being, the more your soul will be allowed by your mind to make the decisions in your life. How you decide in your mind to following the leadings of the spirit determine the quality or "flavor" of your soul. For instance, a leading from the spirit to be charitable may entice you to give money, or on the other hand, to do service. It is a good thing either way, but the "flavor" of your soul is different depending on what you do. People's souls vary in quality depending on how they follow the quiet voice within. The soul is not perfect and can make mistakes. Making the wrong choices by mistake is often painful but it helps you to make the right choices next time and is part of the process of learning by trial and error. A soul is never afraid to make mistakes. It can also be said that there are no such thing as mistakes, only stepping-stones to perfection, if you learn from them.

As a mortal creature chooses to do the will of the Creator, so the indwelling spirit becomes the father of a new reality in human experience, the human soul. The mortal mind is the mother of this same emerging reality. The ancient Chinese saw it as the yang of spiritual consciousness, the old school Egyptians the ka and it is known as the atman to the Hindus. The substance of this new reality is neither material nor spiritual--it is a seamless merging of both. This emerging immortal soul is destined to evolve, transform and survive mortal death.

Spirit - The spirit is the essence of the universe parent, the First Source, the love intelligence of the universe. It seems, aside from materially minded individuals, that the word spirit is intuitively understandable to most people. We may not be able to offer a clear and concise definition, but we know what it is. It is perceived as some kind of driving energy within us and all living creatures. We have phrases such as team spirit, the spirit of teamwork, the warrior spirit, etc., to describe a force that is unseen and dynamic.

Most people in general; especially materialistic scientists often have a hard time understanding and defining spirit. Even those who are religious are often hard put to formulate a comprehensive and well-phrased definition of spirit. To many scientists and analytical minds the word "consciousness" is often used interchangeably with the words "spirit" and "soul". That may be because there really is no clinical evidence that these things even exist. To truly understand these concepts, it may be necessary to venture outside the realm of material science into the noetic – that is, inner knowing.

There are many things in our lives that we believe in noetically without clear scientific evidence. The fact that our own existence is real, for instance, that it is not a dream, is not provable because if our life is a dream whatever proof we come up with would be part of that dream. The fact that there is love between persons is also not provable. There is more, but the point is that on the most fundamental and primal level, there is a knowingness that goes beyond material evidence and material phenomena and is quite difficult to express in words. However I will try.

Wikipedia defines consciousness as:

Consciousness is the quality or state of being aware of an external object or something within oneself. It has been defined as: sentience, awareness, subjectivity, the ability to experience or to feel, wakefulness, having a sense of selfhood, and the executive control system of the mind.

Spirit, in my own experience of my inner reality, is not merely awareness. Spirit is quality, value. Spirit is the qualitative aspect of consciousness. Matter is the quantitative aspect of consciousness. Mind is the coordinating aspect of consciousness.

Spiritual reality deals with value. Spirit is akin to value, religion and quality.

Matter – mind – spirit
Things - meanings – values
Objective fact - interpretation – Subjective truth
Science – philosophy – religion
Quantity - application – quality

Spirit and spiritual reality is not made up of atoms and molecules. It is not matter or physical energy. It is measured as quality rather than as quantity.

The divine spirit within us is the quality that points us in the direction of our eternal destiny, like a spiritual compass. It has been known by many names: the still, small voice; the Christ Consciousness; the Thought Adjuster; the yin of spiritual consciousness; the Brahman; the divine spark; the indwelling monitor; the ba. This is the main driving spirit but not the only spirit influence as there are others.

This leading spirit points the way toward higher values and deeper realizations of meaning and living. It is the guiding light toward perfection! It is not your conscience, as conscience is often dictated by society and culture. It is not so concerned with what you are now, as it is with what you will be in the future. Sometimes it is referred to as the true self. Although most people are not conscious of their divine spirit, they may be led by it on a subconscious level. Whenever you make a new moral decision, one that you haven't come across before, the choice you make will be the result of either following the leadings of the divine spirit or not.

Love

I use the word love to mean the highest, deepest and widest absolute value. The source and center of motivation. It is what makes you act, drives you, centers you, unifies you, supports you and defines your best qualities. This is not love used casually such as in "I love watching movies," or "I love to eat steak." The word love used in this book may go beyond the comprehension of some people. It even goes beyond the romantic meaning of the word, although that is a start. This is love that you would die for, would sacrifice yourself and all your comforts for. It would be the origin, purpose and destiny of your life. Love gives meaning to life. That is why it is often said that God is Love, Love is God. Like God, Love must be experienced for it to be truly understood. If you trace the origin of love in your heart, you will find the Source of all.

A Bigger Picture of You

Is your finger, you? Is your toe, you? Is your leg, heart, or your brain, you? Some people will say "that's not really me, that's my body." But if I step on their toe, they will say, "Ouch, you're stepping on *me*!" If I tickle their body, they will say, "Quit tickling *me*!" So for all practical purposes, regardless of their mystical conceptions, they are their bodies. However, that is not all they are; they are body, mind and soul unified by their personhood. In reality, in those things that matter in daily life, such as in feeding, clothing and sheltering oneself, interacting with others, being creative and loving, your personhood consists of all three as a whole.

So when you say, "my body", you are saying your body belongs to the rest of you; your mind and soul. When you say, "my mind", you are saying your mind belongs to the rest of you; your body and soul. When you say "my soul", you are saying your soul belongs to the rest of you; your mind and body. When you say "my self", you are saying your self belongs to itself, body, mind and soul.

Physically you are an aggregate of your parts. Your material body is a living being composed of many smaller living beings, your cells. Looking at fractal patterns in the universe, it seems that small living things make up large living things. So just as your cells combine to make up you, a larger living being, you in turn make up the larger living being that we call the Earth, or Gaia, a name based on Greek mythology. Whatever name we use, if you can consider that your cells are you, and your finger is you, then we can go up the fractal scale and say that you are also the Earth.

The Birth of Planetary Consciousness

It's been happening over the course of millennia, from drumbeats to smoke signals to carrier pigeons and on. But it's been most dramatic in the past hundred years: From the telegraph to telephone to radio to television to the internet to wireless communications, the physical dendritic structures that are the foundation of Gaia's consciousness have been evolving.

Gaia/Earth is more than just a ball of mud with germ-like creatures living on the surface. We are one, the planet and its inhabitants, and as one, the Earth is a living, loving, breathing organism with mindal and spiritual qualities. Human beings are not apart from Gaia, *we are* Gaia as much as the fishes, trees,

The Gaia Hypothesis

The **Gaia hypothesis** is an ecological hypothesis that proposes that living and nonliving parts of the earth are viewed as a complex interacting system that can be thought of as a single organism. Named after the Greek earth goddess, this hypothesis postulates that all living things have a regulatory effect on the Earth's environment that promotes life overall.

The Gaia hypothesis was first scientifically formulated in the 1960s by the independent research scientist Dr. James Lovelock. He named this self-regulating living system after the Greek goddess *Gaia*, using a suggestion from the novelist William Golding. The Gaia Hypothesis has since been supported by a number of scientific experiments and provided a number of useful predictions, and hence is properly referred to as the Gaia Theory.
Until 1975 the hypothesis was almost totally ignored. An article in the New Scientist of February 15, 1975, and a popular book length version of the theory, published as *The Quest for Gaia*, began to attract scientific and critical attention to the hypothesis. The theory was then attacked by many mainstream biologists. Championed by certain environmentalists and climate scientists, it was vociferously rejected by many others, both within scientific circles and outside them.

Lovelock defined Gaia as:

> *a complex entity involving the Earth's biosphere, atmosphere, oceans, and soil; the totality constituting a feedback or cybernetic system which seeks an optimal physical and chemical environment for life on this planet.*

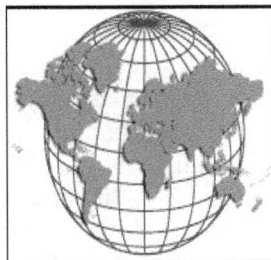

His initial hypothesis was that the biomass modifies the conditions on the planet to make conditions on the planet more hospitable – the Gaia Hypothesis properly defined this "hospitality" as a full homeostasis. Lovelock's initial hypothesis, accused of being teleological by his critics, was that the atmosphere is kept in homeostasis by and for the biosphere. Lovelock suggested that life on Earth provides a cybernetic, homeostatic feedback system operated automatically and unconsciously by the biota, leading to broad stabilization of global temperature and chemical composition. (From Wikipedia)

Gaea rising from the earth, Athenian red-figure kylix C5th B.C., Antikenmuseen, Berlin

oceans, the clouds and the ecosystem. Humans are an intrinsic part of Gaia. We are her "brain cells". We are the beginnings of Gaia's consciousness.

Imagine what the Earth looks like from *out there*, from the alien perspective out in deep space as they gaze at the millions of stars, mostly clumped together as galaxies and globular clusters. We are not even one of those points of light. The Earth is but a speck orbiting one of those points of light.

Getting a closer view, we see that the planet is alive, a holonic entity composed of billions of smaller creatures: bacteria, protozoa, plankton, reptiles, birds, mammals, fishes, and more, plus humans. They all play a vital part in the planetary organism as Elizabet Sahtouris tells us in wonderful detail backed with scientific data in her book EarthDance.

But is Gaia a conscious being? Can Gaia be considered a sentient living entity? Is this little speck of cosmic dust that we call Gaia have a unified mind?

At this point we are not yet a cohesive unit with a single mind. We are divided into nations and separate ideological groups with no center of command, no head, no coordination of the parts which make us up. The planetary mind is as yet unformed. (The United Nations may be an early type of proto-mind.)

What constitutes a planetary mind? What do I mean by saying that the planet Earth is forming a mind?

The mind of a person has as its foundation, the brain. To simplify, a brain functions with intelligence because brain cells – neurons which hold information – communicate with other neurons through dendrites and axons, the "input/output" connections. The more connections are made, and the faster they are made, with better information, plus deletion of clutter (synaptic pruning) the more potentially intelligent we are.

People on this planet are like brain cells in the brain. We are Gaia's neurons. Packages of information. The quantity and quality of our connections impact greatly on the intelligence and consciousness of Gaia.

The neuron is basically a memory cell that hold data. In "The Brain That Changes Itself" by Norman Doidge, M.D., he writes that as far as we know, memory is a stored pattern of connections. It is a record of how that cell related to other cells.

If you think about it, that is also what we humans are. We are stored patterns of our connections to other people and things; a record of our relationships with other beings, things and events. However, looking at the bigger picture, we who are Gaia's brain cells are not yet of sufficient quantity and quality to give rise to a unified consciousness.

At first, the only means of communication between these "brain cells" was word of mouth, now we've got film, television, the internet, and personal wireless communication.

The passage of information that goes on through these connections between people are what constitutes the "thoughts" of Gaia's world mind. In these exchanges of thought, we pass along information that greatly impacts the whole world, for good or for bad. It is important that we nurture Gaia into becoming a good entity, a good "person," if you will. An entity who looks after the welfare of the whole planet, as a single unit.

Just as there are many thoughts in a human mind, there are many thoughts coursing the pathways of the planetary mind. The brief shallow communications between individuals may have little consequence in impacting the world as a whole, but thoughts and ideas from politics, science, and religion are often embedded in film, TV, music, literature and other forms of mass media that circulate around the globe and do influence the course of world events. These are the dominant thoughts of the proto-planetary mind. By dominant thoughts, I mean *those thoughts that directly lead to action which impacts the welfare of the entire unit, whether it is a single human being or a planet.* These thoughts are the foundation for the dynamic self, the self that acts, the object of the word "I" as in "I think."

It is important that the dominant thoughts be peace-generating, healthy, sane, grounded and loving. As we are the basic units where the thoughts originate, we, therefore are the ones who must initiate and embody those thoughts. We are the fractal units which make up the planetary mind. It is important that we increase the quantity of quality thoughts: thoughts that inspire people, thoughts that lead to service oriented action, to harmony, to peace, to oneness.

Obviously, Gaia is not there yet. She does not yet have a cohesive mind. She is not of one mind at all. Some "brain cells" are waking up and realizing the need for environmental hygiene but they are being opposed by others who are unaware. There are pitch battles between cells within the organism. Basically, Gaia is defecating freely into the environment and her limbs are all akimbo, her energies undirected and ungainly. It is plain to see that Gaia is a baby with a consciousness that is slowly forming.

There are difference of opinion regarding Gaia's stage of growth. Some consider her to be at puberty, facing decisions regarding her impending maturity; a planetary teenager. However, even a teenager, regardless of adolescent tendencies, has a unified mind, is toilet trained, and is capable of making relatively rational decisions. From the universe perspective, Gaia does not yet have any of these abilities. She does not have a unified mind, that is, a single planetary authority that determines her actions; is not potty trained, she still soils her environment; and cannot make rational decisions, she struggles to control her own actions. Gaia shows all the attributes of an infant, not a teenager.

We, the ones who are aware of Gaia's budding consciousness are the ones who will play a major role in the development of her character and soul. We are the initial proto-mind that will evolve into a planetary mind.

Our physical bodies are of the Earth. It came from the material that make up the planet and it will go back. The atoms in our bodies have been everywhere. We have literally been the sky, the ocean, the birds, the fish, the rain, the mountains, the trees, the insects, the microbes, and other people.

You are Gaia. I am Gaia. It is this awareness and self-recognition that is the foundation of Gaia's nascent mind and soul. Gaia's consciousness of herself as "I" begins with us. Once there are enough of us in this consciousness, there will be a tipping point when our collective thought of "we are Gaia" will turn into "I am Gaia."

We are, in reality, the initial units of memory that make those choices which constitutes morality on a planetary scale. Gaia starts to know what is right and wrong when we, her brain cells start to know what is right and wrong. And we can see what Gaia is thinking for it is the same thing that we, her brain cells, our thinking. And we can see our thoughts streaming throughout the hyper-media: film, music, TV, wireless communications, internet, books, magazines, person to person dialogue, etc., – the total communication experience of humans to each other. And looking at what is going on in the hyper-media, it is evident that Gaia is but a toddler, her mind not quite unified, and not whole or mature enough to be considered a stable and responsible entity.

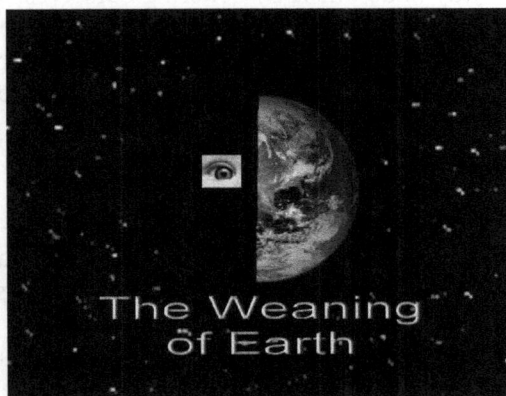

The Weaning of Earth

For Gaia's consciousness to evolve, the individual units of information that comprise its brain, you, I, each of us, must actualize our wholeness as a unified being. There cannot be separation of body, mind and soul. No domineering of one part over the other parts. We must become one and whole, first as individuals, than as a planet, so that we can start our journey of mastery. It all starts from us. Since it is the aggregation of humans that comprise Gaia's mind, as we are, so is Gaia. For Gaia to become a healthy, sane, fit, intelligent, creative, and loving being, those cells that make her up, us humans must individually be healthy, sane, fit, intelligent, creative and loving.

Look at the common person in the street. Look at yourself. Are you healthy and physically fit? Are you free of the poisons of the mind and body? Are you always trying to better yourself by seeking to become more intelligent, more creative, more loving? Do you serve your fellow creatures? It all starts from us. What we are, so is Gaia. And looking at the whole of humanity right now, we are unhealthy, scatter brained, prone to fighting, materialistic, dirty, selfish and without much self control. And that is what you see in Gaia.

But we can change. We are Gaia, but at the same time we are Gaia's parent and child. Let us care for her, nurture her, and raise her as we would a flesh and blood child of our loins. And the best way to do this is by bettering ourselves, to make it a priority to go within and daily connect to the Source of cosmic consciousness, to the maximum holonic entity, the Creator. This means that first we have to learn to connect to ourselves, to be conscious of our whole self: body, mind and soul, not just the intellect, not just the body, not even just the spirit, but our self as a whole person. Many people are starting to be able to do this. And then you can begin to practice cosmic consciousness, to be one with the whole universe through spiritual meditation. This, too, is being done more and more. The next step is planetary consciousness, to be one with the planet's mind, when you realize that you *are* Gaia, not creatures apart from this planet but a brain cell that is an intrinsic part of this living planetary entity. When you connect to this consciousness you will simply *know* in your heart that you are Gaia. You will be as certain of this as the knowledge that you are human.

One disturbing idea of Gaia is that if we humans become too destructive of the environment that she will put an end to us by natural disaster or some such catastrophe. This would be akin to suicide as we are Gaia's mind. If you make some terribly wrong decisions are you going to kill yourself? Most people do not, but some do. If the brain cells that make up Gaia, humans, become depressed and negative minded, suicide is a possibility. That is why it is so important that we human beings evolve spiritually and connect to the love intelligence of the universe. Gaia without brain cells would be Gaia that is not conscious or sentient and incapable of ever becoming a mature, intelligent and spiritual being that will eventually join the rest of the universe.

The True Self

What is your true self?

The true self is the self that you create. It is not the self that was forced upon you, not the self that was a result of circumstances, biology and upbringing. It is the self that you create yourself after attaining free will, volition, self awareness, cosmic consciousness and divine consciousness. After all, how can you say the person you didn't choose to be is truly you?

From the viewpoint of the eternal, your true self is the divine spirit within as it becomes one with your soul. From the perspective of the struggling mortal, your true self is the part of yourself you identify with at the moment; the driver of the unified human vehicle, (which will be discussed later.)

To say that the spirit within, the brahman, the Christ Consciousness, the indwelling spirit, the Thought Adjuster, is your true self is an affirmation of your true state of being as a spiritual entity. However, we must acknowledge that this indwelling spirit is from the Creator and returns to the Creator; it is part of the Creator. If that spirit, by itself, is our true self, and it returns to the Creator, it resumes existence as a part of everything, which means that our identity becomes dissolved into the Cosmic All and becomes as nothing. This goes back to the concept of nirvana and the cessation of all personal identity – oneness with the universe by becoming everything and nothing. If nothingness, non-being, is the result of the culmination of many life experiences and meaningful transformations, it is a vision of futility. It is the same as dying a mortal death and becoming nothing, except on a grand scale.

If, however, we can see the true self as the indwelling spirit fused in oneness with our evolutionary soul, we have conceptualized the creation of a new eternal being, a being that the divine spirit takes up with it in its return to its source. This being will not become subsumed into the whole and become as nothing, rather this being will exist eternally as an entity apart from the Creator but still one with it: separate in form, volition and identity but unified as one in spirit, intent and love. This new being goes in to the center and out again, ministering to the living universe as it respires, taking the love of the Source out and then back in again in the continuous motion of eternal life.

The First Source and Center, God, the absolute, eternal, infinite Creator being omniscient, omnipresent, and omnipotent needs beings to associate with that are separate from it in order to escape from the fetters of unqualified infinity and diffusion of personalities into an undifferentiated whole. We become those beings. That eternal self, an entity created from the merging of the eternal and evolutionary, a being that will never die or become nothing, but will exist in consciousness as a separate but unified associate of God, is our true self. An associate of God, a friend of God. An offspring of God. A child of God. It has been said that "the child is the father to the man." If so, we can say that we are, indeed, unique manifestations of God.

God Is An Artist

Sometimes
he makes incomprehensible works of art.

Incomprehensible to us humans anyway.
Often he makes beauty;
things so beautiful, it makes life worth living.
Beauty that is vibrant with the joys of life.
Beauty that makes you ache with longing,
beauty that melts into your soul
and changes your life forever.

See, God is an artist,
from him comes the light
and we turn it into different shades of darkness:
into color.
You can't have color
if everything's washed in white.
A hot day in the sun needs the cool relief of night.
That is why life is made of darkness and light.

See, God is an artist.
Try to appreciate the whole of what he created.
Not just the scene where your face is painted.
Look at the immense scope.
The awesome grandeur.
The long run, the big picture.

We all have a role,
all important parts of this bigger whole
in this cosmic play being enacted across vast
domains of space
and through eons of time.
So what part do you play in the total picture?
Where do you fit in?

See, God is an artist...
sometimes he makes incomprehensible works of art.

Incomprehensible to most humans anyway...

God

In this book, the word "God" does not refer to a Judaeo-Christian deity, or to the deity of any organized religion. I use the word synonymously with the word "Creator" and also "First Source and Center" and other variations on that theme. The word symbol is used to mean the actual creator of the universe, the cause of all causes.

In any valid exploration of reality, God must be considered, even if he/she/it is to be rejected or dismissed as being superstition. However, any decent exploration of our states of consciousness should give us some inner evidence of the reality of God. In my personal experience, I have found God, but it would be impossible to provide any direct material evidence of that. Even verbal expressions, sung, written, acted out and played throughout history, have not been able to portray the magnificent totality of the eternal First Source and Center, the absolute personality and force that we call God. But it is essential, if indeed God is real, that we figure him in on our exploration of reality in a major way, after all he's the one who created it all. "From him all things come, and to him all things return."

As new discoveries and inventions arise, we develop new conceptual frameworks. Due to the advent of new terms used in computer technology, we can even say that God is like a master server, a mainframe computer that is the source of all the programs that is within each of us personal computers. For those of you who have a dislike for the word God, this concept of the Creator as a master server computer may make it easier to relate to the ideas in this book. In the conceptual framework of holons within fractal patterns, God is the maximum holonic unit of the universe.

There are not enough words to define God for those who have no personal experience with the Creator. For those who have such a personal experience, words are not necessary. Suffice to say that God is the Creator of All. However, here are some thoughts regarding the nature of God:

Is God a person or a force? A being or a law? Personhood, beingness, force and law are all aspects of the universe, of the All. Since God is the creator of All, logically God is all of those but much more.

Is God external or internal? Inside or outside of us? Both. It is a stretch to put spatial limitations on a being/force that is omniscient, omnipresent, omnipotent, eternal, infinite and absolute. Being a transcendent entity, he is the source and manifestation of both material and spiritual realities. It can be conceptualized that physically, he exists at the center of the largest unit of matter, the universe, as well as at the center of the smallest unit of matter, an as yet undiscovered particle. In this way, he exists everywhere, not limited by space and beyond most human concepts of size and location.

Is God male, a female or a thing? A he, she or it? Again, since God is the creator and origin of maleness, femaleness and things, God is all of those and more. Attributing our limited biological concepts such as male and female to God has many shortcomings. However, because of the lack of suitable words, we can't help but use pronouns such as he, she or it to designate the Creator. In this book, the pronoun that seems to best fit the context of the sentence will be used, sometimes the pronoun he, sometimes she or it.

It is also true that God is like a father/mother, a universal parent who has created many creatures that he/she loves as much, actually more than any human parent can love his or her child. The concept of the eternal God having a Son or sons is to instill the idea that we are all one big family. Since the family is our highest concept and loftiest ideal of personal relationships, it is natural that we use words like Son of God to refer to the relationships of our loving Creator and his creations. In this sense, all creatures are sons and daughters of God and God is our divine parent. And by understanding the spirit of referring to the relationships of a loving family to see the relationships between God and us, we can understand the ideal relationship we should have for one another, that is, the brotherhood of man and the fatherhood of God. Again the words are insufficient and misleading, it would be more accurate to say the brotherhood and sisterhood of humankind and the motherhood and fatherhood of God, but that gets rather cumbersome; we must take these things in the spirit of which they are given.

God cannot be truly understood without having a personal relationship with him/her/it, even then it is an understanding that must evolve through time. However, because of the absolute and eternal nature of God, we will never be able to understand him completely or repletely. But that is no excuse for not trying to understand what we can of our Creator. God is the supreme and maximum unit of consciousness of total universal reality. The closer we get to understand the divine nature, the closer we are to understanding true reality.

The Foundation of the Soul

Self-awareness is the foundation of the soul.

If there is a deep part of one's inner self that is shrouded in darkness and covered with a veil, the potential of the soul is diminished. One cannot fully express one's soul if it is under lock and key. It is like giving someone food that is in a locked box. One must open the box before the food within can be shared. The thing that keeps it locked and inaccessible is fear.

For the soul to release its potential, for it to become a vibrant reality in itself, one must be aware of the deepest parts of oneself, the things that are shrouded in darkness and fear. The box is locked for the reason that we lock anything, out of fear or concern. With material possessions, this is natural as in some places there are people who will steal your precious belongings if given the chance. But with your inner secrets, what is the concern there? No one will rob you of your personal secrets. However, there is fear that if they find out your secrets, they will castigate you, hate you, revile you, demean you, and treat you in an undesirable way. Then there are deeper secrets, the ones that you even keep from yourself. You keep those locked away, not from others, but from yourself, so that you won't have to look at them and deal with them. Many people are afraid to see themselves for who they really are.

What are some of those things within a person that he or she may be afraid of even looking at? There are feelings of inadequacy, desires that go against societal mores, bad habits, hatreds, envy, jealousies, greed, even positive potentials. There may be just as many things that can go on this list, as there are people. I cannot go through every one of them, but I can go through several within my own experience, although it was not easy for me to be so candid in the earlier part of my life, for there was a part of me that cringed at revealing myself for all to see. It is only by knowing now that the universe is friendly to those who are born in spirit that all such fear is released.

The feeling of inadequacy was an issue for me that I kept hidden within me for a long time. Because of a brain tumor that I had in my childhood, which was surgically removed, and the ensuing medical challenges, I had felt that somehow I was not good enough. But it was something I overcame as I matured in mind.

I had been conditioned by my circumstances to think that somehow I was abnormal and inadequate. I dealt with this in various ways. One was by reading a lot of books and sharpening my intellect, thinking even if I wasn't physically equal, I could be smarter than most everyone. I kept up a strong front and ignored the deepest parts of myself. One way of propping up my self-esteem was by intellectually overpowering others with logic. I was good at it and used to revel in being intellectually superior, to compensate for my perceived physical shortcomings. I am now aware of that tendency and keep it under control, but this control did not come easy. Back then; there still remained within me something that I did not acknowledge. Something that I had kept locked away in that box within me.

One night in bed, I was tossing and turning, unable to sleep. I might have been a little depressed over something and wondered why I had these problems. Then I started thinking about how my life was shaped by my medically challenged childhood and I began to look deeper until I was face to face with my locked box. I was afraid to unlock it and look within, but a quiet, almost silent voice told me to go ahead. "Trust me," it said, "it's okay." So I did.

What I found were two things. One was that I was not facing up to the incontrovertible fact that I had medical problems and that my life was being shaped by circumstances outside the experiences of most people. (I had surgery when I was a child for a brain tumor that damaged my pituitary gland. I was subsequently treated with hormone shots and other medication.) Although it was mostly in my head, it was a fact that physically I felt inadequate in certain aspects. I was inadequate in becoming a football star and scoring touchdowns: I was not the physically vibrant superhero I liked to read about when I was a kid. I was a nerd wrapped up in my own personal problems. I was who I was. These were facts that I had not faced up to before, always evading and denying it in the core of my mind. But as I grew older these things became easier to face and acknowledge. And once I did, it was not such a big deal. Because the many potentials I had were being suppressed by my fears, once the fears were dissipated, my potentials could be realized. I began to think and act more positively. I worked on my physical health and condition and now, I am in better shape than most people that I know of at my age.

The second thing that was harder to face was my emotional reactions to my condition. The emotions were hate and resentment. I despised being different. I hated to have to take medications. I couldn't understand why I was not born as a sinewy, handsome action hero admired by women and respected by men. I hated this whole situation and blamed God. I had a deep resentment for this and for whoever was responsible for it. I resented my father whom I felt did not do such a great job fathering me, and I resented God, who was ultimately responsible. One of the reasons I kept these emotions locked up was because I thought that it was wrong to be resentful of my own father and God. Another reason was that it was extremely painful to admit those things, to see myself for what I truly was.

But I did. With the help of an unseen hand, I opened that box, spread everything out and inspected it in detail. I cried. Tears dripped across my cheeks and onto my pillow. I wept tears that held within it the essence of my pain and resentment. And with it dropped away the angst that had knotted my insides and had blocked the realization of my inner feelings. And as my hate and resentment vanished, love for my biological father and my Creator returned. I, then, began to love myself for who I was. I realized that the many positive qualities that I have, qualities that made me a unique manifestation of God, was made possible in me only by the experiences of being who I am. If I loved the positive qualities within me, I had to accept the unusual circumstances that resulted in those qualities, circumstances that I did not like at that time but was instrumental in forming the inner core of my spiritual awareness, my soul. I had to take the good with the bad; it was two sides of the same coin. The compassion and empathy I have for others, my knowledge and ability in regards to maintaining health, my spiritual insights, my love and appreciation for life, my creativity, my energy in striving for perfection, my devotion to supreme values and more, they were all a result of my challenges, and I wouldn't trade in those qualities for anything.

Kids want to become superheroes, but in real life, superheroes do not exist. Or do they? Actually, I realized, there are many superheroes from the spiritual standpoint. Those people who secretly do good, saving lives and helping those in need without attracting attention to themselves, keeping a "secret identity". They are all around us, and sometimes we read about what they have accomplished, while their names are unknown. Or some of them may be well known. It doesn't matter. They are the upholders of justice. The champions of goodness over the menace of evil. They are the superheroes. And to be like them you don't have to be physically imposing and have superpowers, but you do need spiritual insight, stamina and the super powers of the soul. Could I be such a superhero? A spiritual superhero? Is that God's plan for me? Then I realized that we could all be superheroes if we just tap into those divine powers within. By realizing the actuality of our divine origin and sourcing the power from which we have sprung, we can actualize ourselves as unique manifestations of the divine. Each of us, with our own diverse experiences and backgrounds has something that is truly original and unique, these are the origins of our "superpowers." The biggest superpower is the ability to transform the negative into the positive, the act of returning good for evil. By empowering this unique ability from within, we become spiritual superheroes.

These realizations happen because even though the mind is afraid to look at the deep seated animal emotions and fear that are repressed, it is encouraged by the leadings from the small, still voice, enabling it to bravely venture into awareness of those darkened thoughts. This awareness then became part of my soul and invigorated my soul. My soul was no longer shrouded in darkness and it was free to realize its true potential. And ever since then, I am able to share every part of me, unreservedly, with God, the deepest part of my consciousness. And by regularly revealing my inner self intimately, to myself and to God, I am in turn able to partake of God's revelations to me, to feel his presence daily. And this also enables me to reveal my soul to others dynamically, revealing truth, beauty and goodness.

Practicing self-awareness is an ongoing endeavor. Being self-aware is not the same as self-analysis. Self-analysis is poking around trying to fix a perceived problem within oneself; self-awareness is just seeing the true reality of oneself. Self-analysis can result in having too much focus on the self, which could make one moody and too self-conscious, while self-awareness merely acknowledges one's true attributes without self-judgment.

While there was only one box within me that was under the lock and key of fear, there were other parts of me that I looked at unflinchingly in order to become more self-aware. I took a close look at my bad habits, my good habits, my energy, my laziness, my sexuality, my reason for hating certain things, my reason for loving certain things, my plans for the future, my childhood assumptions and more. Although these issues were not under a dark shroud, some of them were still things that I was not totally comfortable looking at in my youth. But as I grew more mature, and as I got more in touch with my spirit, I began to be able to inspect them without fear. Truly, through self-awareness, a rock hard foundation was laid for my soul.

A person who is close-minded and intransigent may be that way because their soul is not well founded on self-awareness. They do not have a firm basis from which to steadily evolve. Many people hesitate to look at all aspects of themselves with candor, especially those who may have desires, habits and tendencies that are not accepted by mainstream society. But having associated with people from all walks of life, in various conditions, ages, cultures and backgrounds, I have noticed that often it is not things that are frowned upon by society that festers, it is their childhood insecurities, such as jealousies, envies and unfulfilled hopes that people hate to look at. These early childhood insecurities are the hardest to get in touch with because they are not so much locked away as they are covered over with years and years and layers upon layers of subsequent experiences, emotions, thoughts, and habits. The difficulty of this is that if they were to look deeply and unflinchingly at those early childhood feelings of extreme negativity, they would realize their falseness and would have to acknowledge that for all those years they were living under a false assumption. They fear that all they had invested, so much of their behavior based on those insecurities for so long were a waste of time. It would be a total invalidation of much of their life. They would do anything to avoid looking.

Spirit overcomes this through the soul. The soul evolves experientially and existentially. The soul evolves by learning from seeming mistakes, as well as gaining existential wisdom from the spirit. Once the soul is sufficiently empowered, the soul can look upon all those years of acting under a false assumption as a learning experience. The soul's spiritual point of view can look upon all those mistakes as a treasure trove from which to glean wisdom and truth.

The paradox (there are many wonderful paradoxes in an elliptical universe!) is that for the mind to become empowered sufficiently to get a spiritual point of view, it must become aware of the deepest parts of the self, and it does not want to become aware of those parts until it gets a spiritual point of view. The way out of this paradox is that all negativity will fade and disappear on its own by weight of its unreality, unless it is focused upon, and that all positive values live on for eternity and cannot be destroyed.

Although it may take many human years, a person's soul, unless he focuses constantly on his negativity, will become more and more empowered as his negativity withers away. Eventually, he will have a strong enough soul to go back into his childhood and look unhesitatingly at what troubled him and what those deep-seated emotions did to his life. He can then look further at those subsequent behaviors that caused him so much trouble, and learn from them lessons that would add to the quality and quantity of his soul. Such an experience would indeed be a transforming event and would not be an overnight happening. For it to become a reality would take many affirmative thoughts, many affirmative actions and services, much inner work through meditation and prayer, and a sincere desire for truth, beauty, and goodness. It happens all the time.

A question may then arise such as, what about those who become self-aware that they are oriented in ways that are not accepted by society? What about people who find out that deep inside they have tendencies that are totally reviled by society, like being a masochist, a pedophile or have other deviate traits? By squarely facing up to who they are unflinchingly without guilt or shame, they will realize that God still loves them whatever they are. Societal morality is relative only to that society, and those people who are considered perverted by society are not innately evil, just maladjusted. But if they realize that they have serious behavioral and psychological problems, professional help should be sought. Otherwise, by being self-aware, and by being true to spiritual morality, they can live peacefully within the confines of the societal mores so that they do not intrude upon the rights of the majority who believe differently than they do. In other words, they will have better control of themselves, as that is what spiritual self-mastery is all about.

Self-awareness can also empower the soul to heights of consciousness that are useful in dealing with many of the problems that face society. Through the act of the soul going within, the spiritual pleasure of worshipful meditation can be achieved, and it can become a pleasure that can supersede and replace the stimulative feelings induced by external means such as drugs, sex, food and power. Addictions can be locked away in a box by people who are afraid to face up to it, but it is through identifying and becoming one with the spirit within that one can become aware of and conquer such habits. Then there are people who have relatively minor addictions, which they recognize and confront daily, but they are unable to effectively overcome them because of the symptomatic difficulties inherent in withdrawal. It is just too hard. And it is harder to some extent because they have not hit rock bottom. They still function well in society, and may even consider themselves successful, but they are not realizing their full potential spiritually. An effective way to deal with this is not by trying to take a certain behavior away, but by replacing it with something more pleasurable. It is hard to get excited about taking something away from one's life, it is a negative process. It is easier to get enthusiastic about adding something, for it would be a positive act.

It must first happen by the self-awareness of what constitutes genuine pleasure. There is a difference between subtractive pleasure and additive pleasure. Subtractive pleasure is when we subtract the pressure from the external (even our physical bodies) such as the pressure of hunger, the pressure of the sex urge, the pressure of substance withdrawal. Those things are relieved by eating, sex and re-using mind altering substances. Additive pleasure adds something new and invigorating such as creativity, great relationships, recreation and worshipful meditation. Sometimes I have found that the best form of pleasure is a combination of the subtractive and additive, for instance, relieving hunger through well prepared, spiritually mindful nutritious meals rather than by just stuffing our faces with fast food; sexual relationships that are based on the sharing of soul to soul rather than merely for the act of physical gratification. Even the use of substances, such as alcohol, is more pleasurable when done with mindfulness, control and to enhance social discourse rather than to just drink to get drunk. Pleasure, any pleasure, when had daily and not associated with higher values, becomes adulterated and loses its vibrancy.

Pleasurable activities are the most pleasurable when it is not regular and the gratification is delayed. The animal mind wants immediate and regular gratification. The spirit, conscious of eternity, knows that pleasure is best doled out intermittently to remain pleasurable over the long run.

Spiritual Self-Mastery

Spiritual mastery is, in essence, to be centered, one and whole, by alleviating the inner conflicts of body, mind and soul. This allows effort, reason and faith to act as one.

Self-mastery is often misunderstood. It is NOT self-dictatorship. It is a harmonizing and coordinating of the body, mind and soul, led by the spirit, and not a situation where either the body, mind or spirit, assumes control over the other two. It is NOT the iron hand of sheer will power forcing the body and soul into submission.

Spiritual self-mastery starts when the mind and body, as one, wholeheartedly allows spirit to lead. It is the body, mind, and soul working as a single unit under the gentle and unforced love and guidance of the Creator spirit within us. It is being liberated from the scrutiny of the flesh by realizing the relationships between local convention and universe values.

Industrialized society has conditioned us to think that the analytical mind should be dominant over the body and soul. This has resulted in people as well as the society in which they exist being unbalanced and dysfunctional. It is the analytical mind without the balancing force of the spirit that has produced such horrors as pollution, global warming, and weapons of mass destruction with disregard to the health of the body and soul. We can change this trend but it must be initiated on an individual basis so that it will penetrate into society organically from the roots. It must start from you. When we are whole, the larger holonic unit, which we compose, is also whole.

To accomplish a great task, one must be in the zone of qi: effort, reason and faith united as one, with a singularity of purpose and will in the moment, and carried through in the course of time. All great accomplishments have this in common. Failure results from distractions, from the wavering of intent and focus due to stress caused by conflicts between the body, mind and soul.

Faith must be relaxed – while effort must be exerted – in a singular focus that lasts from each moment to every successive moment until the goal is accomplished. This can be seen and experienced in those moments in athletics, music, and science or in any endeavor when we are in the zone of qi. These are moments of eternity compressed into moments of united purpose, will and faith. This is what gets it done. And you can practice this by being mindful of it each time it happens, and by extending it moment by moment, so that those great deeds that are meaningful and of utmost value can be accomplished.

Consider yourself a committee of three: the body, mind and soul. The mind has free will to do what it wants and the common wisdom of our society says the intellect should take over. For instance, it decides it needs to work and makes the body get up and go. Of course, the body objects to many of the things the mind wants it to do, such as work that is drudgery and activities that cause discomfort. The soul is also often unhappy with where the mind is going. The soul wants to be creative, "smell the flowers" and follow the spirit. But the mind maintains control like a dictator and you work, disregarding the wants of the body and soul.

This creates stress for the body and soul. They don't like the life that they have to live, the life that the mind dictated to them, and they are going to do something about it. The body decides to get sick so it can rest, and the soul decides to be free in order to relieve the stress, which can mean indulgence in stimuli: from substance use to natural activities such as sex, eating and other pleasurable activities, even certain types of meditation can become a drug. Remember, the soul is not perfect and often makes mistakes to learn, in fact it learns by experience and is not afraid to make mistakes. It does not even consider mistakes as being negative, but rather stepping stones to perfection.

So now, we have a situation where there is a war going on inside you. And this is the situation for many people. From the outside they look like whole people but deep inside, they are split into warring factions with lots of blame, guilt, shame, chaos and confusion. With so much energy being spent fighting their own selves, its no surprise that most people are unable to overcome their bad habits. How can you move in any direction if you, yourself, is divided and at a standstill fighting yourself?

The thing to do is to become whole. Become one with yourself. Don't boss the other parts of yourself around. They are equal partners during this part of the journey. When making a decision, achieve a consensus. When you work with other people in a committee, you don't treat them like slaves or peons (hopefully). So why treat the other parts of yourself as slaves? Work in harmony. Be one. Be whole.

To recognize the divine spirit within and to follow it faithfully, without conflict or reservation, is wholeness.

To be not whole is to allow the body to be an automaton, a robot, disregarding both mind and spirit. Habitual drinking or overeating is a good example.

To be not whole is to also be a slave to the overbearing intellect, ignoring the needs of the body and the leadings of the spirit. A materialistic scientist is a good example of this situation.

One can also be not whole by following an illusory spirit, by putting faith in scriptures and religious dogma instead of having faith in the personal relationship with the divine spirit within. In believing in a fear-based deity rather than on a love-based deity. Hypocritical religionists are an example of this.

However, in being whole, there must still be a place of central command, the driver of the vehicle. Since the key is balance of the whole, the soul that is at the focal point between the inner and outer realms of our Personhood matrix is perfect for the job.

Who Is The Driver?

Or, who is the master when we talk of self-mastery?

Who or what is that part of you that is operating your human vehicle?

Whatever, or whomever that is, it is YOU!

The rest of you must obey that part. That part is the central unit, the core of decision-making. Oneness with that core is the beginning of self-mastery, because that core is your Self. When all the parts that makes you up: the body, mind, and the soul are unified in that oneness, then you are whole. You are one. This wholeness, this oneness of being is the prerequisite for self-mastery. Self-mastery is a road, a path that leads to greater and greater control of our self, our environment, and our destiny.

Initially, self-mastery is just learning to control one's self. Being able to control one's body and mind so as to be able to go where one wants and to do what one wants. To take one's own advice. To be able to follow one's highest leadings. It is basically a simple thing. Why can't we control our own body and mind? Why can't someone wishing to stop smoking unable to do so? Why can't some people stay on diets? Why can't people simply make themselves do the things they want to do? Why are people who have mastery over themselves considered exceptional? This shouldn't be the exception, this should be the norm.

Pause and think for a moment or two on this. It is quite appalling. We, humans, can't control ourselves.

Again, lets look at this closely. When we say, "being able to control one's body and mind," whom are we talking about? Who is doing the controlling? Who is the self and what is it trying to master?

This is an important question. Who are *you* that want to be master? You must have a good idea of who you are, your "self", before you can have self-mastery. So who are you? This basic knowledge is crucial to self-mastery and the possibility of eternal life, as we shall see. This is self-awareness, the foundation of the soul, and is the beginning of everything.

So who are you? Who wants who to stop smoking? Who can't stop whom from drinking or eating too much? We all have a body that needs to be controlled but sometimes it doesn't respond to our commands. If you want to stop your car, you step on the brake pedal and you come to a stop. Why can't we do that with our bodies? Once we decide upon a course of action, why can't we stick to it?

We like to change our minds. It is our right, an expression of freedom, and we do it often. But in many things we don't change our minds. Our loyalties, our principles and our values change slowly. Activities revolving around those traits are the ones that we stick to for the longest duration. Activity spurred on by the soul are based on eternal values, they last. Activity desired by the body provides for immediate needs and are often transitory in nature. Activity thought up by the mind can be logical and intellectually appealing but without attachment to long lasting values will fade. That is why programs that work to control substance abuse have spiritual overtones.

So we can control ourselves, as long as we have a good enough reason to. What constitutes good reason? It all depends on who is doing the driving. Who drives the human vehicle determines not only how you master yourself, but also your ability to control yourself and bring out your highest potential.

So who's doing the driving? Taken as a whole, we are an aggregate of body, mind and soul/spirit, the personhood matrix. But the mind within our personhood matrix is the thinking arena in which we make our decisions; how we think and what we think determines to a large degree who and what we are. The mind determines what it wants to identify with, how it sees itself. And how you see yourself determines to a great degree what aspect of yourself you are placing in the driver's seat. How do you see yourself? Do you see yourself as pure mind? Or do you identify more with your body? Or your soul?

If you see yourself as just your body, your mind gives authority to the body's wants and desires over all other considerations. You are concerned only with pleasing yourself and the biological urges of the body. To a person who sees himself as body, self-mastery would mean the ability to get everything the body wants. Satisfaction of basic physical needs such as food, stimuli, sex and comfort would be part and parcel of this life condition. The body becomes the master of the human vehicle.

In the past, many ascetics blamed the body's desires as being an obstacle to spiritual growth. Their error was in trying to totally negate the wants of the flesh in an effort to disenfranchise the body from the wholeness of personhood.

This watch care of the flesh is an isolating and separating practice but was a necessary experiment in the evolution of spiritual self-mastery. It is true that the body must be controlled so that its desires not overwhelm the aims and goals of the spirit led entity. The correct way to achieve this is through love and respect of the whole organism: body, mind and soul. The autocratic demands of the mind must give way to tolerance, understanding, respect and love for the natural desires and wants of our human vehicle. We must be one and whole, not separating, rejecting or repressing any part of us as being evil or unnecessary.

If you think of yourself as your intellect, you live according to the dictates of your mind. You are mainly concerned with doing the things your mind has figured out for you. It tells you what is right and wrong and how to act based on your intellectual abilities. To a person who sees himself only as mind, self-mastery would mean the ability to acquire those things that his mind has decided is desirable. Those things could be philosophical, ideological, symbolic, accomplishments, degrees, glory, and wealth. The mind has power to overrule the wants of the body, given the effort. A person that identifies only with mind has made logic and intellect the master of the human vehicle.

However, the self is composed of more than just the body and mind, there exists a soul and spirit. The existence of the soul and spirit cannot be proven by science. It is a completely subjective experience. Either one feels the spirit within or one doesn't. Either one believes or doesn't. However, one can prove, circumstantially, the reality of spirit by seeing the effects of believing in spirit and living accordingly.

Because science as we know it is unable to prove the existence of spirit, we have to take it on faith, our own experiences, and from the recounted experiences of countless individuals that there is within all people, a divine spirit, the still voice, the Christ Consciousness, a fragment of the Creator that resides within our hearts. This divine spark guides us and leads the way toward unity and harmony in our lives. When the mind recognizes this spirit and follows its leadings, there is created what is often known as the soul. The soul is the direct offspring of mind and spirit. The soul is the very best part of you that was created when you first realized the difference between right and wrong and continues to grow and evolve with each new moral decision that you make. This soul is the part of you that will survive after the death of your material body.

If you see yourself as soul, your mind gives authority to your soul and lives according to the leadings of your spirit. To a person who sees himself as soul, self-mastery would mean the ability to acquire those things that the soul desires; to see the wholeness of life and the interconnectedness of all beings; cosmic consciousness; to be able to find love, joy, happiness and fulfillment in all life's circumstances; to be able to see all of our fellow humans as brothers and sisters, as spiritual siblings; to realize that the universe is friendly to a spiritual individual and that we can lay our defenses down and live in peace. Life becomes infinitely richer, more rewarding, and a fabulous journey full of awe and wonder. However, it does not and cannot happen overnight. The mind slowly begins to delegate decision-making power to the soul. But once it happens, then you have made the soul the master and driver of your human vehicle.

You may get a better idea of the foundation of your soul by being self-aware of your past experiences. If you are a musician, performer or artist, you know when your creative work had soul and when it didn't. A singer that sings with soul or musician that plays with soul knows the part of themselves they accessed when their soul was displayed. Conversely they know when their soul was not evident during their performance. Other artists may also know when soul was present and when it was not during the creative process. For those who are not creative or artistic, you may have noticed your soul coming into play when you interacted with others, in how you dialogued and related with other people. A simple conversation can be very soul centered, especially when discussing personal matters and topics that are of great personal concern. Conversely, you may be aware of those times when your attitudes and conversational approach was coming more from an intellectual or biological source rather than from the soul. Reflect on those experiences and you will gain a better understanding of your soul.

You may ask, how do we evolve from seeing ourselves as body, then as mind and then to seeing ourselves as soul?

It is possible to re-make ourselves; we do it to some degree everyday. However, we can re-make ourselves into what the external world wants us to be, or we can re-make ourselves into what our internal reality wants us to be. We are greatly influenced by those around us. The society in which we live nudges us, pokes us, and coaxes us to value certain things; how we look, how we behave, how to fit in.

If we value the things that society can provide for us, we nurture and support society and try to conform to its wishes even when much of it goes against what we truly want for ourselves. So we set up an accommodating front to face society, while keeping true within to one's soul. We create a face that we use to confront the world and we have our inner face, how we see ourselves, who we are within. When the divergence between the inner and outer is too great, there is no peace of mind and the tension could make life difficult. As we grow more confident of our inner perception of who we are, our soul, we can use the true image of ourselves more often to interface with the world, and we can begin to gain more control of ourselves and our lives, rather than be manipulated by the external pressures of society. However, since we must live in a society of people, our souls cannot be self-indulgent, our souls must be able to keep our inner integrity while at the same time accommodate the souls of others.

The evolution of the soul is quite evident when we become able to make that transition from showing the world our false front to slowly changing our mask and even dropping the mask so that our face on the outside resembles more the face on the inside. An example is a singer who sings and reveals the depths of the heart, and the soul becomes brilliantly evident. It is when we begin to show our real self to the world without fear or favor that the identity shift from mind to soul takes place. The singer may do this only when she's singing, and only when she is singing very well, but more and more, we can all do this in our lives if we move towards it. Remember, though, the soul is not perfect and makes mistakes, but it loves itself more for that because it knows that in experiential time and space, trial and error *is* perfection.

Once we realize who we really are, and which part of us takes precedence; body, mind or soul, and take fearless steps in that direction, then we can enter into the earliest levels of self-mastery and we can begin to safely operate our human vehicle consciously and purposefully. Then we can be who we truly want to be.

Chapter Two
Where Are You Going?

*The destiny of mankind is not decided by material
computation. When great causes are on the move in the
world...we learn that we are spirits, not animals, and
that something is going on in space and time, and
beyond space and time, which, whether we like it or not,
spells duty.*

Winston Churchill

Okay. So where do you want to go?

Heaven? Many people want to go there. What do you
know of heaven, that you want to go there so much? Do you
have any hard data, or even any kind of information on heaven?
Not much detail in the scriptures...and they all seem so
implausible.

So, I would wager you basically don't have any idea
where you're going to and what you would be doing after death,
much less even considering that there may be options on what to
do there once you get there.

You just don't want to die or suffer. And it would be
nice if you could spend eternity in a cushy environment where
all your friends and loved ones are around and everything is a
pleasure.

Okey-dokey. Sounds great.

Or does it?

Doesn't it sound like someone who has had it tough and
just wants to take it easy, at least for a while?

I think we are wise enough to know that with plenty of
satisfactory rest and recuperation, we will get energized and will
want to be more active. Possibly save the world. At least realize
one's full potential to be of value to the universe.

It is evident that with the proper management of our
resources, wise use of technology, social and spiritual

maintenance and development, we can all lead a life free from major want and suffering. Excepting the natural vicissitudes of life, which actually add character and depth to lives that would be otherwise unexceptional, we can have a life that is in the main, enjoyable and fulfilling.

In the past, life has been short, brutish, and a crucible of pain and suffering. But we can now see glimmers of a future when life is no longer synonymous with suffering. We are evolving away from that past.

Instead of just focusing on easing suffering, we can also turn to creating new ways of fulfilling the aspirations of the soul. To ease suffering is admirable, it alleviates a problem. It puts something back that was lacking: health. However, it is not a creation of something that was not there before, such as in art or technology.

A destination should be a wonderful fruition. Not a mere revitalization or an easing of suffering. It is a new creation. A flowering.

In operating any vehicle, we should know where we would like to go. Where is our destination? And conversely, from where are we starting out? (Or from where did we come?) Our destination is tied in closely with the purpose of life. If we can find the purpose of life, we shall find our destination. Let's meander down this avenue.

Destination

What is the purpose of life? Why are we here? To where are we going?

These questions have been asked for centuries and there are just as many answers as there are more questions. The fact is, no answer is provable. There are myriads of books on the subject and none of them can be verified. So let's focus on what we can validate as a result of our own lives; the things that we have personally experienced in the time we have had in this life. As most people, including myself, do not have any conscious memories of past lives, or have evidence that there were any past lives, let us make the starting point the here and now.

As for finding out what our purpose and destination is, we would have to draw upon the experiences of our own lives and the records and opinions of the many people that have lived in recorded history.

Most scientists will simply say they do not know. Science, as we know it, will never be able to discover the spiritual origin and purpose of life. That is in the realm of religion and philosophy. Of course, there are some scientist/philosophers who say that life is an effect of random chance and has no purpose at all. Since there is no scientific evidence for that, scientists who have that opinion are going way beyond the realm of their chosen academic field. That doesn't mean that they are wrong, but that line of reasoning is a dead end and so we will not go there.

Many religionists and philosophers tend to agree that we are in some kind of cosmic school; life is a process of learning. However, the question then becomes, learning for what purpose?

Again, we look at the fractal model.

If you can see into the profound depths of your motivations and reasons for existence now, you can see it in eternity. What is your purpose right now? Why do you get up in the morning? Why do you go to school or work or play? Why do you do the things you do?

The pattern is basically simple, at least on our current level of existence. We learn and grow in order to experience value. To live a life worth living. However, as we grow, what we value changes. As a child we may value candy and toys, in our adulthood we may value gourmet meals and real estate. Our values may also change from the material to that of the spiritual. Hopefully, it does. As we evolve spiritually we begin to value personal relationships, creativity, service and communion with the cosmic All and God over material goods and mundane entertainment. But the basic pattern remains the same. We live our lives to choose paths of value in our own lives and in the lives of others.

As our values evolve, so do we and at a certain point of our progression we are transformed into another form. And we can we see this pattern displayed in nature. The caterpillar transforms into a butterfly, the egg into a chicken, the tadpole into a frog. But how can we know that such natural transformations of animal life work the same way in our spiritual life? We go from being an embryo in our mother's womb to become a child and then an adult, how do we know we will go any further than that? Using our material faculties we cannot and do not know. There is no scientific evidence to prove or disprove of spiritual reality, spiritual evolution and transformation. But our souls know the truth. Our souls know by proof of its very existence and the inference and implications of natural patterns that exist throughout life itself.

Before a caterpillar metamorphoses into a butterfly, does it have an inkling that it will transform into a different form? Does a tadpole know that it will become a frog? Does an embryo have an idea that it will be born? Are we, as humans, like spiritual embryos, undergoing a metamorphosis so that we can be born as spiritual beings? Can we see any indications in our lives that this may be so? At the same time, can we see in human history, a trend of spiritual progress? Is there a bigger pattern within the scope of all existence that points to an ultimate goal?

The Spiritual Evolution of Civilization

In taking a broad look at history, we have come a long way. Although savagery and barbarism is still rampant among some of the residents of this planet, we have reached new heights in spiritual and social behavior. Charitable and service organizations exist now where there were none before. Environmental movements and organizations which were unknown before have been created. Human rights, which were totally ignored in ages past have become a byword for societal morality. Even war is regulated, as much as possible, and imperialism is looked down upon by most governments. There is a trend of people being influenced less by the dogmatism of rigid, autocratic religions and becoming more spiritual in a personal way. So yes, there is evidence that spiritual progress is happening on this world, a movement toward unity, harmony and order, as opposed to separatism, dissonance and chaos.

How would religion and spirituality progress and evolve in our world? What would it be like in the far distant future? If there is a trend, an unfolding plan where humans on this planet slowly become more civilized and more spiritual as well as more intelligent and more technologically advanced, what could it lead to?

In the far future, I believe that religious uniformity will be replaced by spiritual unity. There will be truer manifestations of love, harmony, understanding, compassion and spirituality in our everyday lives.

Religious organizations become less and less God's instruments when they begin to separate God's creatures one from the other, when they lose the element of unity, which is the quality of divinity. Such organizations will disappear. Spiritual unity would be based on the knowledge that we are all extensions of the metaphoric family of God with the same inclusiveness granted to everyone. After all, we are all one. In effect, everyone is, was, and always will be a part of this spiritual unity, even right now, although most people are not aware of it. In the future, this will be acknowledged and accepted as a matter of fact by all. One wouldn't need to *choose* to be a member of this familial organization of God, for everyone will recognize that they are *born* into it.

What one believes or professes to believe would not be important. What traditional faith one is in would not be important. Spiritual reality would be accepted like we accept air, not something separate from life but intrinsically woven into the fabric of everyday personal reality.

This spiritual unity would be the universal religion: the realization, acceptance and acknowledgement of God's spiritual family and reality by all, without creed, dogma, tenets or doctrine.

Everyone would have such a personal religion and they would be the best people that you can imagine. They would manifest universal love, and behave in such a way as to leave no doubt that spiritual reality is just as real as material reality, if not more so. Churches and human religious organizations would not be necessary because spirituality would be a fundamental fact of daily life. Religion would be both personal and universal. God would be an accepted reality, a reality that would be obvious to everyone. People would fellowship together displaying all of the fruits of the spirit in their daily work and play so that spiritual values would be merged into the material aspect of life and would not be apart from everyday practicalities.

Obviously, as we look at the world around us, it is easy to see that such a universal spirituality to take hold among the majority of the world's populace is a long time coming. It may not happen for tens of thousands of years. But as spiritual growth progresses on this planet, more and more people will realize their place within this true spiritual reality. I believe traditional faiths and man-made spiritual organizations such as we know now will, in the long run, fade. It's not that spirituality will go away, rather, it will become central to every aspect of life. All organizations will have an aspect of spirituality. As self-mastery and personal self-government become more commonplace, personal faith and personal relationships with God will be the norm. We can see some of it happening around us now, albeit very slowly and sporadically. When we have a gathering of people who are in that consciousness, a rare event, the energy is extremely uplifting. But since such consciousness will not be universal for quite a while, for the present we will just have to create our own groups in order to enjoy universal spirituality and cosmic consciousness with those of like mind and soul. And this will pave the way for the world to follow.

Currently, in our personal lives, we see a progression of values from the material to the spiritual. However slow it might seem at times, more and more people are realizing that material gain means nothing without the spiritual values of personal relationships. Materialism is still strong but as more people begin to have the basic needs of food, shelter and clothing, and then go beyond to affluency, they will begin to increasingly focus on their inner needs. Historically, it was the creation of leisure time through technological advancements that resulted in cultural developments. When people no longer needed to spend so much time growing food and making a living, they had more time to work on the arts, sciences and humanities. This trend will continue all over the world and more and more people will have time to spend on self-development. Values will evolve over time from the material to the spiritual. From the temporal to the eternal. We will slowly begin to identify less with our material bodies and more with our souls. Could all this be an indication that we are transforming into something else, a material embryo slowly gelling into spiritual solidity?

If this is so, to where are we going? What is our ultimate goal?

Again, I look to nature to see if there is a fractal example. And I see the flower. It sprouts from a seed and grows and grows, until it blooms beautifully, and from which many seeds are created, falling to the ground until the cycle repeats. This pattern can be found in each of our lives, and I think, can also be applied on a much larger scale to our spiritual existence. Human life is but a seed, we are in the stage of sprouting into spiritual reality. Once we do so, we continue to grow and grow until we reach the pinnacle of spiritual evolution, to reach "the right hand of God," so to speak, to be Godlike, and yet not God, and then to go back out to the near infinite universe and become creator offspring in our own right, creators of our own seeds. Like a field of flowers, this will happen not only to individuals but to all evolutionary creatures. Entire civilizations of God's creatures are headed for transcendent transformational experiences in the goal of time, space and spirit. Of course, fractal analogies can only go so far, and as we are but embryos, projecting our futures any further would be like a baby pondering what happens after college. But as we see the small, we see the large. As we see the part, we see the whole.

Traditional Concepts of Eternal Life

There are truths in both the Eastern and Western concepts of origin and destiny, but also some things that seem incongruent and illogical based on my experiences of reality. The Western concepts have us start in this life and progress toward becoming higher spiritual beings in the next life, if we are good, to reach heaven, or hell if we are evil. What we do in heaven and in eternity is not described in detail, in hell I guess we just suffer. The Eastern concepts lean toward reincarnation, some posit that our souls have always been around and after countless lives of being born and reborn is finally released from this cycle to reach nirvana, to escape from the sufferings of life, to dissolve and become one with everything, which would mean to actually become nothing.

Reincarnation

The idea of living countless lives after lives from the beginning of time for the purpose of becoming nothing also seems senseless. And if our souls were around for an infinite time in the past, why does it take so many lives to reach nirvana? Wouldn't an infinity of time in the past be enough to reach nirvana many times over? And if our souls were not around for an infinite time in the past, when and how was it created?

The Eastern and Western concepts of origin and destiny, however, can make more sense if we distinguish the difference in meaning of spirit and soul. The spirit is the essence of the Creator, the soul is the essence of our self. The spirit has been around for an infinite past, the soul is created here and now. The soul evolves and is transformed into higher levels of being through habitation of life vehicles and then fuses and becomes one with the spirit, but where was it created? Why not in this life? If we do not have past memories, this life is probably our first. And when we die, why does our souls have to come back to this planet to live more lives? The universe is immense, why is it conceptually necessary to come back here to Earth? It isn't. But because astronomy and the discovery of interstellar space is a relatively recent development, the sages in the past had only this planet to refer to within their conceptual frameworks. When they said that we will return back to this world, they could not have meant this planet, as they had no idea of planets and solar systems, as we do through the science of astronomy. The "world" was the physical realm, regardless of where it may be, this planet or another.

In the theory of reincarnation, life after death is a given. It is free and a part of nature. We don't have to earn life after death, it happens to everyone. There is a part of this concept that resonates within me. That is the concept of learning and bettering ourselves through living many lives. It sounds like a good plan. It's logical and I have a basis of understanding which stems from my real life experiences. The lessons that I have learned and am learning in this life are so profound, so meaningful, that I can imagine how much wisdom and knowledge I could gain from living many lives. However, the illogical thing about some concepts of reincarnation which makes me doubt their accuracy is that, how can one learn if one does not remember the past lives? For one to learn from one's experience, one has to remember it. To have one's memory wiped clean after each life is like going to school and then forgetting everything that is learned at the end of each grade. How can we be expected to lead life after life and learn from each one so that eventually we will reach a higher state of being if we cannot remember what we have learned from each life? If upon being born in this present life, I had memories of my past lives, I would be so much wiser, so much more intelligent and knowledgeable now. Many of the mistakes I made in this life would not have been made, as they would have already been made in past lives and lessons learned from them as a consequence. Much of the pain and suffering in this world would be unnecessary. Each life would have been like a grade at school, a learning process that could be built upon, layer by layer so that we could achieve a fruition, not a cessation of existence.

If you dig deep enough into reincarnation philosophy, you will find an answer to some of this, such as the "veil" that is purposefully drawn across our memories. But it seems like sophistry. However, the value in the theory of reincarnation is that we look to better ourselves progressively by living continuous lives of transformation.

Reincarnation can be better understood rationally if we look at the workings of the naturalistic world. We are all made up of atoms and molecules that were once part of the Earth. Everything we eat becomes a part of us. When we die, actually even when we are living, as we breathe and defecate, these atoms go back out to the environment. We are not just "bugs" living on top of a rock. We *are* the rock. We *are* the Earth. Literally. When I told this to someone, he said, "I guess so, if you want to think of it that way." My reply was, "How else can you think of it?"

So, given enough time, everything recycles and it is very possible that the same atoms that made us up at one time will be reconstituted in the same way so that we are "reborn" as the person we once were, at least a close enough facsimile. Given an infinite amount of time, we would be recycled over and over, being born as an ant, fish, trees, other people, and our self, again and again. This sheds light to the Buddhist concept of being reincarnated countless times until we can achieve nirvana. The process of achieving nirvana can also be validated and understood by the aforementioned concept that eternal life is achieved by identifying with eternal and spiritual ideals and values. When we identify with material values, we remain material and stay on Earth, being constantly recycled over and over again. When we identify with eternal values, we are able to leave the Earth, our identity becoming able to move on to higher spiritual forms that embrace higher values, escaping the cycles of birth and death on this planet.

Heaven And Hell

Mainstream Christianity's concept of achieving eternal life is deterministic. Life after death is a given, but depending on your moral choices, one could end up eternally in hell or in heaven. But you only have this one lifetime to make the choice. It's unfortunate if one dies early in life and never gained the experience of making the right choices. Or if one's upbringing or circumstances twisted one's morality so that one chose wrongly. It's a crapshoot. One roll of the dice, one lifetime of getting it right, and you could lose or gain everything.

The concept of a hell where the evil exist in eternal damnation makes no sense to me. What purpose does torturing beings for eternity who never asked to be born serve in the cosmic scheme of things? Is there an example of this in nature? Do bad flowers live in a botanical hell? Isn't it more merciful to merely end the existence of all those who do not wish to participate in the divine plan?

On the other hand, heaven seems like a good conceptual destination except it would seem pointless and even worse than hell unless we had a purpose for being there, information that is unavailable in those scriptures

I personally think a Creator with an infinity of time on his hands would be a lot more flexible, but the point of the concept is that we should all try to make this life a life of value. There is much value in the Christian culture regarding the importance of personal relationships and the evolving soul.

Theologies and religions have their differences but instead of finding conflicts in the details the important thing is to look at the similarities, which is that we all desire to improve, to grow spiritually, to make the right choices and evolve closer to the First Source and Center, to become better beings.

It is an innate need. Like the plant seeking the glimmer of light in a darkened room, we are drawn to spiritual light. This then, is our real destination in this life and in the *now*. Fulfillment of destiny may be our goal in the distant unforeseeable future but by fractal analogy, our immediate destination is to fulfill our potentials as human beings here and now. To create, co-create and re-create ourselves with leadings from our spirit so that we can choose the best values in our lives. When we do this *now*, this pattern becomes reflected in larger and larger spheres of reality so that it becomes the pattern of all reality, of all existence. The *now*, when realized and actualized in the deepest level, can become the fractal pattern for the *eternal*.

The Genesis of Organized Religion

To every myth, there is a kernel of truth, albeit sometimes very small. Even the myth of Santa Claus has as its basis the story of St. Nicholas. The myth lasted because it became a tool to teach children the value of being good. So a myth is an exaggerated story that started from a bit of truth and carried on for its social value. Superstition is a behavior that puts stock in a given myth. Organized religion is founded on myth backed by authority such as a church.

During times in history, various enlightened men had contact with the maximum universal intelligence, the First Source, and they were uplifted. They tried to bestow this knowledge to their fellow men but found that their followers lacked the intelligence, imagination, insight and spiritual vision that would make them understand. So, a myth was created, much like the story of the Urps in the beginning of this book; a simplified tale was told in order to make them get a glimpse into universe reality. As time went on these stories became a foundation for a religion based on authority of the organizations, i.e., the churches. These myths then became a part of the social and cultural dogma and parents would indoctrinate their children with them, in order to be socially accepted and also to instill the values of that society.

Atheists came about because some of the children were more intelligent and less gullible than their parents who tried to indoctrinate them in their religious beliefs. These children were too smart to buy into this simplified tale of an absolute, all powerful, all seeing, omni-present, eternal and invisible being, so they rejected it completely and often subjectively and emotionally. Agnosticism is an objective way of looking at the debate as to whether God exists or not. There is no evidence one way or another so being agnostic is an objective viewpoint.

Atheism takes just as much faith as believing in God and is just as subjective. Usually, the God that atheists do not believe in is the one that they were told to believe by their parents (or society) and their atheism is an emotional reaction to their indoctrination since agnosticism would be a more rational approach. The concept of God that is portrayed in this book, that of a maximum fractal intelligence is logical and objective as it follows the scientific observations of the natural world. However, there is one aspect of this transcendent concept of God that is supernatural, and that is that at the foundation of each person and of the universe is consciousness, which science cannot explain and is quite unexplainable by natural laws. So although this *concept* of a supreme being can be objectively explained, since consciousness cannot be so scientifically proven, any claims to achieving contact with this primal consciousness, the First Source (maximum fractal intelligence) would be a subjective experience. But all in all, a subjective opinion, whether to believe in the existence of God or not, does not by itself mean that it is, or is not true or valid. Ultimately, what one believes in or not is up to each person, and is therefore subjective. What is of value, though, is not whether it is objective or subjective, but whether the belief improves one's life and that of the quality of our civilization.

The Religion of Authority and the Religion of Experience

Organized religion may or may not be good for civilization. Good things have come from organized religion but many destructive things have also happened because of organized religions. But is it religion itself that can be destructive or is it because it is often organized by the rules of fallible humans? For this discussion, I would like to separate organized religion from personal or true religion. They can also be designated as religions of authority and the religions of experience; religion by rote versus religion by personal insight.

True religion is a personal relationship with the First Source, a living spiritual experience, rather than something written about in text and endorsed by a church or organization. True religion is an insight into reality, a relationship with the primal love intelligence, and not a mere intellectual assent to any body of dogmatic doctrines. True religion consists in the *reality based experience* of being children of God. True religion consists not in theologic propositions but in spiritual insight and by trusting the underlying love personality of the universe.

When we have such a true relationship with the Universal Parent, this becomes a new religion that is on a level far and above the religions of the major denominations in the world today which are all religions of authority rather than of experience. This would be a religion which is not a religion in the present-day meaning of that word, a religion that makes its chief appeal to the divine spirit of the universal love intelligence which resides in the hearts and minds of all humans.

This new religion has no name, no scripture, and no organization apart from the family of the universal love intelligence, God. It is a real and personal relationship with God that transcends denominations. And just as we don't have an institutional name for our personal relationship with our own biologic father, we don't need a name for our relationship with God, the Universal Father. It is a reality. It simply is. Putting a label on it detracts from its transcendent reality.

Regardless of the drawbacks of organized religion, it is still necessary in this time and age. Most humans are unable to connect directly with the Source. This will change with time, but just the mere act of physical survival consumes so much of our time and energy that most people just cannot relax enough to achieve a transcendental state of mind that would enable them to connect with the universe Source. Therefore, we get religion by rote; a set of instructions that can be followed in order to maintain order and harmony in our society. This requires almost no creativity or initiative, as it just entails following rules and commandments.

When our Earthly civilization advances enough to where the majority of humans have enough time and leisure on their hands to effect spiritual self-development, more people will have a direct personal relationship with the Universal Parent, but until then organized religions must maintain moral order on our planet. However, organized religions must evolve also. It should be the duty of organized religion to entice people to achieve a personal connection with the universe love intelligence so that churches are no longer necessary. Just as a health practitioner with the best welfare of patients in mind should want them to be so healthy that they do not ever need medical treatments at all, churches should want people to have a direct connection with God so that religious organizations would become unnecessary. Just think of a world where everyone has a direct and personal relationship with the Source; true religion, or in terms of the meaning of religion today, no religion, as John Lennon imagined.

Spiritual Evolution Through Time And Space

Internally, within our consciousness, we can be one with the center of the universe through worshipful meditation even right now. Externally, we must go through the course of time and space via the process of life and death – the shedding of previous shells.

To where do we go when we die? Into what new shapes will we be transformed? Does anyone even have a clue? Who would even dare to hazard a guess?

The vision of a fiery hell and a cumulous cloud-studded landscape of winged angels may have worked for simple minded folk in the middle ages but for a more educated and technological world population, such as we are now, a more sophisticated model of continued existence is necessary. I have found only one source worth mentioning (*The Urantia Book*). The only candidate worth considering that has any depth, logic and very importantly, details. Since it is impossible for me to verify its accuracy, I go by its elegance of thought, its logic and ring of truth. This is my understanding of it as I explored it further, sought and received new insights.

It seems that as we evolve from the material to the spiritual, it is not just our essence that is transformed. Our bodies and minds change also. As individuals, we must have a form, whether it is material, supermaterial or spiritual, otherwise we are as nothing. Here on this planet, we have a material body. As we progress, our bodies must reflect our higher minds and souls. We are not instantaneously made into a perfect entity merely by dying. The process takes many, many transformations and millions of years, traversing light years of space, with our bodies and minds becoming more and more spiritual in the process, the magnificent fruition of the results of our experiential adventures culminating in our presence by the side of the Creator.

The physical destination we arrive at, after a number of transformations in which we evolve to higher states of being is the place of supreme perfection, call it Paradise, which is metaphorically, and even geographically and logically, at the center of the universe. The fruition of our spiritual career is arrival on Paradise. Paradise is the center of our material and spiritual universe. Since material reality and spiritual reality is superimposed on each other, the center of one is the center of the other. The seeming paradox here is that by manifesting the eternal in the *now*, we can be one with the First Source and Center anywhere and anytime. Because the Center is removed from time and space, we can in essence become one with it when we ourselves, even for an instant, remove our consciousness from time/space reality to dwell with the Creator.

However, there is importance here in distinguishing between being "in the center of the universe" mystically, and being in the center of the universe in actuality. Being centered mystically is an inner process. Being *actually* in the center of the universe is an external event and is an objective and material reality that takes into account our existence and evolution as a total personhood of body, mind and soul, living within an elliptical universe of both matter and spirit. Our form changes and evolves into a higher state and yet we remain as individuals. It is true that we become one with the All but we can do this without becoming nothing.

We end the cycle of birth and death not by dying, but by being always alive. In the days of old, and even now in other parts of the world, life is miserable and something to escape from. In this spiritually enlightened and resplendent universe, which I believe is the case, life is grand and wonderful and something that we want eternally. We cease the cycle of existence and non-existence by always existing. In such a heightened state, as co-creators, we as individuals can manifest and identify with the All and yet be an autonomous being in harmony with the Creator's will. And as transcendent entities tested by the trials of evolutionary challenges, we will still have a purpose, even after attaining Paradise, which is to go out among the creatures of the universe to minister to them. We can see this in the fractal analogy of our human lives: we get our education in school and then we go out into the world to choose paths that are of value to us and to others. I think this pattern is inherent in our makeup, from the lowest to the highest levels.

This, then, is our purpose, Paradise is our destination. Eternal life is our destiny. But how do we get there? How do we get past this life?

Life After Death

What is the process to achieving eternal life?

To achieve eternal life we choose to identify with eternal values. When we value eternal things, our energies go into identifying with things that last for eternity, so that our eternal soul can evolve. When we value transient material things, our energies sink into things that are temporary, so that we, ourselves become but a temporary occurrence.

In every activity there are eternal values and transient values. The simple act of making money can be for the transient value of gaining more things, but it is not necessarily so. There are eternal values such as temperance, self-control, organization, unity and insight that are necessary to making money. Conversely, even an activity such as being a religious minister can be done with transient values in mind, such as self-validation, self-aggrandizement, anger, intolerance and hatred. It is not so important *what* kind of work you do, as much as *how* you do it.

Temporary and transient enjoyments abound in everyday life. The temporary rush of excitement, the thrill of adventure, the appeasement of biologic desires such as food, sex and stimuli. We chase after them and even when we capture them, they are used up and are gone after a brief moment so that we must begin the chase again. Those transient experiences are not evil, they are a part of life and can be enjoyed without guilt as long as they are not destructive of life, family and relationships. But if that is all that life means to us, then life becomes but a transient and momentary flash in the scheme of eternity. If we can live life so that each moment is filled with experiences that are eternal, then we have achieved eternity in the *now*. If each breath of air we breathe and each sunrise and sunset is a miracle, when associating with everyday people becomes a spiritual experience, when we can look at simple wholesome food as a gourmet meal, when a casual walk becomes a thrilling experience, that is when eternal values have transcended life in the *now*.

Of course, life in the now may not be a bowl of cherries for some. When we talk of life after death and eternal life thereafter, we imply that life is preferable to non-existence. This is an assumption that is not necessarily true. If our present life is full of pain and suffering such as when the body is wracked with a terminal illness, death may be preferable to life. Life is something that we treasure and want to continue only when it is enjoyable, when life has value. We do not want eternal life if it is a never ending time of suffering, that would be a veritable hell. It is when we are living a life of happiness that we seek to extend that experience into eternity. So again, it all comes to the *now*. The experience of enjoying life *now* by identifying with values that can transcend the *now*. Of being so immersed in the spirit so that life is vibrant with happiness and fulfillment.

If the *now* is so important, one might ask, what is the value of even thinking about life after death? Lets just live in the *now* and forget about the afterlife, it's all speculation anyway. We'll find out after we get there, if it's real.

Much of the stories regarding continuous life are speculation. However, through extrapolation and fractal analogy we get something more than just fantasy. The elliptical insight of attaining eternal life as mentioned in the Introduction of this book is one. There are also records of those who have returned, if only for a brief time, such as Jesus. Also, very interesting are the various documents that were ostensibly dictated by celestial beings telling us in exacting detail the transformational process of eternal life. There are more insights on this subject scattered throughout this book.

But why? Why do we need to know?

Creatures are fascinating, we like to move. Even plants move by growing upward. We like to move and we like to know where we are going. By knowing where we are going we can determine what we should do in the here and now. By knowing that we are on an evolutionary path from animals to humans to spirit, our present lives have more meaning and value. For many, it seems futile to live a life that culminates in nothingness, an extinguishing of our consciousness forever. We want the values we have experienced here to extend out further beyond this life, to continue on increasingly, and the idea of eternal life keeps this hope alive in our hearts and our love of living more meaningful.

We humans are also gregarious and treasure our relationships with families and friends. It is not so much our individual deaths that make people sad but the death of our loved ones. The thought of an afterlife where we can once again meet up with those we had such good times with is comforting and provides solace. Therein lies the value of the belief in a continuous life, whether real or not. But regardless, life is for the living, life is for the now. And if eternal life is a fact, the path to it is in leading lives manifested by eternal values. *Now*.

The End of the Beginning

It is only when we come face to face with death that we start living. It is only when we realize that we will be getting off our initial vehicle, the mortal body, that we truly start to realize the significance and value of life. This could happen in a moment of terror, such as on a battlefield, or through an automobile accident, an illness or other similar incidents. Or it could happen gradually, with moments of clarity brought on by insight. Those moments change our lives and makes us more philosophical, but it is when we begin to have a deep inner realization of the life we have spent, the relationship with our loved ones, the fulfilling accomplishments, the appreciation of the good times, the lessons we learned from the bad times, and the totality of the shape that our lives took, that we begin to understand what life is truly about. When we start to live for the quality of time that we spend with each other, rather than the amount of material we can accrue, or how much better than others we can appear to be; when we start to live for the quality of time we spend with ourselves, in the moments of quietness, reflection and meditation; when we start to live for the quality of time we spend with our Creator in love, worship and oneness; this is when the fullness of eternity in our lives have begun to manifest in the now. And by spending this quality time more and more, we begin to think of death, not as an ending but a beginning. Death becomes not an association with the past, but an association with the future. When we begin to live lives in the now, in the fullness of every day's sunrise, there are no regrets, for we have squeezed every ounce of life in each second, in each minute, in each hour, in each day, in each week, in each month, in each year of life, so that there is no hesitation to move on. When such fullness becomes manifest, we are happy and joyful of the life we have led and are leading, glad that it happened and ready to venture forth onto the next ride. It is only when our lives are unfulfilled, when we have regrets, when we spend time doing things not of the essence, when our relationships are incomplete, that we are grief stricken on thinking about death, whether it is our own or of someone we love. And it is by completing our lives, following the leadings of the spirit, to have more quality of relationships rather than quantity of material, to appreciate each and every person and experience, that we truly start to live.

It is unfortunate many people do not start to appreciate life until they have a close encounter with death, or have been inflicted with pain and suffering. It seems in that regard, in that it confronts people with reality and the errors in their thinking, that pain and suffering is beneficial to spurring on spiritual growth. But once a person gets beyond the initial stage, it is not the only way to spiritual evolution.

Perfection

Perfection is not just a goal, it is also a state of being.

From the eternal viewpoint, we are perfect. We are whole, complete, fulfilled, replete and optimized. By experiencing and being one with this perspective in the here and now, we can turn our lives into lives of relative perfection, overcome disease, attain self-mastery, and become embodiments of material and spiritual health, prosperity, and achievement. We experience this transcendental state by becoming more and more one with the divine spirit within, the still, small voice, the Christ Consciousness, the Thought Adjuster, the brahman, the true self.

From the viewpoint of the transient material self, many people perceive themselves as being imperfect. But being imperfect does not mean that they are faulty, lacking in essential parts, or in error. Being imperfect just means that they have not yet fulfilled their full potential. A child is perfect as a child but imperfect and incomplete as an adult. Imperfection is relative perfection. So realize that you are not imperfect but perfect in relation to who and what you are at this time. As we grow, we are relatively perfect in our stage of growth, for everything is happening perfectly for us to learn and transform ourselves.

But there is a danger to thinking of ourselves as being absolutely perfect when our perfection is only relative, which is that we can become too content and laid back, expecting things to happen without making an effort. Effort must always be joined with faith. This idea that we are absolutely perfect in the here and now is a misconception common among New Age aficionados. If we are absolutely perfect spiritual beings now, why do we need to work toward anything? Why do we need to eat? Why do we need a car? Why do we need shelter and clothing? Why do we feel pain and discomfort? If we are indeed absolutely perfect, we wouldn't need or feel any of those things.

We are not absolutely perfect until we have reached our highest state of spiritual evolution. Being absolutely perfect means that all the factors leading to optimization in time and space have culminated into a totality of completeness and repleteness. When we are absolutely perfect, we have no more room for improvement. The Creator, the First Source and Center, is absolutely perfect.

This source of absolute perfection is accessible through the divine spirit within us. The more we are able to maintain the consciousness of this spirit in our daily lives, the more we manifest perfection. The more we are one with the spirit in everything we do, the better our lives are: happier, more prosperous, healthier, more compassionate, more skillful, more artistic, more inspired, more charitable, of more service and just simply more divine. Our relative perfection will become even more perfect. Our growth and learning process will become joyful and fun, without having to suffer pain as a consequence of guilt, shame, anger, intolerance and hatred – poisons of the mind.

Once we have achieved the oneness of mind with the indwelling spirit within and have felt the presence of God, we can build on this until the presence is felt in every activity we do in every moment of our lives. As this eternal presence becomes manifest, every obstacle of mind, body and soul will be removed until the way is clear for total oneness with the divine spirit. Now, we're talking about a mega-transformation here. Shooting for the moon. It's something that we all have the potential for, but which most of us will not achieve in this life, but if we did, it might mean that such a fusion of soul and spirit will make the material body unnecessary. It is conceivable that we will be able to enter the next stage without the experience of mortal death, as far fetched as it may seem.

But why not? We are material creatures on the precipice of spirituality. We are megamorphs, children of the universe on the threshold of a quantum transformation.

Chapter Three
Know Your Neighborhood

Though inland far we be,
Our souls have sight of that immortal sea...

-William Wordsworth

To what distant lands will our spiritual progress and transformations take us? To what unexplored realms will we travel as we rove through the length, depth and breadth of spiritual dimensions?

As the Person navigates its way through various dimensions, it would be beneficial to know the terrain, the universe within which we act out our personal lives. What is the working shape of the universe? What is the composition of the road upon which we travel? We can know who we are, where we came from and where we'd like to go, but we must also know something about our surroundings, the world and universe, how it works, and how we fit in. This chapter deals with three aspects of our environment and how best to interact with them: I. The Universe II. Relationships with Others and III. Relationship with Ourselves.

I. The Universe

One can look at the universe as a whole, or one can look at it piece by piece. One can look at it spiritually or one can look at it materially. One can deal with it pragmatically or idealistically. One can use science and linear logic to understand the universe or one can use religion and faith. What is the best way to deal with the universe? What is the shape and form of the universe? In speaking of the shape of the universe, I am not talking about the physical dimensions, but rather the universe's mode of existence characterized with identifiable features that can be used to understand and manipulate our place in it to a certain degree.

The Elliptical Universe

In going back to the analogy of the automobile, it is as if we are driving a four wheel drive vehicle off-road across an unknown continent to a hazy, unclear destination. We do not have a map, no highways nor a clear-cut road. We must navigate using both our linear faculties like our five senses and logical deduction *plus* our non-linear senses such as intuition, faith, insight and the compass of our divine spark. We use our five senses to navigate by the sun and stars, and by observation and logical thinking, but we must also use our faith, insights and intuitional leadings. Our body, mind and soul is the vehicle and the universe is the terrain we must negotiate.

Originally, humans only had magic, the precursor to religion. We did not have enough knowledge to be able to think scientifically; even simple theories in logic had not been formed. To early man the universe was an unknowable place, and magic and religion was what we used to comprehend it.

After mathematics, logic and the scientific method was formulated, humans began to understand the universe with linear thinking. There was a cause and effect for everything and the logic of science was the key to the mysteries of the world. Mathematics and science became the new way of looking at things.

If a spiritually minded person were to pick a shape to describe how the universe works, a circle may be the logical choice, as a circle encompasses everything within it, and reflects faith in the whole of existence. A scientist may use the shape of a straight line, reasoning that things can best be understood sequentially, cause and effect following itself in linear order as in science. However, in my experience, the conceptual shape of the universe that describes not only its physical but also its spiritual aspects appear not to be either one, a circle or a line, but a combination of the two, it is elliptical. This is an awareness that may not be the same for all, and yet it is obvious if one can open up to the reality that surrounds us, to the reality that we are. The universe is both material and spiritual. It can only be understood using methods that are both science based and faith based. And an elliptical philosophy is a good tool to have in traveling through an elliptical universe.

Elliptic Philosophy

Living life in this world is quite puzzling. We are faced with our material needs (food, shelter, clothing, stimuli) yet we still have to deal with our thoughts (what is right and wrong, our political ideas, our ethics) and our spiritual leadings (our relationship with God, our values, our relationship to the universe). How can we manage to reconcile these things, especially when they are often seemingly in conflict ? What is the best philosophy to have that puts everything in order in our minds so that we can live life in the most fulfilling way?

Reasoning or Feelings?

To base all our life decisions on intellectual reasoning or to act according to our feelings; these are two ways of doing things that may be diametrically opposite. How to reconcile these two? Rational or emotional? They both work at times and at times they both do not work.

Intellectual reasoning works except when the basic assumptions behind the reasoning is not sound. Acting according to our feelings works except when the basic process does not reflect the facts.

For example: To maintain that everything that happens to us is by chance or actualized by what we do, that is, sheer effort, physical cause and effect, assumes that reality is mechanistic and material with no spiritual source. If this basic assumption is not correct, then the reasoning is also not correct and any action taken as a result of this assumption will not be optimum.

To maintain that there is a benevolent God or mystical force that looks after our welfare and that happiness is more than material and achieved by doing his/her/its will assumes that there is such a God. If this assumption is not correct, then the process does not reflect reality and will not work.

In both cases, we test the assumption by making decisions and acting upon them and seeing if the desired results follow, if it does, then there is a high degree of possibility that the assumption is correct. If it doesn't we can safely say that the assumption is probably not correct.

Neither of the two methods seem to work well enough for everybody. However, the most effective philosophy seems to be that we partake of both of them to some degree. This is the elliptic method.

If we assume that God (or the Source) is Love, that this underlying value motivates everything initially, but that reasoning and effort is necessary to implement and actualize what we want to do, then we take the best of both methods. We value the scientific method of using reasoning as a way of staying true to the facts: material reality. At the same time, we recognize the importance of the initial value in trying to achieve more than a material result, a spiritual goal; that whatever we are trying to achieve cannot happen unless we see a spiritual value in it. This value is the beginning and end of all our actions, and this absolute value that determines our personal reality is best described as love, or God.

So, to do the "will of God" means that we are following our basic motivation, the basic love within us that moves us to live, to do what we want to do. And if we follow this *value*, this desire, we will find the right *reasoning* and make the best *effort* to achieve our goals. More and more, I see people doing this, and the reason they are doing it is because it works, and if it works, the basic assumption is probably correct.

When it doesn't work, it is often because we lose faith in our reasoning or we lose the reason for our faith and give in to emotional feelings. Feelings are not the same as values. Nor is it the same as faith. Faith is to have trust in our underlying value of love. Faith is more than emotion, it is spiritual centered-ness, oneness with our basic inner values of love (God). Emotional feelings, impulse and physical urges are not based on this central value, it is but a momentary whim, a distraction caused by a lack of focus on the three motivating factors of love, intelligence and action. All three are necessary to have a good handle on reality. One follows the other. If you are not making the *effort*, it is because you don't have a good *reason* to do so, or even if you come up with a reason, it is not good enough to make you *act* because the reasoning is merely intellectual and not based on motivating love. Also, by maintaining focus on our prime motivating source, the *love* within and its offsprings: *reasoning and effort*, we can avoid being distracted by emotional feelings such as fear and circumstantial momentum (inertia) that can derail us. Essentially, when dealing with people, goodness, truth, beauty, spirituality and aesthetics, i.e.; quality, you must *feel* it. When dealing with machines, numbers, organizations, structures, and material things; quantity, you must *reason* it out.

To have a philosophy that really works in our lives, we have to understand the true nature of reality, otherwise we base our life on illusion. Because science is still incomplete, and religion is riddled with dogma and superstitions, humankind's attempt at philosophy has been insufficient to deal with the uncertainties and mysteries of life. The metaphysical attempt at bridging the gap between the worlds of matter and spirit, when tried without revelation is confusing and largely a failure. Because mankind lacks the concepts that merges religion and science, it needs revelation to enable metaphysics to effectively construct a working philosophy of the universe. Revelation is the only technique that makes up for the conceptual data which people need in arriving at a satisfying integration of the seemingly dual nature of the universe into a singular reality.

Most people have not bridged the gulf between the physical and the spiritual. The reason is because they do not have a clear idea of the true nature of reality. When philosophy leans heavily toward the world of matter, it becomes rationalistic or naturalistic. When philosophy inclines particularly toward the spiritual level, it becomes idealistic or even mystical. When philosophy leans upon metaphysics without the benefit of revelation, it becomes confused. In the past, most of man's knowledge and intellectual evaluations have fallen into one of these three distortions of perception. Philosophy would be illusory if it interprets reality with the linear fashion of logic or with the wholistic way of mysticism. For philosophy to accurately reflect the true state of the universe, it must be able to perceive the elliptic symmetry of reality and all relation concepts as being curved.

People who think linearly are those who are predominantly left-brained: scientists, technicians and mathematicians; they see everything happening as a result of a mechanical and material process; two plus two equals four and so on. This idea of reality says that life is more or less determined by our logical thoughts and mechanistic actions.

Those who are predominantly right-brained such as mystics, visionaries and religionists see reality differently. They see reality as a whole, encompassing the beginning, the end and all of creation. This idea of reality is based on faith, taking it as given that the totality of the universe in space and time is not understandable or comprehensible to humans and will remain a mystery, which means that our own fate cannot be self-determined and must be dependent on the grace of a universal Creator.

Most people's philosophy is based on their perception of reality as being one or the other, and they are both distorted. The mystic who sees reality as being purely spiritual has a philosophy that is often removed from the mechanisms of the physical world while the scientist who sees reality as being merely a "thing" has a philosophy that is mechanical and material and ignores the spiritual aspects of life. Because we are dualistic, material and spiritual, most people have conflicts between their animal nature and their divine nature. Animals are bellicose and self-centered as well as possessing other animalistic habits while the divine nature is loving, self-forgetful and unifying. People spend their whole lives learning how to deal with the conflicts inherent in such a combination of natures and try to create their own personal philosophy that can effectively resolve the two opposing forces. Such a philosophy can only be effective if guided by revelation.

Revelation comes in many forms. It could arrive as a book. Many books have revelatory information in it, however, the information may be useful only to those who can see that particular perspective and are ready for it. The same information may not be suitable for everyone. You can verify its accuracy by applying it to your daily life to see if it reconciles the dualistic nature within yourself. If the information in the book enables you to create an elliptic philosophy that tackles and resolves the issues in your life, you have found a source of revelatory information that works for you.

Another source of revelatory information is personal (auto-revelation), and comes through worshipful meditation, prayer and service. Through these processes, the spirit fills you with insights that gives you an understanding of the dynamics of the elliptic universe and how to combine seamlessly the linear and mystical aspects of your life.

An elliptic philosophy would not be so much a balance but a merging (or morphing) of the linear and non-linear with help from revelatory information; converting dualism into a singularism. To say that we must balance the physical and spiritual in our lives tends to polarize the two and is different from morphing the physical and spiritual. In other words, we can spend time doing something physical and balance it by doing something spiritual, but this is not the same as seamlessly merging the physical and spiritual in everything we do. To use a food metaphor, one can have carrots, potatoes and meat and eat them separately and still get a balance of the nutrients that they contain. However, if we merge them together to make a stew, we get something new that is better than the sum of its parts. Elliptic philosophy is the stew. To eat the ingredients separately would be just as nutritionally sound as eating them cooked together, but a delicious stew would be hearty – it would feed the soul as well as the body.

So what are good examples of a philosophy based on the elliptical symmetry of reality?

Jesus' parables are wonderful expressions of elliptic philosophy. Jesus knew perfectly well the elliptical symmetry of reality when he began teaching in parables. The linear approach didn't work and he was not a mystic so he merged the rationalistic and the spiritualistic into a story, which is an art, really. And true art is a display of elliptic philosophy, a merging of the duality in man, the material; and man, the spiritual.

Another example of elliptic philosophy would be the following lines of wisdom from thinking men and women that came before us. Notice that most of them have some sort of paradoxical element in them which merge the material and spiritual. For instance:

○ *The greatest affliction of the cosmos is never to have been afflicted. Mortals only learn wisdom by experiencing tribulation.*

○ *Stars are best discerned from the lonely isolation of experiential depths, not from the illuminated and ecstatic mountain tops.*

Both of the above reconciles the pain of earthly existence with the rewards of spiritual insight.

Lao Tse's philosophy also is a good example of awareness of elliptic symmetry of reality. He wrote in the Tao Te Ching:

○ *Goodness begets goodness, but to the one who is truly good, evil also begets goodness.*

The above reveals the transcendent and everlasting reality of goodness as opposed to the transitory nature of evil.

○ *The Tao that can be understood is not the eternal Tao. The God that is named is not the eternal being.*

And this above points to the existential nature of true reality and the illusions of labels: names are not the thing itself.

The above examples beautifully merge the material and temporal with the eternal and spiritual. They are all somewhat logical and follow a linear path but twists upon itself in a paradoxical way that encompasses spiritual reality so that what we have is not linear or circular but elliptical.

Elliptic philosophy is very pertinent to solving daily life problems which is a part of the paradox of living in a material body while being indwelt by a divine spark. But this philosophy would not answer a given question with a solely material or spiritual answer, but would rather juxtapose the relationships between the body and spirit in such a way as to reconcile the seeming conflicts harmoniously.

For instance, people are always asking why they have to suffer in life. There has been many attempts at answering this question. The linear, materialistic answer might be that the world is a naturally harsh place and that the only way to survive is by pure strength of arm and keenness of thought. The spiritual, idealistic answer could be that only God knows and that we should have faith in whatever mysterious plans she has for us.

The above philosophies are based on distorted ideas of reality. But an elliptical answer to this question of the necessity of suffering would be:

The greatest affliction of the cosmos is never to have been afflicted. Mortals only learn wisdom by experiencing tribulation.

The above sentences seamlessly merge the idea that the problems in life lead directly to spiritual growth. It answers the question of the purpose of afflictions by making it the price of wisdom.

If we can fashion a personal philosophy that reflects the shape of elliptical reality, it would be ideal for coping with the seeming contradictions and paradoxes of life. Such a philosophy would be one more step toward self-mastery.

Elliptical reality is everywhere and self-evident, and yet most people don't understand it. The reason for this is that people try to figure out elliptical reality using linear reasoning. They live in the conceptual framework of cause and effect and cannot see that one can have both simultaneously. One such case is the phrase now becoming popular in New Age circles that humans are not material beings having a spiritual experience but spiritual beings having a material experience. Elliptically, we are beings that are both material and spiritual having experiences that partake of both realties at the same time.

Some scientists are saying something similar when they postulate that it is not the brain causing consciousness but consciousness giving rise to the brain. Elliptic philosophy would say that the brain and consciousness are simultaneous manifestations of cause and effect. People are so stuck in the concept that one must have cause before one can have effect that they do not see that in the total reality of time, space, and spirit, cause and effect is one and the same. There are some Buddhist thoughts that reflect this.

The Elliptic View

From Singularity To Duality To Tri-Unity

Most of the problems we face as individuals and as a collective are caused by polarized extremism—a dualistic viewpoint of reality. The polarized views of secular materialism versus religious mysticism causes problems in health, prosperity, relationships, security and inner peace. From environmental degradation to conflicts in personal relationships, from individual illnesses to dysfunctions of the community, these problems all stem from a skewed and imbalanced approach to seeing and understanding what universe reality is all about.

The linear, scientific minded materialistic viewpoint has produced a philosophy of material accumulation—where happiness is dependent on the amount and quality of our material possessions. War, pollution, and poverty from an imbalanced economy are some of the results.

The extreme religious and mystical viewpoint has engendered magical thinking, ignoring the fundamental facts, the "nuts and bolts", of the material side of life. This has resulted in intolerance, impractical idealism, persecution, condemnation, insecurity, ignorance, self-righteousness, backwardness, and religious wars.

What the world needs is a philosophy that can turn these dualistic tendencies into a coherent and cohesive whole. This wholeness is achieved by adding a third factor that balances dualistic tendencies into a trinity: the personal aspect. Dualism is actually an illusion as the viewpoint of the person perceiving the dualism must be included, which makes true reality a tri-unity.

Chart of Elliptic Reality

Polarized Dualities	Personal Viewpoint Creates A Trinity that unifies Duality into a Whole	Polarized Dualities
Being	Personal Intent	Doing
The Whole	Personal Awareness	The Part
Eternity	Mindfulness & Purpose	Now
Creator	Co-Creator	Creature
Spirit	Soul	Mind
Intuitive	Creative	Intellectual
Religion	Personal Philosophy	Science
Values	Meanings	Things

May The Qi Be With You!

Linear thinking is the way of science. Mystical thinking is the way of religion. Soul wisdom is the stuff of experience talking. Elliptical thinking is the way of manifesting all together, the part, the whole and the middle.

Elliptical thinking is not just thinking. It is a simultaneous occurrence of being and doing. All aspects are expressed, polarities balanced, thought and action seamlessly merged in body, mind and soul, matter and spirit.

Another way of understanding elliptical philosophy is by saying that it is implied. When addressing an issue one can go directly to the point, or conversely skirt around it and never get to the point. Scientific and linear thinking gets to the point and tackles the issue head on. Mystical and non-linear thinking takes things as a whole and encompasses the totality of the issue, not settling on pointed details. Elliptical thinking implies the point by taking into account the whole, and curving around the issue before settling upon it. A good example would be artistic works. An accomplished poet or a song writer does not get into detailed explanations but rather brings up words that imply the point. Sometimes one is not quite sure what the writer is saying, but one understands within one's soul, the point is received. It is the same with a painting. Too much detail and one might as well have a photograph. If it is too abstract, it becomes mystical and the point is lost. Most outstanding works of art are all elliptical, the point is there but it is implied.

In using revelatory information from personal as well as from various sources, many individuals have experimented with methods of manipulating reality that are elliptical. Just as practices that became the scientific method had been around a long time before it was actually put down in writing and used methodically, elliptical philosophy has been used for a long time, but its methodology is not well known to much of the world and its potential is largely untapped.

To simplify, elliptical philosophy is the effective and coordinated technique of using *faith* and *effort* in our daily lives, but that is an over-simplification for it is a lot more than that, as we shall see. The old school theologians and philosophers used to debate which is more important: faith or good works. It's obvious: faith is all we need to enter the kingdom of heaven but good works (effort) is necessary once we get in, to go further in our journey to perfection.

Now, I don't want to get into some kind of theologic or scriptural debate here. All we have to do is to look at faith and effort in our lives. In every worthwhile endeavor that I've done, or was done by anyone that I've known personally or in books, there was always faith, even if it was simply faith in ourselves that we could do it, which powered the endeavor, and then it was effort that made it come to fruition (with faith constantly shoring it up).

That means that we can't just proclaim our faith once and then forget about it. Faith must be affirmed and maintained in every moment of our lives. We must constantly re-affirm our wills to the universal will in order to keep our faith from faltering. Success in every endeavor requires faith. Effort and good works cannot be maintained in the long haul without faith. It is faith that enables us to venture out into unknown realms, to risk everything for our goals. This is faith that is universal and is accessed at times by everyone, some more than others, even those that are not religious have this faith.

Even a materialist scientist who does not believe in God has faith; faith in science or in himself. But faith does come from a spiritual source! Faith is to believe based on spiritual evidence within our souls; to follow the wisdom of the soul in spite of other material evidence to the contrary.

Faith and effort must both be persistent, reliable, continuous, regular and truly meant for any endeavor to succeed consistently. Effort is linear, faith is mystical. The linear is fueled by the mystical. Effort cannot happen without faith. Unless you think you can do it, unless you have faith that you can do it, you're not going to succeed when met with disappointments and setbacks. With a strong and persistent faith, the effort is also strong and persistent. This joint operation, this melding of the spiritual and physical by the mind unites the spirit and energy/matter seamlessly into action. Then faith becomes action because it is only through our actions that we can reveal faith. Faith without effort is an illusion, a fantasy; effort without faith is hollow, powerless.

The problem with some previous explorations of using faith and effort is that they could not explain how faith and effort can become a seamless force. Nor did they fashion a new word or a new terminology that incorporated these two things into a synergistic new idea. But there are exceptions.

We had faith, and then we put out effort, or we put out effort and had faith that it would work. It was proto-elliptical philosophy. But there were some people who did figure out how to work with faith and effort seamlessly and they led very amazing lives because of it. They were pioneers that formulated practical methods which could be followed by most everyone such as the techniques in the New Thought movement exemplified by the likes of Ernest Holmes, author of Science of Mind, originally titled Science of Mind and Spirit. His approach to elliptical philosophy was from the scientific and linear standpoint, otherwise his book would have been titled Spirit of Science and Mind. Christian D. Larson who wrote the Pathway To Roses was also an inspired New Thought author. His approach was not so linear but was more Christian oriented. These Western thinkers had exceptional insights, and their explanations were for the Western mindset.

From the East, the traditions of Hinduism has been integrated with western medicine by Deepak Chopra and David Simon and should be noted for their elliptic approach, harmonizing practical knowledge with inner principals, transcending dualism into a singular approach. Their success in enlightening the peoples of the world is surely a sign of the efficacy of their methods.

The process of coming up with a way to effectively merge seamlessly the energies of faith and effort was also approached in the East by sages such as Lao Tsu and Gautama Siddhartha. Since they came from the non-linear mystical standpoint, their writings are often very cryptic to the Western mind but their ideas evolved through the ages and by virtue of the many anonymous souls which came after them, there resulted from Eastern thought something that is quite unique. This is the dynamic energy that is known as chi, ki, or qi (pronounced ki). Known also as prana in ayurvedic medicine, qi is the energy of faith and effort seamlessly united and exists everywhere. Qi is used to heal, it is used in martial arts, it is used in business, it is used in everyday life to vitalize, energize, actualize and better our basic life condition. George Lucas has even popularized qi in the Star Wars films by referring to it as The Force. But qi is not fiction, qi is real.

In explanation, one must first understand faith and effort. Faith, taken from a purely humanistic standpoint, is the supreme assertion of human thought. Faith in God is the supreme assertion of our oneness with God; our love of God, our trust in God, our personal relationship with God, the First Source and Center of All.

Effort/action is not merely the outworking of physical activities. Thought/mind and effort/action are one and the same, merely different manifestations of the same thing, just as it is with matter and energy. *The Urantia Book* also describes the Infinite Spirit (known by Christians as the Holy Spirit) as the God of Action and the source of all mind. And Buddhist thought says that cause and effect are actually one and the same also, the relationship between thought and action usually being understood as that of cause and effect. Mind you, these are non-linear concepts and cannot be understood by linear thinking.

An important part of effort/action is the imagination, the mental power within our minds to create. Even Einstein said knowledge is limited while imagination is infinite. Imagination is not just flights of fancy but the ability to create reality with the mind, not just in the mind, but also in external reality, as what is imagined often becomes reality.

So physical energy plus spiritual faith times imagination results in activating qi:

**Accessing Qi = Physical Energy + Spiritual Faith x Imagination
(or Effort/Stamina plus Faith/Spirituality times Mind/Creativity)**

When effort and faith is multiplied by mind we are in contact and in unity with the whole of existence.

It often first happens when we engage in deep worshipful meditation and can be carried out in every moment of existence. It is being superconscious and unified with the Creator and with the universe in all of time and space. When we are one with God and the universe, we take the viewpoint of God and the universe and feel his presence. And this profound spiritual experience results in faith. But in order to direct this force out in the material world, we must have physical and mental stamina. Stamina is not strength. A skinny runner may have more stamina than a muscle bound weight lifter, even if the weight lifter may have more strength. Stamina, in a sense, is the amount of will as embodied in the person. Taken all together, this combination of mindal creative effort multiplied by the infinite and powered by faith and directed by our physical and mental stamina results in a new dynamic force, the qi.

However, reducing an elliptical force into a linear formula just does not convey the fullness of its reality. It is like trying to express a beautiful work of art using mathematics. It can be done but much is lost. Using poetry to express qi works much better:

Qi

Relax.
Connect to the Source.
Be One and be All.
Feel within, feel without
The Energy.
Now dig deep and stream
from the Center
to the outside.

Qi works because when we become one with the supreme mind of the universe, using the power of imagination and faith, we become one with the Supreme's overcontrol of the universe. Just as we can control our own bodies to a degree, we can gain more control of the universe around us. This is also known as power/personality synthesis. Of course, there are things even within our bodies that we cannot control, such as the fact that we must eat, defecate, breathe, sleep, etc., and likewise our control of our part of the universe is also limited. But it is possible to gain more control in both the macro and micro universes by getting to know more intimately what makes things work. Physical and mental stamina resulted in science and technology which is the way we learned how to manipulate the material parts of the universe. Strength of imagination and the power of faith works on the mindal and spiritual realities. The seamless merging of those aspects results in elliptical technology. And it is reflected in the now and in the All. We refer back to the fractal concept again; the eternal that is realized here and now is fractally represented in all of time, space and eternity. What is in *eternity* is fractally represented in the *here* and *now*. One does not happen before the other, as cause and effect are the same and happens simultaneously.

But qi is not just an ethereal mental force. We make it work by manifesting it through our bodies. It has often been used in healing by the laying on of hands, in martial arts by the strengthening of physical and mental power, and in self-control and self-healing by having the qi course through one's body. Because it is an elliptical force, it is not measurable by any known scientific instrument at this time, in a sense qi is not applied but implied, it is inferred by association with divinity. Being elliptical it is also not purely mystical in that it is not faith healing. It is a tangible force that affects reality, just not in either a mystical or scientific way, but seamlessly consisting of both: it is elliptical. And since qi is so dependent on the oneness of mind between us and the Creator/universe, qi will not work to further something that is only of one person's desires if it is not within the framework of universal values. That is why qi can be used for healing, empowerment of the one and the whole, bettering relationships, and other goals that further the relationship of the One with the All. Even in martial arts, qi is used for self-defense and not for personal gain or for getting an unfair advantage over others.

Qi is not a magical force. It is not a substitute for experience, skill, intelligence or ability. However, with qi, one can get a fuller experience, a more finely honed skill, a sharper intelligence and better ability.

To use the power of qi, get into the consciousness of being one with the All and have absolute faith that your endeavor will succeed. Do not apply this force with the strength of the arm, but imply it with the strength of the whole body. Do not *apply* it with the desire of one person but ***imply*** it with the desire of the whole universe. Do not *apply* it with the force of the one but ***imply*** it with the force of the All. Because qi is not a power that originates from the person but rather through association with God, the person is just an instrument. That is why focusing on yourself breeds separation, stiffness and tension, and it leaches strength and power. Focusing on the All unifies us, relaxes us, comforts us, and it taps into unlimited strength and power.

The center of qi in the human body is not in the brain, it is in the *tan tien*, or the point just below one's navel and toward the base of the spine. This is the center of gravity of the human body and the focal point for the mind used in alternative medicine and in some martial arts. By relaxing and letting the whole weight of the body rest on this nexus, one can tap into the source of this power.

Whereas philosophy and religion can only deal in the mindal and spiritual aspects of life, elliptic techniques are able to actually manipulate all things, meanings and values in life in the respective fields of science, health, finances, ethics, the arts and personal/spiritual relationships. It is a system of asserting control of true reality through dynamic and effective processes based on the accurate perception and knowledge of elliptical reality. However, the proof is in the pudding, and words are meaningless unless the technique or process can attain profound results repeatedly and at will. Qi is one of the puddings. It has shown that it can work but its potential is still largely untapped and unfulfilled. By knowing how qi works we can tap into its potential to bring about changes in personal and public life that will indeed be profound. In essence, using the qi is an art form, as is evident by watching a tai chi master going through her moves.

When mind unites spirit and energy/matter seamlessly, we see this displayed in our lives because the result becomes a work of art. In this life, it is only in our souls and in art that we see an even mix of both the material and spiritual. So a life based on elliptical philosophy and elliptical techniques such as using the qi would be well-suited in mastering the art of life.

Vitruvian Man

Humankind has long tried to reconcile the dualistic nature of existence; the material and spiritual aspects of life in the universe. It is said that Leonardo Da Vinci attempted to correlate these two natures with this drawing of the *Vitruvian Man*, the square symbolizing the material and the circle symbolizing the spiritual. The drawing itself is often used as an implied symbol of the essential symmetry of the human body, and by extension, to the universe as a whole. Vitruvian Man remains one of the most referenced and reproduced artistic images in the world today. This may be because people innately recognize the inherent truths of the universe contained in this drawing, as it reflects fractal theory, the golden ratio and elliptic philosophy on different levels.

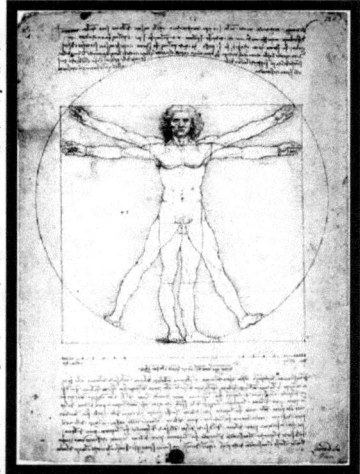

Fractal properties in the human form can be seen in the fact that there are five extensions to the torso: the four limbs and the head, with five digits on each limb and the five senses of the head, (although the sense of feeling is also in other parts of the body.).

The **golden ratio** is reflected in the proportions of the *ideal* human body, as seen on the chart of the divine proportion on the other page. Since there are no universal set of proportions that pertain to each body, the golden ratio is implied here.

Elliptic philosophy can be seen in the circle and square, an attempt at depicting the material and spiritual nature of life. If one were to merge these two geometric shapes into one, the result would be an ellipse. When humankind views the spiritual and material separately, the result is a distortion of true reality.

Science cannot provide evidence of the spiritual. Religion, on the other hand, cannot objectively manipulate the material. It is only when we realize that true reality is elliptical in nature, both spiritual and material, that we can create a philosophy that can effectively negotiate the many challenges of life and fulfill the potentials of body, mind and soul. Attempts in the past have been more of a balancing act, counter weighing one deed with the other. True elliptical philosophy would *seamlessly* merge the two, creating acts that would be neither purely material or spiritual, but both. True art is such a merging.

Life As Art

To live life as an art. To master the art of life. What does that mean?

True art is derived from inspiration. It is not a linear diagram or something based on a blueprint like an architectural drawing. The artist may not even know what the final work may look like as inspiration could come in at any moment to influence the progress of the art.

The lives of all great spiritual leaders were works of art. They had a purpose for living life as a human but did not pre-plan every second in order to achieve that purpose. They did not have a blueprint for life that they followed to the letter. Rather, they constantly listened to the leadings of the Creator as they went along with their daily activities, changing and adjusting their ways and methods as needed. They were flexible and receptive, rarely asserting the thoughts and plans of the human mind over the Creator's. The lives that they led are truly great works of art, filled with light and darkness, with joy and sorrow, peopled with a cast showing friendship and betrayal, love and hatred, truth and error.

Of course, their lives may not be something that we would like to emulate. And we do not have to. Their lives were unique expressions and manifestations of their role as avatars of God and they artistically expressed their personality and mission.

We, as ascending mortals, each have what we want to express. And as co-creators of our art form, the story of our lives, we have some say-so as to how much darkness and how much light we wish to shine onto the stage of our lives. We are able to choose, to a great extent, the amount of joy, sorrow, love and conflict we display in the art form of life that we lead daily. We can participate with God in co-creating our selves, for we are ascending beings in all our beauty, agony, love and travails. But realize that the pattern of the art form has already been set to synchronize with all the other players in this cosmic drama. The part that you play must fit in with the overall scheme of things.

Realize that the script of your story in the fulfillment of your eternal career was written by the infinite author, God. The story is a good one, as God is a masterful storyteller. And have faith and be assured that it is a better story than one that you could possibly imagine. However, God decided to give you a voice in how the story unfolds, a chance to do a bit of improvisation, if you will. You can, through your own efforts change the story to a certain degree, but don't go crazy. Unfortunately, there are people who do not trust the way the story is unfolding so they decide to alter it drastically according to their own limited vision. This can lead to a tale of sorrow and darkness, a story that does not have a happy ending.

To avoid this do your inner work regularly so that you become one with the Creator connection within you, then you'll have a general idea of the story. And once you do, you will realize that all you have to do is to have faith in God and follow the script. Have fun, be creative but keep the improvisations to tasteful limits. Your happiness, prosperity and fulfillment is all written. As it is written, so shall it be.

II. Relationships With Others

What is the best way to relate to people? What is the "terrain" when it comes to personal relationships? Like the universe, people are elliptical: both mystical and logical, spiritual and material, scientific and religious. What is the best way to act toward others? A common concept that is espoused by most religions is the Golden Rule.

The Golden Rule and the Golden Ratio

Every wisdom tradition has its version of the Golden Rule that says: "Do unto others as you would have them do unto you."

Math and Science has what is known as the Golden Mean or the Divine Proportion which may go back as far as the Egyptians and was closely studied by the Greek sculptor, Phidias, hence, it was given the name Phi (pronounced fee). Also referred to as the Golden Mean, the Magic Ratio, the Golden

Constant, Golden Ratio, the Fibonacci Sequence, etc., phi can be found throughout the universe; from the spirals of galaxies to the spiral of a Nautilus seashell; from the harmony of music to the beauty in art. Psychologists have determined that phi plays a role in the human perception of beauty. The human body is said to have proportions close to the golden ratio. The Divine Proportion is evident in the very physical nature of Creation and can be seen as the truth, beauty, love, relationships and organization within the cosmos. It is literally the harmonizing and unifying rule that coordinates the physical unity of the universe.

The Golden Rule and the Golden Ratio are flip sides of the same universal coin; they define the living relationship of the individual to the social group and then to all of the universe (including oneself) - Universal Consciousness.

This is the divine concept that seamlessly merges the rational and the mystical, the linear and the circular, the symmetrical and asymmetrical, the scientific and the spiritual aspects of life into a comprehensive understanding of the true shape of elliptical reality and living relationships.

The Divine Proportion basically says:

"The smaller is to the larger as the larger is to the whole." Or

A_____B_____C_____A_____C
The space between A&B is to the space between B&C as the space between B&C is to the space between A&C .

This is reflected in the natural proportions inherent in some aspects of nature. It is also applied in mathematical proportions in architecture and the aesthetic proportions in art. When applied these proportions seem to be in harmony and pleasing to the eye. They have a sense of rightness.

It can also be applied to personal relationships:

A____(you)__B__(others)____C____A_____(all)_____C
    This is   to this, as this is   to this.

The relationship that *you* (AB) have with *others* (BC) is the same relationship that *others* (BC) have with the *All* (which includes you and others) (AC). This is a threefold relationship which includes *you, others,* and the *All*.

Others in this case refers to those people with whom you come in contact, the personalities that interact with you in your life as you go about doing your daily activities. The *All* is everybody and everything, even those you don't know and will never know.

It is important to note that the *All* (whole universe) includes *you*, so that what *others* give to the *All* comes back to *you* also. So what you do to *others* continues out to *All others* in the universe, *including yourself.* And this continues on exponentially in ever widening circles as you manifest the quality of the *All* towards your relationship with *others*. Indeed, this is how spiritual evolution ripples out to all created beings in the universe.

The misunderstanding that many have of the Golden Rule on this world at this present age makes it more a back and forth action like this:

A_____B_____C

The relationship that *you* (AB) have with *others* (BC) is the same relationship *others* (BC) have with *you* (AB). This is only a twofold relationship which includes only *you* and *others* with the *All* being left out of the picture. And it does not continue on exponentially and does little to enhance spiritual evolution universally.

In other words, *you* do to the *others* what the *others* do to *you*. "You stroke me and I'll stroke you." "Don't mess with me and I won't mess with you."

This is *not* the true meaning of the Golden Rule and is *not* reflected as a Golden Ratio. This line of thinking is bereft of spiritual insight and is reflective of base human emotions.

There was a film a few years before the time of this writing called *Pay It Forward*, which had a philosophical theme of doing good to others and making them promise to "pass it forward," that is, to do some good for somebody else as a direct result of the initial kindness. This is a good example of the application of the golden ratio in personal relationships.

The Golden Ratio shows the potential for the Golden Rule. What we give to the people we know in our lives goes out to the people they know, and as each person does this, the effect flows out in a cascading ripple effect to the *All*, and these things that we have initiated is reflected back to us in the circumstances of our lives and in the world. Rather than have a world where relationships are only between people who directly benefit from each other, this interpreting of the Golden Rule as the Golden Ratio describes a situation wherein everyone in the universe has good relationships with each other, whatever their personal assets.

The Golden Ratio illustrates the Golden Rule in that the proportional relationship that the individual has with *others* is the same proportional relationship that *others* have with the *All*. Since I am part of the *All*, what I get as part of the *All* is the same as what the *others* gave to the *All*, except that I receive it not directly to me, an individual, but as part of the grand whole. This creates a path of giving and receiving that is not one to one but encompasses everybody in the universe. And if for nothing else, that is a good reason to be good to others, to manifest divine love for all the people we come in contact with daily.

This can be seen as the love a parent might have for their children. A wise parent does not want their love to only be directly reciprocated to them, but also out to others. They want to do good for their kids so that their kids can do good to society and to the world and universe.

The hitch in actually doing this might seem that in manifesting love for *others*, a finite being, *you*, have to have the same perspective as the *All*, an eternal entity (God). Which means that one must equal infinity. ($1 = \infty$)

This may seem impossible in mathematics, but not quite. Using time as an example, we can split any second or moment in half, and then half it again, ad infinitum. So in any one finite moment, there is the potentiality of an infinite amount of time.

In spirituality, the finite human being has within the eternal divine spark, and by connecting with this inner source, one can achieve the eternal viewpoint—the love of our Creator.

So, phi, the Golden Rule and the Divine Proportion/Golden Ratio are indeed both sides of the same coin, looking at the harmony and order of the universe from both the linear, mathematical viewpoint and also from the mystical, spiritual side. An elliptical formula, if you will.

To live the true Golden Rule (or the Platinum Rule, as some would prefer to call it) one looks at the big picture from the eternal viewpoint. As more people begin to do this, the more profound the effect will be on our world.

The Golden Ratio or Divine Proportion

The **golden ratio**, also known as the **golden proportion, golden mean, golden section, golden number, divine proportion** or *sectio divina*, is an irrational number, approximately 1.618 033 988 749 894 848, that possesses many interesting properties.

Shapes proportioned according to the golden ratio have long been considered aesthetically pleasing in Western cultures, and the golden ratio is still used frequently in art and design, suggesting a natural balance between symmetry and asymmetry. The ancient Pythagoreans, who defined numbers as expressions of ratios (and not as units as is common today), believed that reality is numerical and that the golden ratio expressed an underlying truth about existence.

The golden ratio was first studied by ancient mathematicians because of its frequent appearance in geometry and may have even been understood and used as far back in history as the Egyptians. (From Wikipedia, the Free Encyclopedia)

Like the illustrations below, the golden ratio can be found in many aspects of nature and art. However, because natural forms and patterns offer such wildly random shapes, the ratios are approximate and will not sometimes fit each and every case, and even when they do, the results are open to interpretation and adjustments. This is because, like fractals, the pure mathematical form can exist as the ideal linear form, but when manifested in nature is influenced by the non-linear aspect of spirit, such as with art and aesthetics, which also cannot be governed by just the linear, mathematical form of phi. They are also greatly affected by the **golden rule**, the spiritual form of the golden ratio. The essence of true art is the inspiration, and inspiration is spiritual. In art, as with life, it is not so much the mathematically quantifiable precision of the numbers that matters as much as the quality; the relationship of the part to the group and to the whole—beauty. (See Chapter Four)

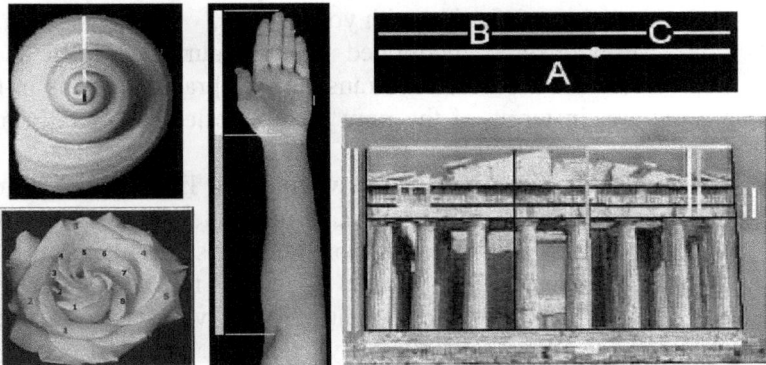

Photos and Graphics From GoldenNumber.Net

III.   Relationship With Ourselves

To propel our human vehicle, we must deal with the universe in which we work, play and live, we must interact with other people with whom we socialize and fellowship, and we must realize, actualize and master our self. In a sense, our self is a microcosm of the All, a fractal universe of its own that we inhabit. In order to master our selves, to drive this vehicle, we must know our own desires.

The Big Picture of Our Lives

What do we want in life? Not superficially, as in we want a life of comfort and enjoyable stimulation, but in the big picture of our lives, what is it that we truly want? If upon the completion of our allotted time here, we look back on our life, what is it that we would be satisfied with having accomplished? Would you die feeling happy if you had a lot of beautiful houses, cars and land? Would you die satisfied with your life if you had completed many works of an academic, artistic, social or spiritual nature? Or maybe your happiness would be contingent on the fulfillment of loving relationships, such as with your family and friends. Looking at life similarly now, what is it about your life you are satisfied with at this moment? And what more do you need to do to further your satisfaction with your life?

Previously, I mentioned that the purpose of life is to choose value. How does that translate into practical terms in the big picture, in terms of the now as it is reflected fractally into eternity?

I think most of us judge whether our life is worth living, its value, by how happy we are. Life may often seem to be filled with adversities and challenges, or life may seem like a bowl of cherries. The key word here is "seems," for it is often our perception that determines how we view the various circumstances that shape our daily existence. Many, if not all of our problems may be imaginary. So many people are distraught and stressed by things in the past and the future; things that have come and gone that are the focus of regret, guilt and shame, and also by things that may never happen; worries and fears of what may or may not come about. Basically, these things of the past and future are unreal in the now, they are not of the now and is a product of imagination. Of course, although they are not real in the present moment, they do affect us as we are now and we must consider their ramifications. We must learn from the lessons of the past and think of our actions now as they may be reflected in the future. For surely, ignoring the signs of the past and present can lead to an unwanted future. But we must not let the memories of the past and our prognostications of the future shape our lives so much that it leads to unhappiness, grief, and negative thinking. We must put the past and the future in perspective, realizing that it is the now that we inhabit. To learn from the lessons of the past, do we need guilt and shame? To bring about desirable things in the future, do we need to fret and worry? No. Through mindfulness of our past mistakes and a sincere willingness to change we can benefit from the errors of the past. Through realistic assessment of our present life coupled with ongoing dynamic and positive actions we can have good prospects for bringing about the desired future. Guilt, shame, fret and worry sap our energies and leads to negative thinking which in turn leads to negative results.

Happiness

When people are asked if they are happy about life in general, there is often a momentary pause, a period of introspection before replying. Of course, if they had just experienced a triumphant event such as in winning a medal in the Olympics or a large sum of money, they do not hesitate to respond in the affirmative. However, most people seem not to know if they are happy in any given moment of time.

What is happiness? Pure pleasure, ecstasy and unbridled joy we can understand and acknowledge during the moments when we are experiencing them. But what does it take to say that we are happy during times when nothing out of the ordinary is happening? For surely, that takes more than just the realization of the perception of invigorating and pleasurable stimuli, more than just the awareness of the present. It takes a certain amount of stillness, a certain amount of transcendence.

Is happiness freedom from want, from pain, stress, fatigue and discomfort? Not necessarily, for there are times when we can be tired, uncomfortable and even in pain and yet be happy. For example, after having accomplished a great deed such as in times of war, by being heroic during disaster, courageous under pressure, and after succeeding in a worthy goal such as in saving a life or helping the needy, we can still be happy regardless of our personal pain and discomfort. People can lose their limbs, their health and their fortunes, and yet be happy if they feel that their sacrifice was worth their loss.

Is happiness to be always ecstatic, constantly stimulated by activities and even drugs, alcohol and other substances? We all know that that is a dead-end street. There is no true happiness there.

True happiness comes from being of value, coupled with the awareness of that value. Without a sense of self-value, we can only consider ourselves worthless to the world, a life with no purpose or meaning. There can be no happiness in such a state. That is why there is nothing so offensive as when one's value is questioned, whether it's one's work or one's character in general.

But how does one value a person? How is a person valued in this world?

There is a perception by some that the value of a person lies in his material wealth. Because money is a measure of material value, the reasoning is that the more money one has, the more value there is in the person who has the money. Of course, it doesn't take long for that person to discover that people who seem to value him doesn't really, he's just there for the ride. There can be no happiness if there is no sense of personal value; he must be valued for what he is, not for what he has.

Some try to be of value by having power, the power to make or break others, the power to conquer countries, create empires, rule conglomerations and take over corporations. They think that if they are feared and respected, they are of value to the world. However, they come to realize, hopefully, that happiness come from being loved, not from being feared. Value comes from sharing freely, from being together in unity hand in hand, not from lording it over others, taking and conquering at will.

So how does one become a person who is truly valued? And to whom should we be valuable?

One can be valued by those immediately around us, and yet be hated and reviled by a larger group. A notable example is Hitler, who was loved and valued by his supporters and many people in his country during his time, and yet detested and condemned by the world ever since. And conversely, there are people who were persecuted by those around them and yet remain a paragon of virtue valued greatly for their teachings, across the world and throughout history, Jesus being a good example of that instance.

When the goal is temporal and material, one can achieve value in the immediate surroundings, ignoring the spiritual goals of eternity. People have done this many times, creating an empire of material wealth surrounded by fawning sycophants intent solely on enriching themselves and their friends, ignoring the plight of the sickly and destitute upon which they laid their stepping stones to opulence. They may be valued by their shallow friends but will have no lasting value in the larger picture of the world, the universe and of time. Do they have happiness? I don't think so.

To be truly happy, sometimes one has to go beyond the company of those who seek transient values. Perhaps not physically, for often they are everywhere, but in mind and soul. To do things of eternal value, rather than transient value, is the key to happiness. To act in the Now reflecting the timeless values of Eternity, to act as One for the enrichment of All is to be of supreme value, and in that lies supreme happiness. To know that one's life is of value to the entire universe in all of space and time is surely sufficient grounds to consider one's self happy.

But even in happiness, one can still weep for those who choose to wallow in the soul stunting ways of transient self-gratification. As we set our sights for the stars, there will be those around us who continue to grovel around in the mud. Try to help them, pray for them, but keep away from being sucked in by the sinking sands of transient lures. To gain true happiness and to fulfill our divine potentials, we must often leave our childhood toys, habits and friends. They'll be fine. Don't worry, be happy!

To get a true picture of yourself here and now, ask yourself these questions: Are you happy with yourself? Are the people around you happy? Is God happy with you?

Are You Happy With Yourself?

When you look at yourself in the mirror; in the mirror on the wall, in the mirror of your mind, or the mirror of your soul, do you like what you see, physically, mentally and spiritually? Your satisfaction or dissatisfaction should not be based so much on where you are now, but how much you've improved from the past, and how much of a progressive trend you see towards the future.

If your life is filled with pain and suffering, you will not be happy and you must *do something about it*. But there are many who cause their own emotional pain. Much of it is due to the importance they place in what others think of them. Get a good perspective on this. Be true to yourself, but realize also that much of happiness or its lack is due to the relationships we have with others.

Are The People Around You Happy?

You are not totally responsible for the happiness of the people around you for they all have their own free wills, but are you doing the best you can to increase their happiness? It is true that some people can make unreasonable demands on you and that you are not beholden to them to appease their every wish but what you can do is to apply the true golden rule (platinum rule) to them. Stick to the highest ideals. Do good to them, not for personal reward but so they can pass the good onto others. To be able to consistently apply the true golden rule to all those in your life is to be doing the best thing that can lead to happiness for everyone.

It is good to be loyal to one's family and social group, but it is better to be loyal to the universal organization, the family of God. It would be ideal if they are one and the same, but often it is not. Which should take precedence, the love of family or the love of God? It depends on whom you are closer to.

As we evolve spiritually, our attention widens from being centered on ourselves, to being centered on family and friends, then to our community, nation and then our universe. The development of unselfishness expands as we grow, our sense of happiness matching it stride for stride. There is more on this in the section on the Personhood performance range of breadth.

Is God Happy With You?

God is always happy with you. It is only your perception that he is not and you may have that perception when you are not doing your best in following his leadings. God knows that you will eventually attain the heights of spiritual living regardless of your mistakes but you may not have this same awareness. You can reconcile your doubts by sharing your inner life with him on a regular basis through worshipful meditation, prayer and service. It is not where you are now that counts with God, but where you are going. If you are consistently striving to better yourself, to sincerely follow your inner leadings, even if you sometimes falter, you will have a better perception of yourself in relation to God. But no matter what you do, he does love you unconditionally.

The above are simple and basic things, but if they are answered in the affirmative, all is well. But all is not so well if you are in physical pain or discomfort, which means you are not happy with yourself, or when you are in emotional pain or discomfort which means people around you are not happy with you, or when you are in spiritual pain and discomfort which means that you think God is not happy with you.

Stress and concern is part of life that may not be avoided, but one can avoid stress that results from imagined and/or unreasoned consequences that is not of the now. One may be totally free from pain or burden at a given moment, but worry and stress can be debilitating and agonizing if there is something in the future that is frightening. For instance, if you are undergoing surgery a month from now, worry may etch its lines upon your psyche. Or if you are unemployed and you know that you will be running out of money in the near future, that may indeed be a cause for concern. Or it may be that a loved one is going to die soon.

The best way to deal with all these things is in the now. If you are facing surgery, or any imminent crisis, make the most of the present moment and take care of yourself physically, emotionally and spiritually, so that you will be in the best state of mind and body to pass through the crisis well. If you are jobless and money is getting scarce, do the necessary things now such as look for employment and watch your spending. If a loved one is going to depart soon, make the most of the now, and spend as much quality time with that person as you can. Take care of the now and there is no need to worry as there is nothing else you can do. The worst thing to do is to become so stressed out and worried that it affects your physical, mental and spiritual health, thereby resulting in making matters worse. Worrying and fretting is letting in fear which depletes the inner resources necessary to using the power of faith and also to giving the best effort. Merge your best effort with the power of faith seamlessly and with stamina. Relax and tap into the infinite source of strength, power and love, the First Source and Center of All, through the connection within you.

Pain and Suffering

From the eternal viewpoint of beingness, there is no such thing as pain and suffering, as they are but the phenomena of cause and effect in the time/space universe. But this is little consolation to those who are undergoing such experiences.

Why is there pain and suffering at all? Why did a loving and benevolent God create the possibility of pain, a tremendously negative experience?

There are many ways to look at this. We can say that negative occurrences are opportunities to exercise our conversion powers of transforming evil into good. The Chinese sages recognized this, as their written character for "crisis" is the same as "opportunity." Everyone is different and everyone needs a different set of circumstances in order to learn how to turn the negative into the positive. It has been said that you are only given enough negative circumstances as you are able to convert into positive effects. Those who are able to handle more adversity are given more of the opportunity. This raises the question, is it more of a blessing to have a life of ease and comfort, with little adversity, with little opportunities for learning how to convert the negative into the positive, a prerequisite for eternal life? Or is it better to have a life full of pain and adversity, which presents you with many opportunities to practice your conversion powers?

Another perspective is similar but more from the world of nature. A beautiful flower starts as a seed that is planted in a very dirty environment, a compost heap, or some other decaying or decayed material, basically crap, a negative environment, one could say. But it needs that sort of fermentation, a volatile stew of compounds and molecules that can provide the necessary nutrients for it to grow. Without the crap, there would be no blossom.

Likewise, those individuals who experience the worst of the worst in this world are very ambitious souls. In order for them to achieve their goals of spiritual attainment, they have to start from the bottom of the bottom. The farther the string is pulled back, the farther the arrow will fly.

The above explanations are partial and are not quite satisfactory. When looking at the suffering of people all over the world, I cannot help but be concerned and empathetic to the pain and agony brought on by hellish circumstances. My heart grieves for them and I cannot minimize their plight by merely saying that it is their eternal plan and/or that they must suffer in order to learn.

Certainly, some suffering is caused by "acts of God" such as natural disasters and diseases. They may indeed be the natural afflictions which we need in order to grow spiritually. However, so much of the worst kind of suffering is brought onto man by man. We are, too often, our own worst enemies. These acts are done through sheer maliciousness, negligence, fear, greed, and ignorance, and they are the results of bad decisions that do not have to be. The downside to having free will.

Giving (relative) free will to imperfect creatures such as humans are necessary for our spiritual growth, for we must have volition in order to love God and each other freely with no strings attached. Free will decisions are what makes us grow, but that means we have to make mistakes in order to learn from them. And the consequences of those mistakes are what causes so much grief and suffering on this planet.

What can we do? Make the best choices, the wisest decisions by the pursuit of service, prayer, and worshipful meditation. In the meantime, take care of those who have to bear the burden of pain and suffering by doing what we can to lessen their agony. And there is so much that we can do that is not being done. The world has the resources to feed, clothe, and provide medical care to all, but the world is not yet of one mind and one heart, unable to act in unity, deterred by the various social, religious and political divisiveness that still engulf the globe. This must change. And it will.

From the purely material standpoint, a person that is suffering can be likened to a car that has gotten into an accident or has a mechanical breakdown. Even emotional pain and suffering is seemingly due to external circumstances such as the breakdown of personal relationships or loss of a loved one.

Chemical and neural imbalances can also be considered as external, that is, physical. Conflicts with the soul and spirit may seem internal, but the problems are reflected by relation to external reality, how it affects personal relationships.

An automobile that has broken down or has had an accident can be fixed by a mechanic. A person who is damaged physically or emotionally is not as easily fixed because although medical science has improved over the past centuries, it is still far from perfect. Psychiatry and psychotherapy is even less developed. There are also many alternative methods that are viable if it works, so we do the best we can using the available methods to alleviate pain and suffering in our lives. Whatever method we use, being centered in the spirit will unerringly enhance and stimulate the healing process.

A person in a impoverished country has a fate similar to a car in the same environment. Lack of good fuel in the case of a car, lack of good food for the person. Lack of parts and mechanics for the car, lack of medical supplies and physicians for the person. The harsh environment also takes its toll equally on the person and the car: rough pathways, exposure, more toil.

The material vehicle, whether human or automotive, cannot last long under those conditions. Time is limited. So the common wisdom is that the only thing to do is to make the most out of the time available: get as much value out of the life of the vehicle before it goes.

Even for those who are in perfect health, even a long life can seem relatively short, so we must make the best out of what we are given. A person with a terminal illness when told that life may end in a few years will make the most of the remaining time. Every breath becomes a joy, every sunrise and sunset a thing of beauty, every walk a dance, every person a friend. In the total scheme of things, a few years or thirty years, even a hundred years is a short time. If we realize this we will make every breath count, every minute meaningful, and every moment eternal.

It seems we all suffer and experience pain to one degree or another. We say that it is a part of life. But is it truly so? Can't we overcome physical suffering through spirit?

Many people think so. It may be just a matter of to what degree we are in the spirit, to what degree our mind has control over matter. Have faith that God does not want us to suffer, that there are mechanisms that she has implanted in the workings of our body, mind and soul that can conquer any and all ailments. People have done this and so it is possible. But it is not magic. It is a combination of faith and effort, science and spirit, linear methods and wholistic ways; an elliptical process. Through faith and regular contact with the divine spark, the brahman, the Christ Consciousness, the indwelling spirit, we are led to various avenues to resolving the undesired situation. We will be guided to people and circumstances that will provide the necessary knowledge and the right techniques.

Again, I reiterate, miraculous physical healing through spirituality may be possible, there is evidence that the mind has powers over the body that goes beyond what was previously thought as possible, but *more reasonably and more often*, I think that one is lead by the spirit to finding the most suitable and efficacious medical treatments and methods, whether allopathic or alternative. Use the powers of visualization, positive thinking, along with research and trial and error– faith and effort. It is important that we keep our minds open and explore as many avenues as we can. It is often the close-mindedness of people that deter them from trying methods that are not familiar to them. A case in point is alternative medicine. Many people keep on suffering because they refuse alternative treatments which have proven effective and could alleviate their pain, just because they are afraid to try something new. Of course, one should always be careful in assessing the qualifications of any doctor, alternative or not, for there are charlatans and incompetents in every field. Follow your spiritual intuition, but also make the effort to evaluate the best option. The internet is an awesome tool for that.

Pain of the body, as a biological phenomenon, was addressed previously in my book *Katsugen – The Gentle Art of Well-Being*. Here is an excerpt:

Physical pain is a survival mechanism. Pain tells us not to do those things that are causing the pain. As an infant, we might unwisely put our hand in a fire. The resulting pain tells us not to do that again. It is experiential wisdom. We learn that fire equals heat, equals pain, equals "don't put hand in the fire"; a very simple equation. Pain is a signpost telling us which paths to avoid. Pain doesn't tell us what is right, it tells us what is wrong.

To use an analogy, think of skiing. To learn how to ski we often fall, which is painful. Falling makes us learn how to ski better, but wanting to fall does not make for a better skier. The purpose is to learn how to ski masterfully *without* falling. When we're not falling anymore, it means we have learned. When we can lead our life so that we do not make ourselves suffer, we have mastered the art of living.

That does not mean that there will no longer be mistakes and errors that might cause some pain. When we become expert at skiing, we may start challenging more difficult slopes, maybe even to the extreme. Then, pain and suffering may again be experienced in trying to achieve a more demanding goal that we have set for ourselves.

To live a life where we experience pain and suffering daily may mean that we are making regular errors in judgment. Whereas to live so that we do not encounter pain at all may mean that we are not challenging ourselves to the utmost. It is a fine line. A matter of balance.

Self-improvement can also cause pain. "No Pain, No Gain" is a masochistic way of achieving goals, but it's easy to see how this kind of thinking came about.

Exercising can be painful, especially when we are pushing ourselves beyond our comfort zone. To acquire knowledge is often painful; studying and researching long hours is a pain. So is finding out a well-kept secret about yourself or someone you love. Pain can be involved when trying to improve in any endeavor, physical, intellectual or emotional. But there is also pain in not improving or staying ignorant. How painful it is to be at a standstill when everyone else is progressing!

Therefore, pain can happen when there is resistance between where you are and where you're going to. From ignorance to knowledge, illness to health, from discomfort to comfort, from stasis to movement, all involves some pain.

So, can one improve without pain? I say, yes. Gradual improvement over time is painless and often pleasurable. I would go so far as to say that gradual improvement is more beneficial in that it is long lasting and is more quality oriented. It is trying to improve too quickly, or gaining too much knowledge too rapidly that produces pain.

Patience and faith is necessary. Relax, and persevere.

Fear

Fear is the thought of the wolf at the door. The actual threat may or may not be an illusion. That is why fear is so fearsome. We can never know if the danger we face is real or imaginary. Sometimes fear is helpful, sometimes it is not. Fear is based on uncertainty.

> Fear.
> Fear can be found anywhere, for it is an illusion.
> With it, we are frozen.
> Without it, we are dangerous.
> It moves us.
> We move it.
> Laugh at fear.
> And fear laughs back.
> With no humor.

The best way and the spiritual way to respond to it is by being certain. By connecting to the source of absolute certainty within.

The two biologically wired methods to deal with fear is to hide from it or face it and kill it. The fight or flight response. Both animals and humans have it. Even animals have courage. But humans can go further if we choose to. If we need to. Sometimes, listening to fear will save our lives. Fear often warns us of physical danger and we would not live long if we disregard this basic survival trait. Those are reasonable fears. The fears that we must avoid are the unreasonable ones. Fears of public speaking, of looking foolish, of seeming vulnerable. Social fears can be debilitating to our egos and keep us from achieving our potentials. As we evolve more spiritually we can manage these fears. We can tap into the higher spiritual agencies and use fear to our advantage. It's like aikido or judo. Instead of directly opposing force with force like boxing or wrestling, aikido and judo uses the opponent's force on itself.

The problem of fighting fear tooth and nail, force against force, is that violence begets more violence. One may kill the wolf, but the blood draws more wolves (so to speak) and it keeps on going. The world trend of war and more wars is a good example.

How else can we deal with fear, besides fighting it or hiding from it? By taming it. By turning it into a dog, a watchdog. The fear is still there but it is no longer something to be afraid of. The fear of fear dissipates. Because of our heredity, as long as we inhabit our human bodies, the electro-chemical response of fear will be a part of us. Even when we evolve from using the spiritual circuit of courage that gives us courage of the flesh and we tap into spiritual courage, we are still dealing with fear. After all, as many people have noted before, courage is not the absence of fear, but the ability to deal with it effectively, to even use it beneficially.

The best way to deal with unreasonable fear, to overcome it and to even use it, is to relax and embrace the result that you fear. Not to embrace the fear so that one becomes more fearful but to look at what it is you hate happening to you and realize it's not so bad. You relax into it, accept it and even begin to like it. The technique of using the qi reflects this well. Fear makes one tense. The body goes rigid preparing for the impending crisis and this weakens us. Strength comes from relaxing and by tapping into the qi, the universal divine energy. We have to be able to relax to tap into this energy, just like worshipful meditation. And when we can do this well, we are flowing with qi, and fear cannot have a hold on us when we are relaxed and in oneness with the universe. After all, fear is a separateness. It is anxiety about the safety of our body, this unit of matter, as opposed to being one with the entirety of the universe. When we are at one with the universe and God, fear has no effect on us. Fear is doubt of our own safety. And the opposite of doubt is faith. And faith is something we choose and is facilitated by relaxing.

Of course, it's not all that easy. Faith can be very strong in us and sometimes it is not. We may at times, seemingly, have no fear. When we are rested, at peace, well fed, emotionally secure, happy, etc., we can relax and be at one with God. But being human, we must undergo times when we are tired, sleepless, fatigued, emotionally drained, energies pent up, and sad. These are the times when the wolf rears its ugly head. When the watchdog turns on the master. When, for whatever reason, we cannot relax, faith is eroded, we are tense, rigid and cannot tap into the qi efficiently, fear will again come knocking.

So the problem we must deal with is this: How can we relax and have faith when circumstances are making us tense, self-absorbed and separated from universal oneness?

By making a habit of using the qi, by practicing elliptical disciplines such as aikido, tai chi, yoga, etc. or worshipful meditation all the time, we can be relaxed no matter how stressed we are, no matter how sleepless, hungry, emotionally drained we are. A master at using qi, or a master of faith may be able to maintain the oneness regardless of all external circumstances, regardless of all stress and pain, even torture. It's something to ponder and work towards.

In the meantime, I just try to stay away from all activities that will stress me to the point where my connection with the Source becomes cut off. Stress can take one further and further away from being relaxed. As being relaxed is key, the fatigue erodes the tenuous connection that we have with the Center. As stress builds up, the line gets garbled more and more.

The danger is that as we get more distant from the Source, we adapt to the conditions and tend to become unaware of how much of our thinking process is compromised, how much of our connection is lost. So the inertia keeps us working and building up the stress until the body or mind breaks down and we get ill or make a huge blunder, which forces us to go back to square one.

So we don't have to be a master of qi to control stress. Just be mindful of how stressed you are and take frequent naps, plus go on vacations regularly. Relax and spend quality time with the Universal Father, the Earth Mother and your family and friends. Keep the connection clean and clear. No amount of money, status or validation is worth being cut off from the Source of the Universe.

Having discussed the terrain on which we travel, the road stretches before us endlessly. What are the options on moving forward? How can I facilitate my exploration of this grand and wonderful universe?

Chapter Four
On The Road: Shake, Rattle and Roll

Self-reverence, self-knowledge, self-control,
These three alone lead life to sovereign power.

-Alfred, Lord Tennyson

Free Will Choice

Although we are like the plant that is naturally drawn to the light, we are also much different. Like the plant, we do not have *absolute* free will. We cannot turn ourselves into birds, reverse gravity or go against the universal laws of the Creator. However, we are imbued with *relative* free will. We have a choice not to go toward the light, not to following the leadings of the spirit, if we wish. We have free will choice to smile or to frown, to be happy or sad. We are not automatons, not like robots that are programmed to follow and obey rigid commands. Why? Because we are creatures that are the children of the Creator. And like children, we must grow up to become responsible adults, and not just tools to be used without our own free will. The Creator wants our love freely. Not by being hard wired to slavishly follow each and every wish that she may have. If we didn't have the free will to love or not love, whatever feelings we have toward the Creator and toward each other would be meaningless, a result of pre-programming. So free will choice is a gift, but a gift that can be abused. Giving such a gift to evolving mortals such as ourselves may seem unwise by human standards, but without such freedom of will, spiritual children can never grow up to assume full responsibility as cosmic adults.

In our journey towards our destination, we will be faced with many choices. Some will be based on the needs of our body. Some on the wishes of the mind, and some on the leadings of our spirit. We must be considerate of our body in supplying it with the proper nutrients, shelter, security and exercise. The needs of the mind with its desire for stimuli and knowledge is also important. However, it is best to keep in mind that the leadings of the spirit are what will guide us to our destination. How we follow the spirit's leadings, so that it is harmonized with the wants of the body and mind, is the job of the soul.

Choosing value is the key to following our spiritual leadings and arriving at our destination. We *choose* value, not create value. There is no intrinsic value that we create in anything. An ingot of gold has material value because our society *chooses* to value it. Otherwise it is a piece of yellow rock. An old photograph of a loved one may be of value to us because we *choose* to treasure its sentimental worth. It may not be of value to anyone else. Friendships and loving relationships have value only when we *choose* to value it. It is the same with all relationships, including the one we have with our Creator.

The question becomes, what do we value more, our relationships with others and our Creator, or material things and intellectual ideology? Do we choose eternal values over temporary values, or are temporary things more important?

If we choose eternal values, spiritual values, we reach our destination, we become eternal. If we choose transient material values, we are sidetracked and are lost, our souls die. It is our free will choice.

The Neurons of Positivity

There are exciting new discoveries in neuroscience, the study of brain cells.

In "Train Your Mind, Change Your Brain" (2007) by Sharon Begley, she documents the collaboration between neuroscience and Buddhism in which monks with up to 50,000 hours of deep meditational practice were hooked up to various instruments in order to see what was going on in their brains as a result of the meditation.

The results were amazing and the details can be read in her book. The bottom line is that yes, we can change our brains by using inner mental techniques. Other discoveries in neuroscience have confirmed this. We have much more power to change our brain's wiring and structure than we had previously thought. There are still many things that, by nature, we cannot control, but it seems that are a lot more that we can, by nurture.

These new discoveries give us a material basis for free will. If we can create new neurons, how will this impact your life?

Experiment! If you are an experienced meditator, meditate on certain behaviors or traits that you want to strengthen, such as being more friendly. Then meditate on increasing the brain cells that give rise to friendliness. The purpose for this is not to prove a point and publish it in a scholarly magazine. See if it will substantially improve your life. If it works for you, use it and include it in your arsenal of self-mastery techniques.

Of course, this is what meditators have been doing all along, we were creating new brain cells and new connections which contributed greatly to the well-being of the whole. Now we have the scientific data to back us up.

Positive thinking, in its most powerful form, is similar to meditation because it comes from personal faith.

Positive Thinking

In its many guises, whatever you call it, positive thinking has been a boon to mankind. The fact that it has been through many marketing incarnations and is constantly being re-packaged and re-sold is in itself proof that it works, at least to those positive thinking marketers who make it work. Positive thinking is a powerful tool to achieving success, wealth, health and prosperity, and it *is* a big secret, to the negative thinkers!

Positive thinking does not work if it defies reality. Faith is at the very root of positive thinking, and as previously explained, effort must go hand in hand with faith to keep a cosmic balance, if you will. Faith rests on the ocean floor – in the depths of your soul. Thoughts – positive or negative, are like waves rippling on the surface.

Rather than positive thinking, which can sometimes become implausibly optimistic and unrealistic, I like *reality* thinking. Not positive or negative. It is seeing things for what they truly are. So that, if necessary, we can change it for the better.

So what is real for you? What do you really want out of life? What the heck are you doing here in this manifestation anyway?

Material wealth is a goal for many in our industrialized societies and positive thinking has been highly touted as a way of achieving this end. In determining your relationship with material wealth, you have to dig deep into your soul, connect with the Master Server, God, if you will, and think, is unearned wealth good? Do you want to live like Paris Hilton? Or conversely, why is it necessary that we make money the old fashioned way, by earning it?

Most of us have these values. We think that we should get what we deserve by virtue of what we do. What is the value of success if it is so easy and everyone can get it without any directed effort?

If we dig deep enough within ourselves, we realize that it is the process that is important, smelling the flowers and enjoying the adventure. The goal is merely just one step, the last step. To want the last step without taking the previous steps is a sign of immaturity, fatigue or illusion.

Conversely, to be born into wealth without earning it, as more and more people are doing in the wealthy countries, can be just as trying *for the soul* as being born poor. And I don't necessary mean the very rich. Even middle class America is very rich when compared to the rest of the world. In either case, it is a personal journey of discovery and exploration, both externally and internally, for which a positive mental attitude is most useful.

The Principles Of Attraction, Repulsion and Conversion

Attraction is not an incontrovertible law but a principle. Positivity does not always bring positivity, contrary to new age thinking. Look at your life experiences: have you ever laid "pearls before swine" and have them turn and rend you? Have you done things in the most positive way and yet be rejected and even attacked? Jesus is considered by many to be one of the most positive people in history, and yet his positivity was returned negatively by being tortured to death. Indeed, many people will often take advantage of your goodness for their own personal benefit. And often, those who are negatively minded, when faced with your positive traits, will not like you because, in their eyes, you make them look stupid and selfish, and they will react to your goodness in the most negative way.

However, in company of positive minded individuals, in the realm of the spiritual universe, your positivity will be noted, appreciated, and returned. And regardless of the negativity that you encounter from some people, having a positive outlook is crucial to happiness and health. One just needs to be careful not to be discouraged when one's goodness is returned by bad, as this can short circuit your positivity.

The seeming paradox of the principle of attraction is that sometimes negativity will bring positivity. One common example is that of some women being attracted to men who have the "bad boy" attitude. Another example is that of highly evolved individuals who will return your negativity with the positive, returning good for evil.

The principle of repulsion is that negativity will bring negativity, but not necessarily so. In addition to the previous examples, revealing your negativity can sometimes make people feel sorry for you and do you a good turn. Also, stewing in your own negativity can sometimes bring on a reaction in your soul that will make you determined to start doing the right things. Reaching "dead bottom" as in those who have experienced alcohol or drug addiction is a good example. Sometimes you have to initially go in the direction that is opposite to where you want to go. When jumping up, you have to first bend down. In order to breathe out, you have to first breathe in.

The principle of conversion is the crown jewel of the three. This is when everything is converted to the positive, regularly and consistently returning good for evil. Whatever negativity that is within you is converted into positive thinking and doing. All negativity that comes from outside is also transmuted into the positive. You suck up the dirt. The rain and the cold translates into gold. You become a clean machine. You realize that all negativity is just an illusion.

Negativity &The Clean Machine

Watch out...watch out!
Here it comes...
At you with a roar
Or slipped quietly under the door
When you least expect it..

It may hurt like hell, it may sting,
but you deal with it, and learn from it
until it no longer has a hold on you.

You suck up the dirt, and the dirt become diamonds.
The rain and the cold translates into gold
when you least expect it. You are the clean machine!

Wholeness

Many of you are already whole, at least some of the time. Some of you may be whole most of the time. There may be some who are whole all the time. But for most of us who have embarked on this voyage, it is an ongoing process, with moments of wholeness punctuated by moments when we are distracted, unfocused, torn, and unwhole. By regularly connecting to the Source, we become more and more able to maintain wholeness in our lives.

What is wholeness? It is being one with the deepest part of our consciousness, the I Am, the part that originates from the Prime Source, and to lead a life based solely on this consciousness.

To be not whole is when you have to fight yourself. When you have to force yourself to do something. Just the words in the above sentences imply that there are more than one of you, that you are split: "Fight yourself?" "Force yourself to do something?" Who is fighting who? Who is making who do something? If you are one and whole, you just do it, without the inner struggles of a divided personality.

If you have a habit that you are fighting to overcome, such as overeating, overdrinking and overanything, you are not whole. If you are stuck doing work that you hate, you are not whole. If you are negating an aspect of reality, such as a material scientist scoffing at spirituality or a religionist ignoring scientific facts, you are not whole. If you disregard the needs of your body; by not exercising and/or taking in healthful nutrition, you are not whole. If your emotions and the biological urges of your body control you, you are not whole. If you do not regularly connect to the Source, you are not whole.

If you are not whole, there is fighting within. When you force yourself, you are committing violence upon yourself. This fractal pattern extends out to the world around you. If there is fighting and strife within each person that make up the world consciousness, then there will be strife and conflict in the world at large. What happens in the part manifests itself in the whole.

The greatest obstacle to becoming whole is duality. As long as people are fighting an external factor, they cannot be whole. The external factor may be the rules of your own society, a religion or tradition, or a belief based on hearsay without your inner confirmation. As long as there is tension and a conflict of interest between what you want and what the external factor wants, the eventual result is inner conflict which becomes externalized as violence, ignorance, strife, chaos and lack. The duality is this conflict between the inner spiritual and outer material realities.

Government and traditions try to control the people in order to have peace and harmony in the society. They are successful only to a limited degree and they also cause more conflicts. This can be remedied by becoming whole within ourselves. By attaining self-mastery, we can have a world of self-governing individuals; a world where each individual is so in tune with cosmic consciousness that everyone behaves with utmost spirituality and love so that no laws and no government would be required. The inner and outer realities become one. There is no one left to fight.

This is quite a ways off, but that is the goal, and it starts right now, right here and with each one of us. First there is one, then two, then three. Then we have a community that is self-governing, then a town, a city, a nation...the world!

But before we can proceed we should know why there is such a schism, how and why such a duality was brought about.

Governments attempt to create social peace and harmony by maintaining control of our external lives. Religion should achieve peace and harmony in each person and society by inspiring us to bring out the spiritual qualities within so that we can manifest it externally. The religions that are the most divisive are the ones that act like governments, trying to exert control over our lives through external means, such as social pressure, persecution and laws based on scriptural beliefs as well as spreading the fear of eternal damnation and the threat of going to hell. External standards that are imposed causes hypocrisy as most people have their inner standards which are often not in harmony with those that are arbitrarily placed upon them from outside. This makes people have two-faces: one for dealing with external authority and the real one, which is the face of the inner self. When this dualism becomes evident in action, we see it as hypocrisy.

It is understandable that government cannot bring inner wholeness to the people by external means. Authoritarian government may naturally breed hypocrisy, but why is it that religion, an institution which purpose should be to propagate oneness and wholeness rather than the opposite is also rife with duality, divisiveness and hypocrisy?

The key may lie in the way we understand the word faith.

What Is Faith?

In talking about faith in this book, I do not mean faith as it applies to any external thing. I do not mean faith in a church, a religion, a book, a philosophy, a science, a discipline or a way of life. What I mean by faith is the loyalty to one's own spiritual ideals gained through spiritual experiences. It is the conviction of the reality within. Faith is what initializes all action, by believing that you can do it, even with no external evidence. Faith is not theory, it is based on inner empirical evidence, experience with spiritual reality – consciously or not.

One does not need faith to believe that the sun will rise tomorrow morning. This is simply a deduction based on observing the same thing happen day after day, year after year. We do not need faith for things that are in the material world. We need faith for those things that can't be seen. Such as spiritual reality and God.

A major fraud was committed upon mankind when faith was interpreted as something placed upon the organization, scripture and hearsay, external sources, rather than on the personal experience of God within. This is the root of all hypocrisy and fragmentations of the soul, of division, schism and schizophrenic mentality – of not being whole. This is the underlying cause of most of the problems facing the world today. The Earth, Gaia, is not whole because most of the people which comprise her thinking and reasoning faculties, her brain cells, are not whole.

To have to negotiate with a deity mandated by society or religion is dualistic and the cause of all divisions within the inner self. To be told from an external source, such as institutions and "holy" writings, that the Source of All, the Creator, wants you to be something that you have no natural desire to be, that you have to negate your personal understanding of the deepest part of yourself, is like a wedge that can split your soul asunder. It causes a vast gap to form between the true inner God and the false outer God: the God that you have a personal relationship with versus the God that other humans says is out there. Unfortunately, because not many people are conscious of their own personal relationship with God, they buy into the preachings of an organized religion. This results in duality and hypocrisy, with actions not matching the inner standards and values.

A good example of hypocrisy that has resulted from faith being placed upon the organization rather than on one's inner religious experiences is the behavior of the many members of organized religions that have used coercion to proselytize and convert others into joining their denomination. These organized religions have created patterns of behavior, not only within their organizations but in their society itself, that regards hypocrisy as something to be shrugged off, as "business as usual." This can be seen in clergy that violate children and are shielded by their organization, as well as the terrorists that kill and destroy in the name of their religion, all members of organizations that have historically used force and the threat of death and punishment to coerce others into joining their religious group.

In the book, *The Closing of the Western Mind*, by Charles Freeman, it is clearly seen that early Christians, even after baptism, did not wholeheartedly adhere to the values and beliefs of their newly found faith. This passage demonstrates this: "The true commitment of Christians to their faith came after baptism, but many lingered for years as catechumens, in effect living in a no-man's land in which they would continue to attend pagan festivals." In other words, they paid lip service to the religious authority but still believed and worshipped their pagan religion when they can. Historical facts that prove this point are many.

It is fairly obvious that when one is given a choice to either join a religion or is tortured and/or put to death, most will renounce the old religion for the new state-endorsed faith, while at the same time practicing the old religion on the side, often in secret, hypocrisy by necessity, if you will. And if a large percentage of the members of a given religion was forced into accepting the new religion, this hypocrisy becomes a socially normal part of that religion, something that is not overtly condoned but accepted as a necessary evil that one tries not to look at too closely. After thousands of years, this becomes ingrained in the society which formed around that religion, and so we see it now in modern times, in politics, in business, in the military, in all our institutions and in our personal philosophies. True religion should counter the hypocritical attitudes which are reactions to governmental authority by teaching wholeness from within, not become another external authority to react against.

Faith became synonymous with religion because faith was placed in religion rather than in religious experience, in the church rather than in God. Charles Freeman writes of Origen, a theologian in the early centuries of Christianity who said, "'As this matter of faith is so much talked of, I have to reply that we accept it as useful for the multitude, and that we admittedly teach those who cannot abandon everything and pursue a study of rational argument to *believe without thinking out their reasons...*' Here the concept of faith has shifted, from being a state of openness to revelation (or directly to the teachings and personal charisma of Jesus as recorded in the Gospels) to one of being ready to accept what is authoritatively decreed by the church hierarchy."

This perversion of the word faith resulted in coercive conversions, for if one is *forced* to believe in the church or a theology, it is not necessary to have a personal relationship with the inner spirit. It just required an external show of allegiance – which was gotten through sheer force and intimidation, with people being converted like a country being conquered, their allegiance only a façade to what they truly believed within, a sure path to hypocrisy. It became a numbers game, similar to the way the American military in the Vietnam War gauged success in the battlefield, by body count. In religious terms, success was measured by how many people were converted, or rather, how many publicly renounced their former faith to proclaim their acceptance of the new one. Whether they were truly converted within, in their souls, was immaterial to the state endorsed religion.

This interpretation of the word faith has also turned many scientists away from religion. To have to believe in the authority of the church hierarchy and scriptural writings without question makes no sense. To accept faith as a conviction of one's inner understandings of spirituality is more acceptable to reasoning minds.

The dependence of the masses on church authority was necessary in the olden days, as the printing press was not yet invented, books were rare, and most of the people were illiterate. They had no access to scripture, and the ones who did, the religious organizations, interpreted it sometimes accurately, sometimes to suit their agenda. Now, in the modern era, knowledge is available to anyone through inexpensive books, the internet and the media. We no longer need to be dependent on an intermediary, we can go straight to the source and accept it or reject it accordingly using reason, our own insights, experimentation and experience. The religious institutions no longer have a monopoly on spiritual knowledge. Spiritual liberty has come of age.

Unquestioning faith in the religious institution, in scripture, in the church, rather than in the faith of true spiritual experience is what derailed our world, and we must get our world back on track. We have the tools to do this. By accessing the storehouse of information that is now available to us, we can now freely experiment with the various methods used by past masters and sages, as well as the cutting edge techniques now being formulated to empower and optimize our minds and souls.

Wholeness of being is the key. Embrace everything that your inner spirit leads you to: Science, religion, philosophy, service, research, the arts, analytical thinking, sincere prayer, exercise, nutrition, meditation and more. Try them all out. Have fun. Experiment. Do not take this book on faith. Reserve your faith for the spirit within.

Be one with the deepest part of yourself and be one with the biggest concept of the universe. Be whole.

Insecurity, Guilt, and Shame

It's all a big ball of dirty laundry that needs to be dumped into the "clean machine", the part of you that converts the negative into the positive.

Our personal feelings of insecurity stem from our feelings of inferiority and superiority in relation to others. Ego, basically, but more than that, because we do need a sense of self. Normal egos are fine, but egos that are inflated or deflated are the cause of our feelings of insecurity and the stress that results from it.

A false image of ourselves is what we're talking about here. A person who can't see his own limitations and projects an image he can't possibly live up to, or conversely, a person who doesn't realize his own potential and so doesn't even try. Being locked in to such an image of oneself that is apart from reality can be very stressful.

If we didn't have such entrenched egos, we wouldn't be so insecure. Drop the illusions of false identity and all feelings of shame, guilt, insecurity and fear melt away.

Just see yourself as you really are. If you see darkness inside, bring in some light. If you see light inside, bring it out and share. Get out of your sense of being inferior or superior. You are fine just the way you are!

There is a school of thought that says that we are never inferior to others as we have within us the divine spark of the Creator. This is essentially true for we are all equal in the eyes of God, but this is an eternal perspective. In the total picture, from the standpoint of the omniscient, omnipresent, omnipotent, absolute and infinite mind, none of us are better than anyone else. We are, in the transcendence and fulfillment of the vast potentials of time and space, brilliant spiritual beings, all unique and magnificent in our own ways.

However, in the moment, as we live our lives on this planet, each of us are inferior and superior in different ways. I know that I am inferior in calculus compared to many who are better at it than I am. I have no qualms in admitting that I am much inferior in basketball compared to the professional athletes in the NBA, not to mention even the kids at the playgrounds. I am inferior to many people in many respects. That is a reality.

But I am also superior to many in those things that I am good at. I am superior in surfing than most people on Earth. I am superior in my knowledge of philosophy than many people. My imagination is superior to many who lack such creative faculties. That is also a reality. I am unabashedly inferior and superior in ways beyond my own comprehension.

So in existential reality we are all equal, but in experiential reality we are decidedly unequal. True reality is a merging of the two. To maintain that inferiority and superiority does not exist among people is to deny the superior traits which come from hard work, effort, and natural talents. To maintain that such a hierarchy of inferiority and superiority is the only reality is to ignore the innate value of each person.

It seems one of the biggest obstacles to achieving cosmic consciousness and oneness with all creatures wherein we nurture and help each other instead of playing a game of one-upmanship is insecurity, a lack of self-esteem, a sense of inferiority.

I see insecure people all around me. I used to be very insecure myself. Insecurity often breeds defensiveness and a tendency to compete, to self-aggrandize and strive to be better than others at their expense, to be superior. A father, because of his security in being an adult, does not need to compete with his child to prove that he is superior. A child, insecure of himself, will fight with others and do whatever he can to proclaim himself worthy. The sense of unworthiness results in action that tries to raise self-esteem, and/or in action that tries to diminish the value of others.

People hate to appear less than others, less attractive, less capable, less rich, less intelligent, less physically fit, less in status. People hate to be thought of as inferior. It seems it's not so much what one actually is, as how one appear to others. You can be stupid and ignorant, but as long as people think you're smart, you're okay. Or you can be very intelligent and tell yourself that it's not important what others think, but still, you do not want to be perceived as being stupid. However, when you have achieved a certain oneness with the universe and have gotten an idea of your eternal self, what others say about you become less and less important. You know that you are a child of the eternal Creator, a magnificent spiritual being, and you know that God, as well as the people and beings that really matter see you in your true light. By seeing yourself from this eternal viewpoint, your self-esteem becomes unimpeachable. You take the viewpoint of the father, secure in your spiritual maturity. People can call you whatever they will, it is like water off a duck's back. Rather than being offended by their childish name-calling, you smile at them knowing that they will soon outgrow their infantile ways. At the same time, you do not ignore their opinions because at all levels, "children" are sometimes very perceptive, and sometimes they strike a chord, they push a button that you didn't know you had. And if that happens, it is a good time to take good look at what that button is connected to. Why did a certain comment bother you?

Words have power, but only to the extent that we allow it to have power. To be labeled as stupid, inferior, and lacking in intelligence and/or physical abilities can be extremely hurtful and can stigmatize one's life. Especially if one has a history of being taunted. We all experience it to one degree or another when we are children, as children can be cruel in taunting each other. As we grow, we learn to ignore these hateful labeling and manage to continue with our lives, but they do influence us by limiting our self confidence and giving us a sense of powerlessness. One of the ways we combat these negative influences is by self-programming ourselves with positive affirmations that counter the thoughts of inferiority and lack. However, this is only part of the solution, as affirmations only deal with the surface and not the underlying reality of why and how we are who we are.

No matter how many times we affirm to ourselves that we are smart and intelligent, it doesn't help much if our actions are stupid. No matter how much we affirm our positiveness to ourselves, it is useless if our negative attributes are entrenched in our behavior patterns. The only way to truly turn this around is to come face to face with our negative attributes and turn them into positive attributes. If we do this, we won't need to even affirm our positiveness because we will be positivity incarnate. Just as we don't need to affirm to ourselves that the sun is shining when it is shining. If you are truly positive, you don't need to remind yourself of that, as it would be obvious.

So how does one counter negative conditioning? A lifetime of being told that one is stupid, lacking in higher qualities and generally inferior? Affirmations are only partially effective, if at all. What other methods are there?

We all have free will. Once we know what we want and given the motivation, we can use the faculties of our brain, through meditation and newly discovered techniques, to create new neurons which will enable us to overcome insecurity.

We can rewire and restructure our brains to become more positive. We can make it a positivity machine that can turn any negative cause into a positive effect.

But it starts from knowing who we are and what we are. And that can only happen through mindfulness. What do you really want? Is it really that important to be a super achiever? To be considered superior? And is it that bad to be inferior? We are all superior at something and inferior at something. Inner security comes from knowing that we have the power to improve ourselves in any endeavor that we put our minds and souls into. To realize that we have volition, that we have free will to chart our destiny, is the foundation of both material and spiritual liberty.

Life and Death, Happiness and Despair

Life seems to be so full of ups and downs. There is poverty, then success, illnesses, triumphs, downfalls, deaths, victories, wonderful love affairs, disastrous breakups, failures, mistakes, joy and prosperity -- over and over again in lives upon lives. It seems few are able to settle into a life of total unbroken happiness and well-being. Is such a thing even possible in this life? Can happiness last forever? The immediate answer seems to be no. Loved ones are going to die. Bad things are bound to happen. Inevitably, the facts are that we are all going to face material death.

However, in the cosmic balance, good is measured by the bad, the bad by the good. How high you rise is relative to how low you sink. How good you feel is relative to how bad you felt. All lives in all of history have had good times and bad times. We are caught in a cycle of highs and lows that it seems we cannot transcend. No matter who you are: king, queen, president, rock star, movie star, business executive, billionaire, guru, street person, ordinary guy -- pain and suffering, doom and despair is going to be at least a part of your life, or so it seems.

The sages had an answer to this. Don't be enticed into leading a life of ups and downs. Don't be happy when good things happen to you, and don't be sad when the bad comes into your life. Lead a life where you can be aloof from judging things that happen to you as good or bad. Make the graph of your life less wavy, diminishing the extreme highs and low. If you don't get happy you won't get sad. If there is no joy, there is no sadness.

On an intellectual level, this may not seem like such a good idea because it would mean leading a peaceful but boring life without the contrasts that make life exciting and worth living. It would be a drab life with little color, highlights or shadows; a life of mediocre sensations. Of course, this may be desirable if you have led a life of extreme happiness and misery – a veritable roller coaster of a life which you have found too intense.

It is by looking at this from a spiritual level that we get a better perspective. Material life is dominated by cause and effect, by ups and downs. To every action there is a reaction. In a sense, karma. It is by going to the spiritual level that we can transcend this. From the material standpoint, we take an eye for an eye, from the spiritual perspective we can return good for evil. In the material world, every cause and effect is inextricably linked. We light a match and a flame results as a product of chemical combustion. We pound our fist on a table and everything on it jumps up. To those who live a life based on this material reality, they respond similarly. They get hit and they hit back. Evil is done to them and they do evil back. They receive good and they give back good. It is only by manifesting the spirit that we learn to give good back even if we receive evil. It is only within spiritual reality that we can abrogate the limits of cause and effect, of the highs and lows, the ups and downs of material reality. It is by choosing spiritual values that we can transcend the cycle of ups and downs. And our Personhood has the power to do this.

This is accomplished by going within and being one with the spirit. Many religions have formulated a technique for this at one time or another, even though some of it has been degraded into becoming merely a ritual. It's something that I like to call worshipful meditation. A process where a person begins to identify with the All, to become one with the universe and its universal personality – the Creator. All major religions must have or once had this practice at their core, and maybe it is still practiced in those faiths by the members who have transcended the fear, guilt and narrow mindedness associated with dogma, but it is rare to see them display its fruits much in the world.

True worshipful meditation is manifesting the *eternal* in the *now*, the *now* in the *eternal*. Initially, it may happen for only a split second, but constant practice can lengthen the time you can be in that state. The methods to accomplish this will be discussed later but suffice to say for now that this transcendence of the present and the material to become one with the eternal and the spiritual creates the fractal pattern which can dominate your life for all eternity. It can overcome pain, suffering, grief, depression, and all ailments of the material state of being, all the up and downs, even if it is just for that one moment. I personally experience this state for some moments every day and the time spent in that state is increasing. During the time I am not in that state, I must still experience the ups and downs to a certain degree like most people. I do find that the better I get in maintaining that state during my times of worshipful meditation, the more control I have throughout the day over the highs and lows of my emotional and mental state, which results in increased levels of self-mastery. The effects of the moments I spend in that state flow over into the rest of my day more and more. Also, the inspirations and promptings that I get while in that state lead me to find elliptic solutions to any physical, material or emotional problems that I may encounter.

A reasonable question may be asked, "can I just experience the highs but not the lows?" In a way. The deepest levels of worshipful meditation is beyond high or low. It is the greatest pleasure that can be experienced, as it is being one with the All, direct communion with the source of all creation. It transcends our feelings of good or bad, high or low, as those are words that describe existence in a time/space universe. When we can go to a place, even for a split second, that is beyond time and space, it is a feeling that "passes all understanding." But it is not the high of material gratification. It is a pleasure that is experienced with the soul, and not the flesh. The lows will be when we are not in that state, but we can all eventually attain the personal growth level where we are always in a high state of spiritual consciousness.

Experiencing the eternal, now; spiritual paradise in the material life, is our immediate destination. That is our short term goal: Transcendence.

Experiencing the now eternally; material life evolving into spiritual reality, is our ultimate destination. That is our long term goal: Perfection.

Now

In movement, there is growth.
In stillness, there is being.
I open my pores, breathe in the air,
the clouds drift by, the wind ruffles my
hair.
I experience fully the moment.
I am alive!

Gladness for existing melts into gratitude.
I banish the desire for more;
more money, more things,
into infinity, where more has no meaning
nor value.

I possess nothing and so everything,
I accept and enjoy the now,
with no question of why or how.
Not even an answer, not now!

Mastery

How many ways are there for you to be perfect? Externally, you can become better physically; more fit, healthier and stronger. Mindally, you can become more knowledgeable, more understanding and wiser. Spiritually, you can become a more loving person exhibiting an abundance of the "fruits of the spirit". How about as a total being?

Are you, as a person, making any headway in becoming perfect? Are you even getting better everyday at something? Can you tell if you're going anywhere?

Now is a good time to discuss how the human vehicle can negotiate the terrain that was discussed in the last chapter.

In driving an automobile to arrive at a destination, we get there not by just driving straight, but also by making turns and going downhill and uphill. A person has a similar range of cosmic dimensional performance and they are all relative to each other. Even in just trying to go straight ahead, a car cannot. If one looks closely at the movements of a car, or any vehicle for that matter, one will notice that there are minute course changes happening all the time. At the same time that one goes forward, one is also going either slightly right or left, and at the same time up and down. It is the same with the range of movement of a person.

The person has the ability to master itself in three dimensions:

I. **Mastery of Destiny**
    (Relationship with God - Length)
II. **Mastery of Self**
    (Relationship with ourselves -Depth)
III. **Mastery of Environment**
    (Relationship with other people and things – Breadth)

The body, mind and soul changes and evolves in quality as we move in these dimensions and the person keeps them together and moving as one. The explorations of these dimensions are often facilitated through worshipful meditation (length), prayer (depth), and service (breadth). The next three sections will discuss the person's range of movement in these dimensions.

These concepts are derived from the only source available that has details on such things, *The Urantia Book,* with added insights and connections based on my experiential auto-revelations.

Mastery of Destiny (Length)
Direction and nature of progression--
movement through space and according to time--evolution.

Progressive Evolution of Our Form	Ascension Thru Time, Space	Mindal Progression (Our connection upgrades)

Soul Spirit

Human Mind

Animal Matter

Higher
(Spiritual Circuits)

- Soul Philosophy
- True Worship
- Spiritual Relations
- Soul Intelligence
- Spiritual Realities
- Soul Reason
- Faith and Insight

Standard
(Human Mind Circuits)

- Wisdom
- Worship
(added to animal circuits below)

Lower
(Animal Mind Circuits)

- Counsel
- Knowledge
- Courage
- Understanding
- Intuition

I. Mastery of Destiny - Length

The person's movement in cosmic length represents 1. The direction and nature of progression 2. Movement through space and according to time--evolution. 3. Upgrading from lower spiritual influences to higher spiritual influences.

This is the lengthy progress of our bodies, minds and souls unified by the personhood matrix in the upward movement towards the universal *First Source and Center*. By analogy, this would be the ability of the car to move forward to get closer to the destination; the positive forward progression of the body, mind and soul in this life and continuous life afterwards. This forward progression is greatly influenced by the dimension of depth of self-realization. A car goes faster forward when it is going downhill.

1. Direction and Nature Of Progression

The concept that as we evolve spiritually, we are transformed, not just figuratively but literally is not that fantastic to those who have considered what may come after this life. That we turn into angels is one idea from the past, an idea that is still held by some. A winged human being is not that unreasonable if we consider that a butterfly is but a winged caterpillar. But the image of a human being with wings made from feathers such as a bird's seems rather incongruous. It works as a metaphoric symbol but nothing more. Describing what form we would take, even if we knew for sure, would be rather pointless, as without proof it would just become another jaunt into the realm of the fantastic. However, we can explore the nature and progression of our evolutionary forms.

The direction, of course, would be towards perfection. We would become more and more perfect as we draw nearer to God. We have progressed from the material, the substance which composes our body, to the animal and to becoming human. Our soul is the embryo for the next stage of existence. Without going into what that form may look like, I think we can logically deduce from looking at natural evolution that even as we evolve spiritually, we will change in little increments, by taking baby steps. In our next stage of being, we will be more spiritual than we are now, but we will still have many of the attributes of the animal, but only those attributes that we have not yet mastered. Using the same logic, it would be natural that those people who have totally mastered their animal heritage on Earth would be transformed into forms that are commensurate with their spiritual status.

Each level, each stage of our evolutionary progress would hold lessons to be learned, as there are in this stage of existence. It is after completion of each level that we would be upgraded to a new form, becoming ever more spiritual as we progress. The road to perfection is long and may take millions of years, as we measure time with our limited perception, but it cannot be anything but a joyous and fulfilling one, although not necessarily easy, for much of our learning will still be a result of overcoming challenges. The learning curve is probably the steepest here on Earth, where the energy of the Creator first imbeds itself into a material form, nurtures and evolves it into a creature of spiritual potential and yearns to become one with it and journey back to its place of origin. No matter how much we evolve and into what form we change, I think we will always remember fondly the experiences we have here.

2. Movement Through Space and Time

Presently we are here on Earth. Paradise is our destination. The word paradise conjures in our imagination a utopian land of perfection, harmony and fulfillment. It is that but much more. Think of Paradise as the perfect center of Love consciousness. It is accessible within our own personal consciousness right now, right here, but in the course of time and space it will take some time and effort to get there. It is naive to think we are going to die and instantly be transformed into a perfect being without earning it. If there is anything I've learned here on Earth, it's that anything worthwhile has to be earned. It will take many transformations, possibly millions of years of spiritual evolution and a journey through millions of light years to get there, as

Paradise is not only a state of spiritual consciousness but also a real geographical location in the center of the universe.

This is a concept that may not be readily acceptable to many people. Paradise, a real geographic location in space?

Heaven and paradise has been in the consciousness of humans for thousands of years. At certain times in the past, some cultures have thought of Paradise as being in a land far, far away across the ocean, above the clouds, or in another country. After the Earth was explored to its fullest, people began to think of Paradise as a mystical, ethereal place, a non-material, dreamlike domain of uncertain composition.

The universe is elliptical, which means that it is both mystical and rational, spiritual and material. So that would mean that spiritual reality is not a totally separate realm from material reality but a domain that is superimposed upon the foundations of matter. Or looking at it from the spirit perspective, material reality is a domain superimposed upon a spiritual foundation. So Paradise, the center of spiritual reality, would also be the center of material reality.

As we are transformed through spiritual evolution, we traverse the spiritual domain, getting ever closer to the center. At the same instance, we, as transformed entities in our personhood matrix, are moving closer to the center of space through time, gaining experience and learning the lessons of the ages upon sphere after sphere, stage after stage, level upon level, getting spiritually and physically closer to God.

There are thoughts that the divine spirit manifests itself in physical beings then eventually moves back to where it came from. This evolved into thoughts that the spirit manifests itself into the time space universe and stays there. These thoughts are both correct. The perfect divine spirit manifests itself into the imperfect time space universe, uplifts, animates and makes conscious inanimate matter into a person, then carries this new spiritual personality back to the Source and Center for divine recognition and acknowledgement. This new, spiritized personality does not rest on its laurels in Paradise. Having progressed in the ascension career to become spirit, it moves out from the center to minister to the farther reaches of the universe, bestowing the love of the universal parent to uplift and bring back more spiritized persons back to the Source and Center, repeating this circular movement until the entire universe is ultimately transformed into perfection, both materially and spiritually.

3. Upgrading From Lower Spiritual Influences To Higher Spiritual Influences

What process in the mind can be said to be totally from an inner source? All acts and thoughts than stem from memory – past causal events in the external world – are of external origin. What comes solely from an inner source? And can we be sure that they are indeed from the inner, and not merely a delayed memory function?

We can see our inner workings when Personhood disrupts the normal chain of cause/effect events of the material world to create something outside those processes, such as when we convert the negative into the positive, that is, return good for evil. Animals cannot do this as they have no choice in the matter. They are hardwired to respond like a machine. Humans have an inner switch that enables us to break away from the material chain of events. Spiritual urges like intuition, courage, and understanding are also derived from that inner source.

There are natural stepping stones to going from material reality to spiritual reality. These graduated steps are not readily discernible and not identified by most people as such, but they are there. It merely takes looking at it from a certain perspective to see that they exist.

As our body grows, our nutritional requirement changes. We start from mother's milk, then to baby food, then as we become able to chew, we begin to eat solid food, although even then, our childish tastes continue to change as we grow older, from sweets, pizza and hamburgers to more refined dishes.

Similarly, the spiritual nutrition that is required by our human vehicle undergoes changes also. We start from animal needs to human needs, and then to what our soul requires.

All life has an innate guidance system that seeks perfection. A plant put inside a darkened room with but a crack in the roof will unerringly grow towards the light shining through the crack from outside. A human being endowed with spirit on a darkened world will also consistently seek spiritual light. The spiritual light, however, shines from within the human being for it has an internal source rather than an external one, and this spiritual light is tailored to fit our stage of growth. We have spiritual baby food, the lower spiritual influences that are right for us in the beginning stages of spiritual growth when we are mind centered, and then as we advance, we are given adult food, or higher spiritual influences when we are soul centered. These spiritual influences, our "spiritual food", are received by our minds.

The common understanding among scientists of our day is that our minds are but a product of our biologic mechanism, i.e., our human bio-computer, that our thoughts are merely the computations of our physical hardware. However, there are some scientists who are exploring the concept that there is within our brains a receiving mechanism which connects to a universal mind, that apart from the adding up of data, our brains have access to a higher "overmind" through certain unknown circuits.

The Seven Adjutant Mind Spirits are these circuits, they are the standard spiritual circuits that influence the mind of humans. These non-material circuits in our mind gives us the urge to reach for a higher consciousness that our materially based logic and intellect alone cannot achieve. By analogy, it is like baby food when we are teething, so that we can grow to ingest solid food later on.

To say they are spirits or merely circuits may be misleading. The word "spirits" tend to connote ethereal entities, while the word "circuit" makes it sound as if they are but electronic components. They are similar to both but are neither. Think of spirit in the context of "team spirit" or the "spirit of friendship". And think of circuit in the context of "connection." The words will be used interchangeably to refer to the same phenomenon.

They are ministers of the lower levels of experiential mind, and they are as follows:

Lower and Standard Mind Circuits
(Animals have the first five, humans have the five plus the two circuits of Worship and Wisdom)

Intuition
Understanding
Courage
Knowledge
Counsel
Worship
Wisdom

These circuits or spirits are resident in our minds through the biologic hardware in our brains that can receive and transmit spiritual information. The brain must have evolved the necessary hardware in order for these connections to happen. The spirit of Courage bestowed on an electronic computer will not result in a courageous computer because the computer has no components that can manifest courage. An insect without the biologic development of an advanced brain that is capable of receiving the circuit of Understanding cannot be bestowed with that spirit. That is why insects are non-teachable, they simply are not wired to understand some things. It is the same for all of the seven adjutant mind spirits or circuits. Intuition, Understanding, Courage, Knowledge, Counsel, Worship and Wisdom are possible in the mind because we have evolved the necessary receiving hardware in our brains that make these functions viable.

It is up to us to empower these circuits. We have a choice in the matter. Some people are courageous because they choose often to use the circuit of courage. Some people are more understanding because they choose to empower this circuit. We must recognize these leadings in our lives and choose to use them everyday.

The Spirit Of Intuition urges us to look beyond the mere logic of linear thinking. The Spirit Of Understanding transcends the complex arranging of concepts and begets results that partakes of a coherent whole. The Spirit Of Courage overcomes animalistic fear and self-interest to higher values of bravery. The Spirit Of Knowledge reaches beyond the mere adding up of data so that we can really *know*, rather than to just store information. The Spirit Of Counsel establishes relationships for higher reasons than to just gain material benefit. The Spirit Of Worship leads us to look for causes that are not evident in the material world. The Spirit Of Wisdom enables us to see the total picture beyond what is readily discernible.

If the purpose of our minds was merely for biologically hardwired survival and species perpetuation, why do we use functions such as courage that is often self-destructive? Why be able to understand complex concepts in mathematics and science that do not materially benefit our immediate survival and comfort? Why be led toward relationships that do not result in material gain? Why get involved in worshipping an unseen God that seems to do nothing to ease our physical wants? (Intuition and wisdom may be the only functions that help us both in our immediate needs and our unseen future.)

If we were not spiritually evolving creatures we would be like insects, surviving individually and as a species but not progressing to a higher cosmic state. These circuits enable us to reach upward, from the material realm to the spiritual by urging us to become more intuitive, understanding, courageous, knowledgeable, counseling, worshipful and wise, to go beyond our basic physical faculties in search of higher answers. If we did not have these circuits, we would be unable to grow spiritually by following the leadings of the spirit.

By using the connections of the seven standard circuits, we begin to realize that there is more to life than matter. As we learn to make decisions based on these spiritual circuits, our souls are quickened to the reality that there is more to our existence than meets the analytical eye. The perception of how we see our lives begin to head in a direction away from its biological and material origins to its spiritual origins, and the focus shifts from having external reality as the center to a more balanced outlook taking into account the reality and importance of the inner life.

As we follow the urges of these early spiritual influences, we are weaned away, more and more, from dependence on material reality. As we make, with increasing frequency, the moral decisions that contributes to our soul's evolution, at a certain point the soul becomes so empowered in quantity and quality that the mind identifies with it fully and begins to delegate authority to it. We start to become transformed, not only outwardly but also inwardly. This is when we start reaching for a higher reality. And as we evolve into higher cosmic levels, we identify with our souls more often throughout the day as opposed to identifying with our body or mind, and when we do this, we respond to our daily challenges by connecting to higher spiritual circuits in addition to the seven circuits. Relatively few humans have achieved this level of empowerment.

Higher Spiritual Mind Circuits

Faith and Insight
Soul Reason
Soul's Convictions of Spiritual Realties
Recognition of True Relationships
Soul Intelligence
True Worship
Soul Philosophy

The mind spirit of intuition gives way to soul intuition: Intuition is a quality that even animals have. But as our soul is empowered, we upgrade from using animal intuition to spiritual intuition – faith and insight, by tapping into the cosmic mind and our divine spirit. Animal intuition is self serving, while spiritual intuition is selfless. This ability for quick perception evolves from selfish purposes to the soul's concern with the welfare of the whole.

From the mind spirit of understanding to soul understanding: A dog can understand the command to fetch upon being taught but no amount of teaching can make the canine understand art or music. A human can understand art because of the soul, as understanding evolves from the purely mental level to the soul level. True art is partially material and partially spiritual. The materialistic levels of mind can comprehend only the material components of the artwork but not the spiritual; it takes the spiritual leadings of the spirit as allowed by the soul for the mind to understand and enjoy art, whether it is visual, musical, formal, dramatic, etc. However, just because a person cannot understand a particular art form does not mean that person has a deficient soul. Physical abilities to discern nuances in color in art, differences of timbre, tone and harmony in music and other such mechanical functions must be also present in that person's anatomical makeup for that person to be able to understand that particular art form.

From the mind spirit of courage to soul courage: Courage is often said to be not a lack of fear, but the ability to overcome the fear that we do have. Courage of the flesh is the lowest form of bravery. Mind bravery is higher, but the highest form is uncompromising loyalty to the convictions of profound spiritual realities – bravery of the soul. Courage of the flesh is a struggle against the debilitating affects of fear. But soul bravery is an acceptance of our spiritual convictions. There is no struggle, no clenching of our will, but a relaxation into the rightness of our actions. So our soul does not use the spirit of courage to overcome fear, but rather bypasses fear through spiritual convictions.

From the mind spirit of knowledge to soul knowledge: To know something intellectually can be as simple as just having data in one's bio-computer, the brain. But, how often do we know something and yet cannot access it or cannot apply it? Our brain is a complex instrument and sometimes we cannot immediately withdraw the information which it contains. For instance, we can memorize the words to a speech, a poem or a song, but when we are ready to deliver it under pressure, we forget the words. To know something with our soul is to know it by heart. There is no intellectual process in withdrawing the information when it is contained within our soul. However, we must be relaxed enough so that we are one with the soul in order for the soul to perform, otherwise we are left with the intellect with it's penchant to get flustered under pressure. Also, human knowledge is often derived from recorded works, soul intelligence is first hand and is based on personal experience as well as existential spiritual leadings.

From the mind spirit of counsel to the soul's desire for spiritual relationships: The mind spirit of counsel urges us to get to know our fellow creatures. Our mind leads us all to be with our fellow humans in camaraderie but the soul goes beyond shallow relationships to having relationships with the spirit within all creatures. The soul desires to know more about others than casual appearances and things on the surface. The soul desires contact with the souls of other men and women, to come together as spiritual siblings on the deepest level.

From the mind spirit of worship to the soul's urge to worship: The intellectual urge to find the source of all creation, the cause of causes, leads us to worship. This urge has made humans worship anything from rocks to trees to other humans to anthropomorphic deities and eventually to a concept of the Universal Creator. As we become more and more our souls, we worship the Creator as a reality, without need of a personal name or institutional denomination. To paraphrase Lao Tsu as he wrote in the Tao Te Ching, "The Tao that is understood is not the eternal Tao. The name of God is not the eternal being." The soul interacts with the reality of God, not with just an intellectual concept of God.

From the mind spirit of wisdom to the wisdom of the soul: Much of human wisdom is based on philosophical works, a compendium of human experience that is recorded verbally and/or orally. Soul wisdom, like soul knowledge is based on experiential trial and error and existential spiritual consciousness. The mind spirit of wisdom coordinates and articulates the first six mind spirits, the lower spiritual influences, while soul wisdom coordinates the higher spiritual influences. Soul wisdom is the acme of spiritual performance. Soul wisdom is the goal of a material existence dominated by spirit. Intellectual wisdom is straightforward and linear, soul wisdom is often paradoxical and elliptical, as it must operate within the duality of both the material and the spiritual.

The following may enable you to get a better understanding of the Seven Adjutant Mind Circuits (Spirits) and how they are augmented and eventually superseded by the higher spiritual influences.

1. **The Circuit Of Intuition**--quick perception, the primitive physical and inherent reflex instincts of the mind, the self-preservative endowments of all mind creations; the one circuit that also functions largely in the lower orders of animal life and the only one that reaches down to contact the non-teachable levels of mechanical mind, such as insects.

Do you have the ability to perceive things quickly without reasoning it out? Not reflex instincts of the physical body, for they are bio-mechanical, but quick mental perception such as hunches that often come true? Do you sometimes surprise yourself because you seem to know things before it happens? Do you seem to have a knack of ascertaining some things that goes beyond mere reasoning and logic? This is the act of an adjutant mind spirit of intuition ministering in your mind. Reflect on this ability that you have.

Then, as you become more aware of the influence of the spirit of intuition, think of those times when your perception transcended intuition. As you identify more and more with your soul, you will experience the soul's way of quick perception and use less and less the spirit of animal intuition. Identifying with the soul, you will begin to perceive things quickly not by mindal intuition but by spiritual faith and insight. Reflect on how faith and insight can supplement and then sometimes even replace animal intuition.

2. **The Circuit Of Understanding**--the impulse to coordinate and associate ideas automatically and spontaneously. The ability to coordinate acquired knowledge, the significant occurrence of agile reasoning, keen judgment, and prompt decision.

When you were first taught mathematics such as the addition and multiplication tables, you merely memorized the numbers. You put into your mind that certain combinations of numbers resulted in other combinations of numbers. As you grew older you began to *understand* why the first set of numbers resulted in the second set of numbers.

When you are driving and see that the stoplight is red, you stop because you were taught that that is what you do when the light is red. But, when you realize that this system of red, yellow and green lights is necessary to have an orderly system of managing traffic, then you begin to truly *understand* why you must follow the system of lights. The mind spirit of understanding is what urges us to go beyond mere learning by rote. Take a moment to experience consciously the presence of this mind spirit.

Treasure this spirit and recognize that understanding with the mind is followed by understanding with the soul. With the soul, understanding comes from spiritual reasoning, not from intellectual reasoning. If you see that the light is green, but that there is someone still walking across the road, you yield right of way even though the green light says you can go. If you yield because you realize that running over the person may get you in jail, it is merely intellectual understanding, if you yield because your soul feels empathy and compassion for the person and realize it is the right thing to do, a moral choice, then it is soul intelligence.

3. **The Circuit Of Courage**--the urge of loyalty to personal values, the basis of character, moral stamina and spiritual bravery. When enlightened by facts and inspired by truth, this is the route of spiritual evolution by intelligent and conscientious self-direction.

Courage to defy being physically hurt is courage of the flesh. Courage to reject unreasoned fears is courage of the mind. Falling on a grenade to protect your buddies in times of war is courage of the flesh. It has been said that people fear public speaking more than anything else in the world, even death. This fear is often unreasoned. But whether unreasoned or not, public speaking does require courage, as does many things in life. Even to stand up and give your seat in a crowded bus for an elderly person, to get out of bed in the morning when you know you will have a trying day, to have to go against the status quo, requires courage. It has also been said that courage is not a fearless state, but of overcoming fear that you have, a struggle against an invisible foe. The ability for the mind to fight off the paralyzing effect of fear is due to the mind spirit of courage.

Acknowledge this spirit of courage within yourself. Then think of the times you have transcended this spirit of the mind to allow your soul to bypass fear through your spiritual convictions that gives you transcendent faith. All is well. It is not a struggle but an embracing. Not a clenching but a relaxing. Faith in God and insight into our eternal destiny bring forth the highest type of bravery: loyalty towards spiritual realities. See if you can differentiate in yourself the courage of the flesh, the courage of the mind, and the brave convictions of the soul.

4. **The Circuit Of Knowledge**--the connection towards adventure and discovery, the scientific spirit; the complements to the spirits of courage and counsel; the urge to direct the endowments of courage into useful and progressive paths of growth.

As you go about your daily life you pick up tidbits of knowledge, from the books and newspapers, from television, movies and other people. Your brain is a storehouse of data, much like the hard disk on a computer. But the computer is not aware of the data it contains. You are, however, aware of the information that you have. You know that you have knowledge because of the function of the mind spirit of knowledge. Seize on this awareness.

And now think of what you know in your soul. Your soul knows things existentially as well as experientially. It was nurtured by heartfelt experience, but as it begins to ascend, it gains knowledge from the spirit, knowledge that transcends experience. And your soul is aware of its own awareness. The soul knows that it knows. Reflect on what you know with your mind and what you know in your soul. Knowledge from the mind results in beliefs, knowledge from the soul results in faith.

5. **The Circuit Of Counsel**--the urge to socialize, the willingness to cooperate; the ability to harmonize with others; the origin of the gregarious instinct.

Most people enjoy socializing. We benefit greatly from the interaction as we gain information and make friends through social relationships. As a member of a bigger group, the exchange of ideas and assistance increase the welfare of the whole. Appreciate that the spirit of counsel provides your material mind mechanism with the urge to socialize, to gather together, sometimes even in animosity.

The soul goes beyond mere socializing, it seeks spiritual relationships – becoming one with the family of All, to see the divine in all creatures. As your soul seeks to become a member of the universal family, your relations with others become more than social, they become loving.

6. **The Circuit Of Worship**--the religious impulse, the inner demand to seek out and understand spiritual origins, a primal urge separating animals from humans. The spirit of worship forever distinguishes the creature with which it is endowed from the creatures without it. This urge is the first step towards spiritual ascension.

The wonderful urge to worship, to find the origin of life itself can be mysterious. Think of the many things that are worshipped by the various religious faiths in the world. This urge to communicate with the Creator comes from the mind spirit of worship. Recognize and appreciate that the spirit of worship provides us with the urge to worship...anything suitable.

What is the difference between worshipping a rock or an idol with the true worship of the Universal Creator? Could it be that soul worship achieves the reality of communicating with God? The soul does not need the adjutant spirit of worship for the urge to worship. The inexpressible longings and unutterable aspirations of the human soul is directly communicated to the divine Creator. The soul has a personal relationship with the reality of the First Source.

7. **The Circuit Of Wisdom**--the inherent tendency of all moral creatures towards orderly and progressive evolutionary advancement. This is the coordinator that makes the work of all the others intelligible. Through this circuit comes the urge of mind creatures which initiates and maintains the program of transformation – continuous life; their ability to coordinate all their past experience and present opportunities. Wisdom is the acme of intellectual performance. To be wise is the epitome of human mental and moral existence.

When, as a child, you were given money, you might have initially spent it all at once. As you aged you might have learned to save some of it for a future time. This growth in wisdom was facilitated by the coordination of the six other mind spirits. Through intuition, understanding, courage, knowledge, counsel, and worship, you learned the wisdom of delayed gratification. The mind spirit of wisdom may even have urged you to make it into a hard and fast rule of living. Appreciate the mind spirit of wisdom urging us to orderly advancement by coordinating the other six adjutants and formulating human philosophy.

Then reflect on how your mind's wisdom is rooted in the linear material world, while your soul's wisdom partakes of spiritual reality. The soul's wisdom transcends fixed rules and human experience and taps into the existential wisdom of spiritual realities. Human wisdom is often rigid and rule oriented, the soul's wisdom is characterized by spontaneity and flexibility. Human wisdom focuses on the illusions of this life, while the soul's wisdom encompasses the destiny of eternal life.

Mastery of Self (Depth)
Organismal drives and attitudes, the varying levels of self-realization and the general phenomenon of reaction to environment.

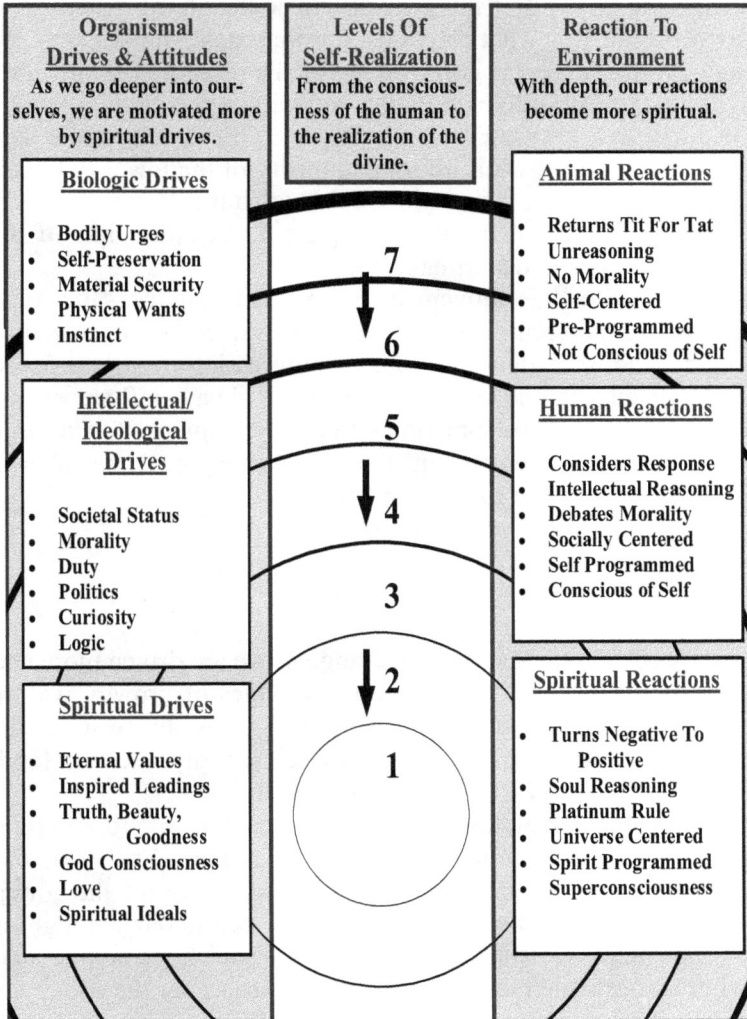

Organismal Drives & Attitudes	Levels Of Self-Realization	Reaction To Environment
As we go deeper into ourselves, we are motivated more by spiritual drives.	From the consciousness of the human to the realization of the divine.	With depth, our reactions become more spiritual.

Biologic Drives

- Bodily Urges
- Self-Preservation
- Material Security
- Physical Wants
- Instinct

Animal Reactions

- Returns Tit For Tat
- Unreasoning
- No Morality
- Self-Centered
- Pre-Programmed
- Not Conscious of Self

Intellectual/ Ideological Drives

- Societal Status
- Morality
- Duty
- Politics
- Curiosity
- Logic

Human Reactions

- Considers Response
- Intellectual Reasoning
- Debates Morality
- Socially Centered
- Self Programmed
- Conscious of Self

Spiritual Drives

- Eternal Values
- Inspired Leadings
- Truth, Beauty, Goodness
- God Consciousness
- Love
- Spiritual Ideals

Spiritual Reactions

- Turns Negative To Positive
- Soul Reasoning
- Platinum Rule
- Universe Centered
- Spirit Programmed
- Superconsciousness

7 6 5 4 3 2 1

II. Mastery of Self - Depth

The person's movement in cosmic depth embraces 1. The organismal drives and attitudes 2. The varying levels of self-realization and 3. The general phenomenon of reaction to environment. It is what drives us, our innermost motivations. By analogy, this is the car going downhill. Think of this as the inner work that we must do in realizing our spiritual leadings. Depth is the dimension of progression in Psychic Circles attainment as a result of the progression from the ministry of the lower to higher spiritual influences. Psychic Circles attainment is not merely spiritual growth, but balanced progression in the realms of the material, mindal and spiritual.

Again, this movement is happening at the same time that we are traveling forward and sideways, in the dimension of length and breadth. Although progression may proceed predominantly in one dimension, there are always influences that affect the other two, sometimes minutely, sometime in a large way. Inward movement in the dimension of depth always facilitates movement forward in length.

1. Organismal Drives And Attitudes

As we evolve, our basic drives change as we are driven more and more by deeper leadings. In the early stages of growth, we are mainly driven by our biological bodily urges: the instinct for self-preservation, our need for material security such as food, clothing and shelter and other physical wants.

After our biologic needs are taken care off to a certain degree we start to become less self-centered so that our intellectual and/or ideological drives can focus on the group rather than just on the self. This is manifested in our willingness to implement societal mores, political, social, economic and religious work and other projects that we see as our duty.

As our perception of universe reality evolves, we reach higher levels of self-realization which results in the outworking in our lives of transcendental values brought about by inspiration. More and more truth, beauty and goodness, cosmic consciousness and unconditional love become manifest daily as we begin to be led more by our spiritual drives.

However, this does not mean that the lower drives are erased and done away with. As long as we live in the material world with a material body, we must still keep the drives that keep the physical organism alive. The same is true with our intellectual and ideological drives. But as we reach higher consciousness and begin to manifest the higher spiritual drives, those drives and attitudes begin to take precedence. When a choice has to be made between acting on our bodily urges, our intellectual thoughts, or our spiritual leadings, we choose the spiritual over the intellectual and physical. For example, the urge to eat can be stifled if there is not enough food for all, and the spiritual leading of letting others eat over one's own wants, if strong enough, should be able to overpower the personal physiological drive for sustenance. The mental drive to do one's duty as understood intellectually can also be suppressed by spiritual drives. A good example is the military officer who is ordered to execute a prisoner without due process. The officer's spiritual drives stemming from love and cosmic consciousness may forestall the action that was based on a purely intellectual level.

The depth of organismal drives and attitudes are not manifested as steps that are left when completed. The progression is more like ever deepening circles of behavior with the deepest circle of spiritual drives taking precedence over the shallower circles of intellect and biology.

2. Levels Of Self-Realization

The levels of self-realization that we progress through could be described as animal, human, and divine. It's relatively easy to see the animal within ourselves. For some people that's all they see. In fact, to be like an animal is seen as something good in certain circles, namely for some members in the military as well as athletes, and in other activities where the "macho" mentality is desired. In many primitive societies, the warrior identified with wild animals for their strength and ferocity and even now we name our more dynamic sports teams after them: Lions, Falcons, Raptors, etc. The truth is that we are not very much removed from the animal and it doesn't take much to realize this. But it is okay to acknowledge our animal heritage. We need to know and realize that we are not very far from being animals and that we have to be mindful of this background so we can be always watchful in maintaining our humanity over our animal tendencies. And there may even be certain times in our lives when our animal traits can come in useful; possibly in times of dire physical difficulties when animal instincts under the watch care of the mind and spirit can be used to assure survival.

To realize that we are humans and not animals require knowledge and understanding of the difference. What differentiates you from an animal? What qualities do you have that puts you a step or two above a dog, cat or monkey? The ability to communicate complex thoughts, to think ahead, to create technology, are some of the things we can do that animals cannot. We also have to ability to contemplate the universe and question our purpose here as well as to formulate a philosophy of living. And we can have cosmic consciousness. And be aware that we are aware. When we begin to realize these things, we can get above the level of identifying with animals and start to see the value of being human.

As humans we contemplate our purpose here and begin to realize that there is more to the universe and our lives than what is readily visible. We begin to see with our "inner eye," that is, we begin to feel with our minds and souls the existence of spiritual reality and start to realize the divinity within us. This opens up realms of new potential. Is it possible that we do not have to die? Can we exist as something more than human? What is it within us that can transcend material life? Upon determined and persistent seeking, these questions are answered in varying degrees to the soul and they are largely realized through faith garnered through spiritual experiences and spiritual insight.

The Seven Cosmic Circles

These circles are also known as the Psychic Circles, referring to the levels of the mind. It is a conceptualization of the fact that as we move forward in transformation, we also go deeper inward into our minds. These levels of development happen in the total progression of the physical, mindal and spiritual selves; it reflects the development of the person as a whole; body, mind and soul. Since there are areas that overlap as well as times when a person may regress as well as progress, it is difficult to say exactly in which circle a person may be in at a given time.

Imagine seven concentric circles, the seventh being the outermost circle and the first the innermost. One enters at the seventh level, which is just above the animal stage, empowers the soul around the third level and can communicate directly and constantly with the divine spirit after reaching the first level.

The following areas are where the unified human vehicle must make improvements in order to progress in these levels:

Material and physical – The inner resources necessary to deal with one's material environment, the body being part of this environment. Progress in being able to handle problems of material need as well as the vicissitudes of physical health is important.

Mindal and emotional - Progress in clear and reasoned thinking. Inquiry, study and action. Developing a philosophy to manage the problems of life.

Soul and Spirit - Progress in following the leadings of the spirit. Identifying with spiritual and eternal values over material and temporal values.

Advancing in the above areas constitutes inward movement - depth, however, since the way we advance through these levels is by upgrading from the standard mind circuits and to the higher spiritual circuits, this also results in forward movement - length.

3. Reactions To Environment

As we immerse ourselves deeper into self-realization, we progress from the consciousness of the human to the realization of the divine. This results in changes of our reaction to our environment. It seems the deeper we go, the better we get. Our animalistic reactions such as returning evil for evil, unreasoning fear, and self-centeredness are replaced by such human reactions as intellectual reasoning, being socially centered, and making conscious decisions. Then we go deeper to spiritual reactions such as unconditional love, returning good for evil, selflessness, and being universe centered.

The urges from the mind circuits and the leadings of the higher spiritual circuits play an important part in this progression of self-realization and reaction to our environment.

Our animalistic reactions are purely biological and is part of us through the millions of years of physical evolution that we had to undergo in order to become who we are now. We have been conditioned to respond animalistically because our bodies are animals. But since we have developed an intellect, and through the intellect the means of receiving the urges of the standard mind circuits and then the leadings of the higher spiritual circuits, we can progress to displaying human reactions and then spiritual reactions, overcoming the bellicose tendencies of the animal within us.

Animals return tit for tat, as in getting bit and biting back. Humans consider what is the best response. The spiritual reaction is to always do good, even return good for evil. Animals are unreasoning, humans react with intellectual reason, our soul reacts with spiritual reasoning. Animals have no morality, humans react by debating what the best morals are and create societal mores, the soul knows that all human morality is relative and reaches for spiritual morality. Animals are mainly self-centered; humans are socially centered, their perception by society being important; the soul is universe centered, recognizing our place in the whole scheme of things. Animals are hardwired to act in certain ways, they are pre-programmed;

humans can change their programming, they can self-program themselves; the soul seeks to be divinely programmed by the spirit. Animals are not self-conscious, they are not aware that they exist; humans are self-conscious of themselves, they are aware of their existence; the soul is superconscious; the soul is aware that it is aware.

These transformations of behavior in our everyday lives do not happen instantaneously. From the human standpoint, we have to be ever vigilant of the animal sneaking through, and we must strive to allow the spirit to become more dominant. When we are weak, tired, fatigued, intoxicated, emotionally overwrought, hungry, etc., the animal raises its ugly head. It is much easier to be nice and civil when one is energetic, cheerful and clearheaded. I often see people in public places that seem to be in an evil mood, that is, they are surly and not very loving. Rather than condemn them for being bad people, I try to understand why they are that way. And I begin to understand their point of view by looking at myself when I am sometimes in a bad mood. Most often, it is because of a pain or a discomfort, whether physical or emotional that causes me to be irritable and in a bad mood, and I began to realize that that is how it is for most people. Having a bad headache can make people act animalistically. Physical discomfort can force us to act in ways which we normally would not.

The trying times we have when we are physically tortured by our health are one of the challenges that we face in the material plane. The way we maintain our spiritual ideals and treat people with love and grace when we are undergoing pain and suffering is by allowing the spirit through, thereby overcoming our animal and human reactions with our spiritual reactions.

This is one of our goals in the now: to overcome physical limitations through spiritual oneness and insight. To attain the peace and tranquility of the eternal in the now.

There are those who act like animals because they are in pain. Then there are those who act like animals for other reasons. In other words, their reaction to environment is to return tit for tat, unreasoning, immoral, self-centered, pre-programmed, and not conscious, not because they are suffering from physical or mental pain but because they have made the wrong choices using their gift of free will.

There are circumstances, such as upbringing, culture, societal environment and education that predisposes some people to disregard spiritual values. They have been led by other humans or negative circumstances to think that reacting to the environment with animalistic reactions is the only way to live. Some even think that their animalistic reactions are spiritual because they have been taught this way by a theologic ideology. There are many people who are of this ilk, some in high places in government and in organized religious institutions. Many of the problems in the world can be attributed to such people.

Then there are people who react in a typically human way, and it is varied because humans react by considering their responses, intellectually reasoning out their reactions, debating the proper morality, reacting according to societal norms, reacting according to the way they programmed themselves, and with self-consciousness.

The spiritual reaction is to always do good, to return good for good, and even good for evil; to use soul reasoning, and not just the intellect; to see that human morality is relative according to culture and circumstances; to react by being centered in the universe; to be spiritually programmed; and to be superconscious of the self as well as the universal environment.

Returning Good For Evil

To return good for evil is not easy for most people. The immediate reaction upon being struck is to strike back. To receive negative energy and to be able to convert it into positive energy is truly the hallmark of a dynamic soul.

To refuse to defend ourselves is difficult for the animal mind to understand. Our instincts tell us to fight back. That if we do not do this, that we will lose our integrity, our faith, our rights, and everything we've worked towards. The materially minded person cannot get beyond this as this is where spiritual reality departs from material reality.

Indeed, in defending material possessions, we will lose our property if we do not defend against aggression. We will have our families killed, our land taken, our freedom curtailed, our lives destroyed. Spiritually, though, it is not so. Refusing to defend ourselves will not destroy our faith, our integrity, our values, nor the ground gained by our evolving souls. These values remain in the universal mind and cannot be so easily negated. Rather, it is by trying to defend such eternal values that we tarnish them. For, if we have faith in ourselves and our righteousness, in those values gained through life's experiences and the resultant good that is stored in the Supreme, then there is absolutely no reason to defend them. What is eternal needs no defense.

The ideal is to turn an evil committed onto us into good. This ideal is difficult to attain because we live in a material world where things are decidedly eye for an eye. It may be that the original thought of an eye for an eye was gleaned through observation of the physical laws of the universe, the physical laws of our time/space reality. The world does not return good for evil. If we err in falling off a tall building, gravity has no love that will gently float us onto a soft cushion. The mechanical system of cause and effect is often harsh and seemingly without love and tolerance. But love and tolerance is there in the hands of the Mother Spirit. For it is only through such baptisms of reality that we learn and evolve. It is only by being faced with the consequences of our deeds that we can start to take responsibility for our actions. The eye for an eye system of cause and effect is inherently necessary in the way the material time and space universe is created.

So when do we return good for evil? And when do we act with an eye for an eye? I have struggled with this at first but now I am convinced that if we wish to identify with our spirit-led soul in the realm of spiritual values, we must return good for evil, while the eye for an eye approach can be used in applying ourselves to physical and mechanical systems or on the animal level. But as we evolve spiritually, more and more we respond in terms of the spiritual, and less and less we base our reactions on the animal level.

How can we relate this to real life situations? To the daily confrontations with negative energy? To the strife between nations? The little conflicts we face everyday are all about material things, they relate to the comfort of our material shells: our bodies and the attached ego. They are important in their own right, but not more important than the relationships we have with each other's souls and the relationship we have with the Creator. They are not more important than the values by which we spiritually evolve. It is okay to defend our material possessions, but never at the expense of the soul values that we have struggled so hard to attain.

A piece of land is non-spiritual, a car is non-spiritual, a house is non-spiritual, money is non-spiritual. They are all means to an end. The end itself is the relationships between people, between all creatures and our Creator. So why kill ourselves, hurt each other and sacrifice this community, this relationship we are building with each other on this beautiful planet over non-spiritual things?

There are many reasons. Mostly insecurity and the mental poisons of fear, hate, anger, envy, lust and lack of self-esteem, which all stem from being separate from the universal consciousness. Then there is our age-old animal heritage of always wanting to fight and defeat an enemy, to create one if necessary because we are biologically hard wired to kill the latest saber-tooth tiger in the neighborhood. Some people simply like to fight.

Even intellectual sophistry can lead us away from spiritual thinking. One of my more seductive thoughts was that if we do not respond to an action mechanically, that is, returning tit for tat, that the offending person will not learn that his actions were harmful. "If I don't smack 'em upside the head, they're not gonna learn!" Why should we, as humans, abrogate cause and effect, the teaching method of nature?

I think the answer to that is that the ascending child of God learns an eye for an eye from the physical laws, but that the spiritual laws must be gleaned by being a recipient of good for an evil that we have committed to another. First hand experience of the manifestation of love leads us to grow spiritually. The offending person does not evolve his soul by being retaliated against. The evolution occurs only when his negative act returns as a positive response thereby causing him to reflect on his spirituality, which often creates a desire to make better moral decisions.

However, the purpose of returning good for evil is not to change the actions, the attitude or the morality of our fellow mortals. Its intention should not be to manipulate others into fitting into our agendas, however benign and spiritual we think they are. We return good for evil just because that is the quality of our indwelling divinity which is reflected by our soul. We return good for evil simply because that is the way of the spirit, because it is the right thing to do.

As material beings slowly evolving into spiritual entities, returning good for evil represents our growth into the higher levels of spirituality, like marks on the wall that record our incipient growth as cosmic children. Upon what fond memories will we reminisce when we have evolved into a much higher state and look down on those old scratch marks on the walls of our first home?

Mastery of Environment—Breadth
The domain of coordination, association, and selfhood organization.

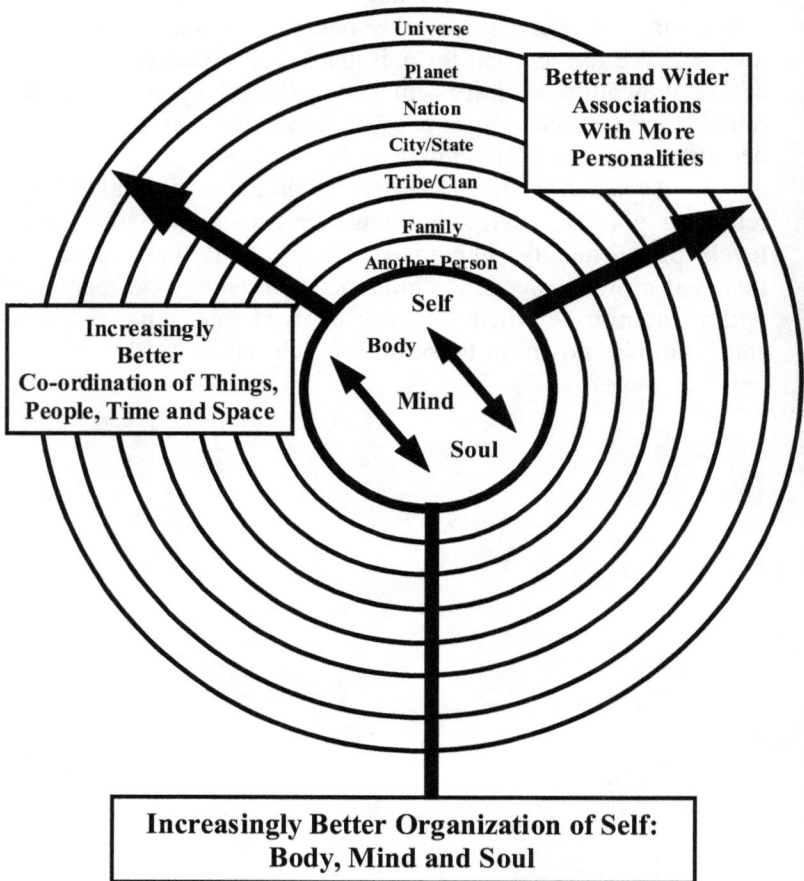

Universe
Planet
Nation
City/State
Tribe/Clan
Family
Another Person
Self
Body
Mind
Soul

Better and Wider Associations With More Personalities

Increasingly Better Co-ordination of Things, People, Time and Space

Increasingly Better Organization of Self: Body, Mind and Soul

III. Mastery of Environment - Breadth

The person's movement in cosmic breadth embraces the domain of 1. Co-ordination, 2. Association, and 3. Selfhood organization: how we work with other people, things and situations. Think of this as the car turning to the side. This is the ability of our body, mind and soul to go out into the world to actualize our spiritual leadings. Moving in the dimension of breadth does not necessarily get a person to the destination quicker, but it will make the quality of the journey better. Breadth is the realm of our activities during the journey, appreciating and enjoying ourselves and the company we keep as well as the quality of our experiences.

1. Coordination

As we evolve, we widen our sphere of influence and consciousness so that we become increasingly better at coordinating things, people, time and space. We start to become adept at arranging events so that we do the right things with the right people at the right time in the right place.

We see a lack of coordination of things, people, time and space very frequently in the world. Some people cannot do the simple act of being at a certain place at a certain time; they are always late. This is a measure of not having a handle on time. Difficulties in relationships is a symptom of a lack of coordination of people. Financial problems stem from a lack of being able to coordinate things and people, while not being aware of one's place, whether it's geographical, social or spiritual is due to the inability to coordinate space. The ability or non-ability to coordinate one's own being also has a bearing on all the above.

Individuals who are unable to coordinate things, people, time and space have something in common. They do not realize its importance and do not care to focus on these things. It is not uncommon for many people to look down on "things" as being too material. There are those who do not value other people and their relationships suffer. People who think that being on time is of small matter may think, "What difference does it make if I'm half an hour late?" But doing this constantly can result in that person being out of synch with life in general. Their timing in the circumstances of life become skewed. And those who disregard the importance of space become more than geographically lost. They become disoriented in the direction of their life, unable to realize where they are, where they came from and where they are going.

Learning how to coordinate things, people, time, and space enables us to have material wealth, good relationships with others, synchronization with the circumstances in life, and a good working idea of our origin, our present, and our destiny.

One of the more essential aspects of exploring the personal performance range of breadth is the coordination of people. Coordination of people through service will benefit almost all aspects of one's life by bettering personal relationships. Personal relationships are paramount to life. Without the interaction of one's body, mind, and soul with the body, mind, and soul of others, life has no meaning whatsoever. All of our endeavors, work, play, worship, creativity, science, philosophy, sports, art, everything is based on relationships with other personalities, some even divine. Self-maintenance and solitary activities may be two exceptions, but even those things have meaning only within the larger context of associating with other people. It you are unsatisfied with any part of your external life, it is probably due to the lack of service you give to people. Service that can coordinate your relationships with them.

Again, service is to act on behalf of the whole rather than the part. On behalf of the group rather than the individual, the individual most often being yourself. This does not necessarily mean self-sacrifice, because you are also part of the group. So service must serve not only the interests of others but also yourself. Therein lies the seeming difficulty and the paradox which is inherent in an elliptical universe.

One of the things that make it more difficult than it is are the mental toxins of Fear, Anger, Envy, Jealousy, Suspicion and

Intolerance. These mental poisons are just as insidious and harmful as physical poisons, maybe even more, because the physical poisons are visible and we are warned about them in magazines, television, books and even on bumper stickers. But mental poisons are taken for granted as being a part of us, as something we have little or no control over. This is in error. We can and should work on ridding ourselves of these terrible toxins of the mind.

If you take a close look at all the relational problems you've had with other people, you will notice that they were all directly caused or influenced by these toxins within yourself or within others, but most of the time within all parties concerned. (Unless it was caused by physical toxins.)

People indulge in these mental poisons voluntarily, just as they may indulge in physical toxins such as nicotine or alcohol. The indulgence is usually caused by insecurity. We get Fearful when we are insecure of our health, status, self-esteem, possessions, and love. We get Angry when we are insecure of our point of view, of being right, of being understood, of being taken seriously. We get Envious when we are insecure that we are not having as good an experience as others. We get Jealous when we are insecure of our worth because others are having a better experience. We get Suspicious when we are insecure of our faith in others. And we get Intolerant when we are insecure in our perception of truth and goodness in other people.

Kicking these mental habits would certainly be doing a service to ourselves. The way to banish these poisons from our minds is to be secure. Secure in the safety of our body, mind and soul; secure in being fallible and not taking ourselves too seriously; secure in the value of our own lives and personal experiences; secure in our self-worth, without comparison to others; secure in our faith of others; and secure in our minds of the existence of truth and goodness in other people. But where do we get such a powerful sense of security? There is only one place, one source of absolute security, and that is the Creator of All, and the connection to that source is within us. By regular contact with that source, we can achieve security of the body, mind, and soul.

2. Association

Our levels of association also grows with our self consciousness until we reach cosmic consciousness. Step by step, we grow from thinking about the welfare of just ourselves to thinking about the welfare of larger and larger groups. From the one to the whole.

If the "whole" that we are dealing with is one's family, it is quite probable that we know what is good for it. But as we deal with an ever increasingly larger whole, be it school, organization, city, state, nation or planet, the harder it becomes for us to know what is good for the entirety.

When we consider the ultimate whole, the universe of universes, not only in space but in time, how can one mere mortal possibly know what is good for such a mind-bending aggregate of matter, mind and spirit? And if we cannot know what is good for the whole universe, how can one individual do anything for the whole rather than for oneself? Because of this conundrum, most people will only act beneficially for the whole that one can see around them and know intimately such as one's family and friends. The wider one's sphere of influence and consciousness, the better the understanding and acceptance of what the whole encompasses. Some behave for the good of the whole family, some for the good of the whole city, some for the good of the whole nation, and some for the good of the whole planet. Not many human beings can see and know what is good for the whole universe. But that is our target: increased levels of spiritual perception and cosmic consciousness.

This development of cosmic consciousness will eventually happen to the group, starting from families to churches to small communities to larger groups, cities, states and nations, and then to the whole planet. Individuals, however, can proceed at their own pace. It is entirely possible for an individual to identify with the entire universe and to have loyalty to the whole of creation regardless of their group's inclinations. This is made possible by connecting to the spirit within, the divine fragment of the Creator with which we are all endowed. This contact is made possible because the soul initiates it, the mind consents to it and the spirit conducts it. Once the individual achieves such a contact, even for a second, a oneness with the universe ensues, and regular contact results in a peace that passes the understanding of most people. This is when identity with the whole of the universe begins and faith/insight becomes a tremendous force when having to decide what is good for oneself as related to the whole.

However, in achieving such lofty states of perception and consciousness, one must start from the individual's center of being, we must be able to organize our self-hood efficiently.

3. Self-hood Organization

Coordination and association starts from our self-hood. We must organize well our body and material environment with our mind and consciousness together with the efforts of the soul and the leadings of the spirit. Self organization is where it all starts. We must organize our self so that we allow the soul to be the driver of the vehicle. The soul is coordinated by mind and takes direction from the spirit and is the most qualified to take our vehicle to our destination. However, the soul is not infallible. It does make seeming mistakes. But the soul learns from the mistakes and is not afraid to make them. It can even be said that that is the only way it learns. So in spiritual reality, the soul cannot make mistakes, as all "mistakes" are but learning experiences that are necessary. So always be kind to yourself, to your soul. If you make a seeming mistake, it is quite all right. Rejoice in it! Be happy that you now know what not to do, and that now you have the knowledge to do the right thing.

It is often hard to be happy with our mistakes as we get pressured from the external world to kick ourselves, to be ashamed and guilty; society does not like our mistakes and wants us to feel bad about them. But remember that all external pressure is detrimental. It is only the internal pressure from within ourselves that can take us to our destination. This is because our souls learn from our own decisions and from our own thoughts and experiences, as well existentially from the spirit, not from second hand sources. Not to say that we shouldn't listen to suggestions and advice, but to be pressured into following other people's advice without the benefit of evaluating them using our own wisdom is pure folly. When you have made a seeming mistake, when it seems that you have done wrong, it is good to become aware of where that judgment comes from. Is it something that comes from society, from what others may say? Or is it something from within yourself? If it is from an external source and if it is not agreed upon internally give it little weight, as it is but someone's personal opinion. If it comes from deep within yourself, acknowledge it, learn from it, let it go and move on. This is a part of self-organization that is very pivotal in being able to move forward efficiently in knowledge and experience.

In a sense we can say that our body is the animal quality, our mind is the human quality and our soul is the divine quality. So in organizing our body, mind, and soul, we are organizing the animal, human and divine qualities within us. The ideal is that the animal is subordinate and follows direction, the human coordinates direction, and the divine gives us direction. But the human mind is the arena of choosing, this is where we have free will, so this is where we can accept or reject the directions given us by the spark of our divine creator.

Why would we even think of rejecting such divine direction? It would seem to be a no-brainer. But because the minds of most people are still affected greatly by the animal body, we are torn apart by self-interest and self-gratification versus universe interest and universe gratification. In other words, the divine spirit may direct us to give and share but the body may want to keep and not share our blessings, and so the mind is caught in a tug of war and sometimes the body wins. Sadly, it is *too often* that the body wins in the case of many people in this day and age. We can change this. It is through the regular practice of becoming one with the universe and the Creator: worshipful meditation, prayer and service, that we can begin to accept more and more the direction of the spirit within us. It is by transcending the material that we can transcend the wants of the body and allow the mind to follow the spirit's directives. That is how we can win this constant tug of war for our souls.

We move in the dimension of breadth in conjunction with our inner work in the dimension of depth and our progression in the dimension of length. It is the harmonized and seamless progression in all three dimensions of length, depth and breadth that moves us closer to our spiritual goals. In relation to our destination, we are always moving forward, sideways and up and down, simultaneously, to a lesser or greater degree, even when we are focusing on moving in one of the above dimensions.

Chapter Five
Care & Maintenance / Customizing

The one fact that I would cry out from every rooftop is this:
the Good Life is waiting for us – here and now! . . .
At this very moment we have the necessary techniques,
both material and psychological,
to create a full and satisfying life for everyone.

- B.F. Skinner

Spiritual Technology

There are many technological inventions that make our bodies mobile such as the cart, wagon, bicycle, automobile, train, airplane, rocket, etc. Our ingenuity has created many devices for transcending our physical body's limitations, and this same ingenuity has created methods and processes for furthering our spiritual growth.

Some of these add-ons are like vehicles in their own right, and there have been religions formed in the past based upon using such devices, while some are just inspiring thoughts to guide us. Some have become ritualized. Whatever their level of complexity they are all devices that optimize the mobility of our unified human vehicle, our Personhood, in the mastery of our destiny, our selves, and our environment.

Basically, this is "spiritual technology".

The most important thing necessary in order to get our vehicle moving in the right direction is the ability to follow the spirit's leadings. Although the body and the mind are equal partners in this adventure, they have their jobs as does the spirit. The body's job is to stay alive and be healthy, to be the material platform for the mind and soul. The spirit's job is to lead, to give us direction in the course of our lives. The mind's job is to make decisions, to follow the directions of the spirit and at the same time to keep the body healthy and happy, but sometimes the body and the spirit have conflicting desires, they want to go in two separate directions, and sometimes there is garbled reception of the leadings of the spirit. There can be many problems associated with running the human vehicle efficiently and purposefully and there have been many techniques created on how to reconcile these difficulties. These techniques are your custom upgrades. For your human vehicle comes with standard components that are essential to everyone, but it is often desirable to add a few additional devices to suit your own needs.

Because of the ritualization of some techniques for mobilizing our human vehicle, there are age old methods that have become adorned and encumbered with unnecessary baggage and stifling practices. So first, a word on rituals.

Got Rituals?

In the early days of mankind's history when we use to be foragers, the whole tribe would travel in search of food. When the tribe got lucky they would find a stand of wild grain or a flock of wild chicken and they would settle down for a time until all the food was eaten. Then they would move on. One day someone thought of planting seeds to grow their own food and raising animals on their own. This enabled the tribe to settle down permanently in one place and start a civilization.

The same goes for spiritual food, that is, spiritual experience. We could live our lives hoping that we would come across spiritual experiences, or we could be proactive and create situations that lead us directly to them. People have been doing this for ages.

A creative individual would have an enlightening experience seeing an inspiring sunrise and would try to duplicate it by having a bonfire lit on top of a hill at all times. Once a day the people would go to the hill to pray and worship. This worked great for a while until the novelty wore off and it became a meaningless ritual, but the people found it difficult to abandon the practice when it became a superstition. They feared that ceasing to honor the ritual would bring them bad luck. Consequently, they still keep practicing the senseless ritual to this day, empty of all meaning and value.

The moral of this story is that rituals can be an effective and beautiful way to remind ourselves that we are in the presence of God at all times, by utilizing it to open our minds to a fresh realization of God's love for us and each other, but when the original meaning is lost, there is no value to it and should be discarded. Then, new meaningful rituals can be created which will give us new ways of having a spiritual experience.

Techniques to further our spiritual explorations have been around a long time, unfortunately, much of them has devolved into meaningless rituals awkwardly supported by dogma and tradition. Some of them are effective to a degree but there is so much baggage attached to them that they do not charm or attract those who seek to get away from the rigid doctrines and limiting creeds that surround those traditions. All rituals will eventually fade and disappear, but we must take care not to throw out the baby with the bathwater. We must keep the drive to seek out spiritual experiences on our own, rather than to adhere to obsolete practices or to just wait for new ones to appear. And we need to lighten up our attitude on rituals. Have fun with them and not take them so seriously.

Having mentioned how methods of receiving spiritual inspiration have devolved into rituals, we must keep that tendency from crystallizing and ritualizing our practices that enable us to keep in touch with spirit. By realizing that these methods are personal and that what works well for one person might not for others, and that the practices must change and evolve as we ourselves change and evolve, we can maintain an atmosphere of objectivity and openness in our efforts to create and work on progressive devices for stimulating spiritual activity.

What follows are some tried and true methods. There are more, some that I know of and probably more than I am not aware of, many of which may be in the process of being created right at this instant. They can all be described under the general heading of soul work.

Soul Work

Soul work can be described as any process where we explore the length, depth and breadth of our inner and outer reality in order to ascertain and to do the will of our Creator. In this section we will cover 1. Connecting to the Source - Worshipful Meditation 2. Connecting to Our Self - Uplifting Prayer, and 3. Connecting to Others - Service.

God is within and God is without. The universal Creator created all realities, internal and external, so therefore he must simultaneously exist in both. To say otherwise is to put human conceptual limits on an omniscient, omnipresent, omnipotent, eternal, absolute and infinite being. Some thinkers in the past relegated God only to the external or internal, just as they limited it to being personal or impersonal, male or female. The Creator of All, by definition must encompass all of those realities, and more.

The effort to get closer to God in the external world as we progress in space and time and as we upgrade in form and levels of mind toward Paradise is the movement of the person in cosmic length. The superconscious reflections of *worshipful meditation* is an effective tool to optimize this movement. During this process, we allow our souls to consciously recognize the external reality of total space, time and spirit as discovered by science and informed by revelation, and are drawn by the Creator's energy to increasingly make physical reality perfect. By manifesting divinity in our lives we change for the better the world around us, including our own form.

The effort to find God in the internal world as we delve deep into our inner life is the movement of the person in cosmic depth. The uplifting power of *prayer* is an efficacious method to fully empower the divine resources in the depths of our being. By praying to manifest in our lives our deepest drives and most spiritual reactions, we bring our most profound qualities to the fore.

The effort to find God in the souls of other people and in his creations is the movement of the person in cosmic breadth. The loving ministry of *service* is a tried and true way to achieve such divine relationships with God's creatures and creations. By coordinating, organizing and associating the various things, systems and personalities of the world around us in uplifting service, we transmit the love from God to each other in a network of divine harmony.

These efforts by the person to find God in all three dimensions is soul work. Through soul work we optimize the performance of our unified human vehicle. The vehicle can function without conscious soul work, but it will be sluggish and performance will be mediocre and unexceptional.

Through our natural and inherent desire that draws us toward the source of all creation, we allow the spiritual ministry of our Creator to draw our imperfect animal selves toward becoming perfecting spirits. This ministry is reflected in the Seven Mind Spirits of *intuition, understanding, courage, knowledge, counsel, worship and wisdom.* As we become more tuned in to the First Source of creation, we give more credit to intuition, we want more understanding, we value courage more, we gain more thirst for knowledge, we desire better relationships, we wish more fulfilling worship, and we gain more wisdom. This results in steadily advancing through the psychic circles of universal attainment, and when the quality and quantity of our soul reaches critical mass, we begin to allow the soul to have more authority in the direction of our lives. The soul, having escaped the animal heritage, cannot use the seven mind circuits and must tap into a higher source of empowerment, the spiritual circuits, which replaces *intuition* with *faith* and *insight, understanding* with *soul reason, courage* with *the soul's convictions of spiritual realties, knowledge* with soul *intelligence, counsel* with recognition of *true relationships*, the urge to *worship* with *true worship*, and *human wisdom* with *soul wisdom.*

For many humans in this age, the soul may not be fully empowered, or if it is, only briefly and sporadically during the course of one's life, so that these higher spiritual influences are rarely used. But through regular soul work, we can progress dynamically in all the personal performance ranges of length, depth and breadth.

1. Connecting To The Source: Meditation

I have experience with three very different types of meditational states: worshipful meditation, mindal meditation, mystical meditation.

Worshipful meditation is the act of reaching out to the Creator of All. It is an attempt to contact and to be unified with the First Source of all creation. A superconscious state; connecting to the Source.

Mindal meditation is the mind becoming aware of and changing the basic programming of its mental software.

Mystical meditation is an exploration of the subconscious through dissociating with external reality and fixating on a fragment of inner reality.

At any given meditation session, I mainly explore the primary states of spiritual and mindal meditation. I avoid delving into mystical meditation now as it is a subconscious process. It is more productive to nurture superconsciousness rather than subconsciousness, to be totally aware of one's awareness rather than to focus one's awareness on a segment of one's mind.

How can we discuss a state that is totally internal? We can't see meditation, can't touch meditation. How do we know that what we are talking about is the same thing? Intellectually, we can't. But the senses of the soul will know if there is an incongruency.

From talking to various people, meditation does not come easy to them. They just don't understand it.

There is a reason for this. It's like the system folders in a PC computer. You don't want inexperienced users messing with the delicate parts of the software. And that's exactly what meditation is; getting into the very root of our mind's operating system and making changes. And that's why meditational techniques are laced with rituals and age-old processes that somehow manage to structure the exploration into inner space in order to keep it from getting out of hand.

And it can get out of hand: Religious fanatics, overzealous proselytizers, doomsday scenarios, and paranoid delusions are results of a mind with corrupt software. The effects of meditation gone wrong.

Some faith traditions have found ways to meditate safely, but all too often, their meditation turns into a mindal or psychological technique rather than a spiritual one.

True worshipful meditation is simultaneously a local and non-local connection to the Creator of all. Being connected and centered in the First Source is like a computer that is always hooked up to the main server, with any changes being immediately recognized and harmonized into the total network.

One of the ways people fail at this is by trying too hard, by making too much of an effort. They think it is a grasping, like we grasp new knowledge; a task, like accomplishing a job; or an accomplishment, like graduating from school. It is not. It is more a letting go, a relaxing, an opening up, an unfolding. It is more like riding a wave than riding a bicycle. Like parachuting, more than climbing a mountain. Like gently floating downstream, more than swimming against a current. Making an effort to grasp it is like trying to grasp air. To best feel the presence of air, one just relaxes and lets the breeze gently waft across one's skin. When you make an effort in feeling the presence of God, the effort contradicts the reality that God is all around you and that no effort is necessary to sense him. To feel his presence, you must be like a receiving satellite dish. Or an ear. They do not make an effort, they do not have to send out signals. They receive by just being. To many people it is difficult because it is so simple.

Maybe a recounting of an early childhood experience will help.

When I first began to learn to swim, I was very tense. I would jump in the water and immediately begin to flail about with my arms and legs, making lots of splashes but resulting in little forward movement. In fact, I sank like a stone.

What I was doing wrong, according to everyone around me, was that I was not taking the time to relax and float first, before moving my limbs. So I did as suggested and I relaxed. I took a breath and floated on the water, feeling its buoyancy all around me, then I gradually started to move my arms and legs. And hey! I was swimming!

Similarly, when a bird flies off of a cliff, it does not always begin flapping its wings immediately. Often it will glide first, feeling the air currents, before making a few well-timed flaps to make it soar through the sky. It becomes aware of its external environment before taking action.

In meditation, we must become aware of our inner environment through a total relaxing of internal and external tension. This awareness is the foundation of superconsciousness. It is being aware of your own awareness. This is where it begins.

This act can begin by simply setting aside time everyday to spend with God, so that one can share one's life with him. But in sharing one's life fully with God, one must be aware of one's inner self, aware of the soul yearning to contact the spirit. The mind allows this contact to happen and worship begins.

The techniques of contacting the Creator have been draped in much mysticism. Some people have difficulties in effectively negotiating this process. The problem may stem from false preconceptions and the tendency to confuse mystic meditation with spiritual meditation. One of the more common reasons some people cannot meditate for longer than a few minutes is "mind chatter" and the inability to simply sit still doing nothing. Mantras and chanting are two methods that were developed to counter these problems. Newer methods and updates of old practices based on new experiential sources are constantly being developed. Mystical meditation is gradually being replaced by spiritual meditation.

Worshipful meditation is awareness of the superconscious contact of communing with the divine spark that dwells within the mind. It is the act of the material mind's assenting to the attempt of its spiritualizing self, under the guidance of the associated spirit, to communicate with the Universal Creator. It is the superconscious, joyous and loving act of recognizing and acknowledging the truth of the intimate relationships of the Creator with us as we are connected through our indwelling spirit to the First Universe Source in the center of space and time. We are attracted by the love gravity of this all powerful source so that we are drawn to evolve in form and consciousness through time and space.

Being superconsciousness, true worshipful meditation is not a trance state or any state of consciousness where we are only dimly aware of our body, mind and surroundings. It is not a state of lesser consciousness, but a state of heightened perception. It is the awareness of communicating with the divine Creator spark within.

By tapping into the source of all sources, one can gather strength, wisdom and energy for the ordinary problems of life. It is also good for drawing the spiritual energy necessary for the solution of the higher problems of a moral and spiritual nature. By becoming one with the All, one can transcend the material world and its lures as well as its pains.

The regular regimen of worshipful meditation and prayer keeps the channel to the Source open and clear. It is like flushing a water hose to keep it from clogging. This makes it possible for spiritual experiences to happen at any time. By always having a clear channel to spirit, one gives the opportunity for spirit to communicate with you wherever and whenever the moment is right. The quality of your worship is determined by your depth of perception; your organismal drives and the realization of your divine nature. As your knowledge of the infinite character of the All progresses, your act of worship will become so all-encompassing that it will eventually attain to be the highest delight and the most exquisite pleasure known to creatures.

Meditation can be beneficial to the soul, whether it is spiritual, mindal or mystical, but there are ways that it can be abused. Be extremely aware that spectacular "fireworks", states of ecstasy, pleasurable vibrations, etc. are only signs of validation, signposts, not the goal itself. Take care not to be fooled by them. True worshipful meditation is being still, giving your full attention to the Source and Center of All. It is a very simple thing and a simple feeling, that, when repeatedly made manifest, becomes a very powerful force.

Dangers of Extreme Mysticism

In attempting any type of mystical meditation as the technique of contacting the consciousness of the Creator, one should take care that such practices do not lead to social isolation and result in religious fanaticism. We know enough of the human mind to know that much too frequently that which the so-called mystic interprets as divine inspiration is coming from his own deep mind. One can be much more sure that one has contacted the divinity within when one has wholeheartedly and lovingly been of service in unselfish ministry to one's fellow creatures.

The point is to have the awareness of the Creator on a superconscious level, not on the subconscious level. There is also danger associated with the habitual practice of spiritual daydreaming; it can become a method of reality avoidance, notwithstanding that it can also be a source of genuine spiritual insight. The essence of divinity is unity, to be one with everybody, that is why prolonged isolation is not conducive to spiritual growth of the entire personhood.

Signs of Extreme Mystical Meditation

o social isolation
o religious fanaticism
o gravitating toward sub-consciousness rather than
    superconscious
o mental dissociation
o abnormal mental manifestations
o making it a technique of reality avoidance
o prolonged isolation of personality
o cultivation of trancelike state
o diffusion of consciousness on a passive intellect

Spiritual, Mindal, and Mystical

Mindal meditation is a wonderful technique that is as important to our health and well being as physical exercise. Recent scientific discoveries such as documented in "Train Your Mind, Change Your Brain" by Sharon Begley show that our external brains can be rewired through an inner process - meditation. We can actually create new brain cells by willing it. The implications are immense. Free will is not a fantasy, we can be who we want to be given the effort.

However, the Buddhist meditational practices mentioned in that book are strictly mindal. It is not *worshipful* meditation because those Buddhists do not believe in a divine Creator. They do not worship. They meditate on feelings like compassion, on being, on thought. When monks with tens of thousands of hours of meditation were wired up to appropriate machines, the data confirmed that brain cells were being created in the part of the brain that was responsible for generating the feeling of compassion, or whatever the focus of the meditation was.

In spiritual worshipful meditation, the mind is not so much concerned with itself and its processes, as in allowing the soul to contact the Creator. But why not use the methods and techniques of mindal meditation to create new brain cells in that part of the brain that reaches out to the Source, the Creator, God? By meditating on the Creator of the universe, can we strengthen that part of our brain that connects with the Creator, by creating more brain cells there? There is no clinical evidence for this, yet, but my personal experimentation has given me results that support that conjecture. I encourage clinical researchers to explore this avenue.

So mindal meditation can easily lead to spiritual meditation if the focus of the mind transcends to the spiritual. In other words, worshipful meditation will not happen unless the mind recognizes spirit and allows it to happen.

In a sense, spiritual meditation is consciousness of connecting with everything – the internal and external realities; yourself, others, the environment and God. Mindal meditation is consciousness of the body, mind and its processes. Mystical meditation is consciousness of selected parts of inner realities. Mystical meditation disassociates the mind from external reality in order to go into a trancelike state. Spiritual meditation associates the mind with inner and outer reality to go into a heightened perceptive state. Spiritual meditation is unifying, mystical meditation can be isolating. Spiritual and mindal meditation focuses the consciousness on a dynamic intellect, mystical meditation diffuses the consciousness on a passive intellect. In order to keep from straying from the consciousness of the external and internal to just the internal, keep your consciousness of the external world awake. To keep the meditation from being just mindal, put God into the mix. Be always conscious of yourself, where you are and the universe around you, from the micro to the macro, and from the personal to the impersonal, from just yourself to all the personalities in the universe.

As there are various ways for attaining this state, the following are only some of the many methods created for worshipful meditation. These deep meditational states take practice. If you have no experience in such things don't expect amazing results right away. (Transcendent results may occur immediately but they are the exception and not the rule.) Regularity and persistence is key. Designate a place in your home for this activity, or not, some people just like to take walks. Some people hang an inspirational picture on a wall and sit in front of it, using it to focus their mind. I have a small Buddhist altar, a remnant of the time I spent in Buddhist practice. Feel free to be creative or to use traditional methods, do what makes you comfortable.

Begin with just a few minutes every day, getting into the habit of sitting down and devoting a hundred percent of your being to accomplishing this. Remember, this is a pleasurable experience. Come away from each session with something positive, even if it is just the appreciation of having time to spend relaxed, unhurried, and devoted to self-improvement. Think of your personal spiritual growth as of the utmost priority, because it is. Realize that the rest of your day is based on these moments of inner work.

This can be as simple as setting aside time everyday to be with God, so that you can share your inner life with her. Sharing your inner life can mean speaking to her as you would to someone next to you, out loud or in your head. Or it could mean just the opposite, being silent and one with the stillness. There are a variety of ways to express your true inner being. Remember, she is there, in you and all around you. The only way you will be unable to feel her presence is if your receiving mechanism is clogged by your own interference so that it is jammed with static. This interference may be caused by a having too many locked boxes inside. Unlock the boxes, learn to let go, open up and relax. It is easy as basking in the sun.

The following exercises do not have to be done exactly as is written. Use them as reference so that you can create what works best for you.

Converting Mind Chatter

One of the greatest obstacles to being mentally still is mind chatter. Thoughts come unbidden, seemingly out of nowhere. Try to think of nothing and everything fills the mind.

It is possible to convert this noisy energy into peace and tranquility. Instead of fighting this flow of thought, relax into it. Go more deeply into each and every thought that appears. Become hyperaware and superconscious of the internal and external; inspect and analyze every little sound that you hear, every irritating itch on your skin, every reminder of your past. Delve fully into each and every chattering thought until you are mentally exhausted. Then, suddenly, think, what is left? Take away all of those conscious thoughts and see into the core of your mind. Look beyond into the space behind the mind chatter and what will you find?

If you have found even a split second of nothingness, you will have found a basis for the stillness. For in nothingness, there is everything. Practice going to this space everyday until you can transport yourself there at will. From that stillness will come a feeling of the eternal presence, the First Source.

Sourcing Love

This is perhaps the easiest way to find the God within. Just reflect on the love you have in your heart. Then meditate on the source of this love. When you trace it all the way back to its primal origin, you will find God. You can do this with all the positive qualities within you that come from God: creativity, altruism, compassion, and more. Follow their trails. They all come from the same place. Spend some time there.

Exploring the Universe: The One and the Whole

Place yourself somewhere quiet where you will not be bothered. Relax and settle in to yourself.

Use your imagination and think of your spirit inside your body. Realize who you are on the deepest level inside: your ideals, motivations, your desires. Think of the people closest to you: your family members, your friends and loved ones. Then think of your body in the room you are in. Think of your body in the room in the house. Think of your body in the room in the house in the neighborhood. Think of your body in the room in the house in the neighborhood in your part of the city or town. At the same time think of all the people that inhabit each geographic level of your awareness. Send out your appreciation and love to them all. Continue with this and increase the scale by increments: the city to the county, the county to the state, the state to the country, the country to the continent, the continent to the planet, the planet to the solar system, the solar system to the galactic spiral arm and on and on until you come to the entire universe as you know it, but always keeping in mind that the myriads of personalities are what really gives meaning and value to the material universe.

Identify with the whole universe. Imagine the countless beings all connected together through the Universe Creator. Imagine the waves crashing on countless shores. Winds whistling through a billion forests, love flowing through a multitude of hearts. Know that you are one with them. That the universe is friendly. Be at peace with everything. Become everything and you can become as nothing – still and in harmony with all. And then realize that it was created by a divine being, the First Source and Center, our Universal Creator, God.

The above is a little exercise that you can do on a regular basis without preparation. There are many more out there that you can find in books. Use the one that speaks to you. I used to do the one above quite often until it evolved into the spiritual treatment below that I occasionally offer people. It is a bit more extensive and entails either memorizing the process or having cards beside you with the written words. When used by yourself, just make it first person by changing the appropriate pronouns and adjusting the phrasing ("I appreciate my life," rather than "thank you for living.")

Although affirmations to oneself can be very effective, when you use affirmations on others, it has more power, as it is always more empowering to have someone else tell you positive things about yourself. When doing the below process, have the person you are treating lie down in a comfortable place and sit right next to the person's head. Gently place your index finger or your palm on the person's head. This soft laying on of hands generates qi energy which keeps the person's awareness attached to the universe, rather than having it become isolated. Take a few moments of quiet time to relax and then softly speak the words to the subject. (It is not necessary to mention the titles in bold print.)

Spiritual Treatment For Cosmic Health

1. Affirmations
    You are, in your true form, a brilliant spiritual being. You deserve the best that the universe has to offer. You receive freely and give freely. Everything is fine. You are master of yourself. The rewards from your efforts increase everyday. The universe is friendly and God loves you. You are fine. You are happy. All is well.

2. Appreciations

Thank you for living! Thank you for having the unique qualities that help make the world a better place! The world rejoices in your life and we are glad of your existence! You are truly appreciated! You make a difference just by being alive!

3. Relaxing

Relax. Health, strength, power, love and peace of mind come from knowing how to relax. The more you relax now, the better you will be later. Each time you relax to your deepest level, you have the ability to re-create yourself. To re-make yourself into a better person: stronger, healthier, smarter and more spiritual. Right now is the time to relax.

4. Soul Identification

In your relaxed state, casually look at the part of you which is the heart of your heart. The very best part of you: your soul. Your soul is free and has purpose and volition. Which means you can do what *you* truly want to do, coming from the very best part of you: your soul. So feel your soul. Be your soul. You are your soul. What does your soul desire in life? No need to think deeply because your soul already knows. Put your soul's desires in an imaginary envelope and set it aside.

5. The Part & The Whole

In your mind, see yourself as you rest here. Now, see your home. Home can be the house or building you live in but also the home of your heart, where all the people that are close to you, your family, friends and loved ones live. Appreciate each and every one of them. Now see your neighborhood and the people you know that live there. Send them your love. Now, do the same with this city and its people. This state and its inhabitants. This continent, this planet, this solar system, this galaxy and then the whole of the universe with all the billions and billions of warm, loving personalities in various shapes and forms. They are your spiritual brothers and sisters. Now you are seeing the universe of personalities as God sees it. He is the creator personality. Meet him on that level, and greet him! Now hand him the imaginary envelope which contains all your soul's desires and give it to him. He takes it and acknowledges your deepest desires. All is well.

6. Thanking God

Now, let us thank the Creator. Thank you, God, for our lives! Thank you for all the creatures in the universe, thank you for making our lives a joyful one! Thank you for the good experiences, for making our lives enjoyable. Thank you for the bad experiences, for allowing us to learn and grow wiser with the experience. Thank you, God, for all that we have and all that will be given us. We truly appreciate our lives!

7. Receiving

Now, be ready to receive an answer. Imagine yourself as a satellite dish pointing to the center of the universe. Or a flower opening its petals up to the sunshine. Be completely relaxed and receptive. Your whole being is tuned in a state of relaxed openness to receiving God's love. God's emanations may come to you in various ways. It may be just a warm feeling or a loving thought. Just be assured and have faith that your soul is soaking it all up. Enjoy this moment of loving and being loved by God!

8. Total Health Of Body, Mind And Soul

Now it is time to narrow our perception from the whole of the universe to clusters of galaxies, then to the galaxy we live in. Then to our solar system, planet, continent, state, county and down to our city, building, room and then to our body. Now, narrow your perception to the parts that make up your body: your face, hands, feet, arms shoulders, your organs. Your blood and bones. See and acknowledge the cells that make up your body. To your cells, you are God. They want your love so that they can love you in turn. Give love to your cells as God gives love to you. Treat your cells as you would want God to treat you. And feel the love from your cells. They adore you. And you adore them. Consciously reach out to them with your mind and bestow to them your highest and deepest love, the love that you received from God. Now realize the importance of your cells getting along well together, and appreciate the importance to God of you getting along well with your fellow creatures. This circulation of divine love and energy from the highest to the lowest, from the largest to the smallest is what empowers the total health of your body, mind and soul.

9. Maintaining The Consciousness and the Circulation

You have relaxed to a place where you are virtually one with God and the universe. Health, strength, power, love and peace of mind are yours. You have relaxed to your deepest level and with God's help, have re-created yourself. You are now a better person − healthier, stronger, smarter and more spiritual. The circulation of divine energies has cleared away all blockages and has revitalized and reinvigorated all your cells. Your mind is now more in tune with God and your soul is empowered and inspired. Maintain this circulation of consciousness in your daily life. Keep the energies flowing everyday. Whatever may happen, know that you can always energize the cycle by tapping in to the peaceful inner space within, where lies the divine spark, the source of total health for your body, mind and soul.

2. Connecting To The Self: Prayer

Prayer mobilizes our unified human vehicle in the performance range of depth. But before we can go further into exploring this process, we need to define what is meant by prayer here, as I have noticed that people use this word to mean different things. Some use the word prayer to mean any process in which we go within our non-material self. What I defined as worshipful meditation is prayer to others. Sending out good thoughts to other people, whether such mental emanations are real or not, can be thought of as prayer.

Affirmations, whether to oneself or to others, are a form of prayer. Mantras, chanting and singing songs of positive intent can be prayer. All of the above may be considered as prayer, but in the main, the word prayer is meant as an appeal to our Creator for intercession in our lives. Through praying, we ask God for assistance.

It may be arrogant and even ludicrous to think that God, an eternal, omnipotent, omnipresent entity will grant the request of one human being just for that person's sake, especially if there are others who are praying for just the opposite result, such as in a war, a conflict or even a sports event. Even when all humans are in agreement that something should be done to alleviate a disastrous condition, their request may be but a shortsighted solution and counterproductive in the long run, in the whole scheme of things in time and space.

We have been given a body, a mind, a spirit, an evolving soul, and many supportive personalities to enable us to lead a fulfilling life. We have been given sufficient tools for the task and one of the values of living this existence is in learning how to use those tools wisely and efficiently in our ascension career. God will not change his plans for creation just because a perfecting mortal who cannot see the big picture is dissatisfied with the way things are going in his small circle of perception. Prayer is not a substitute for clear thinking, work, imagination, and productive effort, nor a way to escape reality. However, prayer does work and prayer has immense value in our lives.

There is a spiritual current that ascends toward God and prayer is a way to stretch out our spiritual wings so that we can catch these updrafts to higher levels. By praying with heartfelt sincerity, we can enhance spiritual growth, change our attitudes, and feel the satisfaction of communing with God. Through prayer, we connect and empower the best part of ourselves.

Our prayers are answered when we receive a better comprehension of truth, an appreciation of the beauty of our lives, and a heightened awareness of goodness. Prayer is a highly potent stimulus for spiritual growth because it must deal with concrete objective realities by reaching out on spiritual levels. Through prayer we transcend human values in search of spiritual values.

The soul's attitude is paramount, not the words themselves. Words are just the conduit in which our spiritual yearnings flow. However, there are psychological values of using certain words that may be important to individuals. Other words may have similar impact during group worship.

It is better to pray for values and not for things. But sometimes we pray for things that are needed for growth and spiritual gratification. To pray to have a house and material wealth for solely selfish purposes would be self-gratification. To pray to have those things in order to raise a family and to contribute to society would be for values that would support growth. The priority should be on the health, happiness and well being of the family and the bigger whole, rather than in the selfish desires of the individual, for sometimes material wealth is not necessary to achieve those worthy values, but can be an impediment when it becomes an obsession.

Understanding this is vital in exploring the statement that prayer mobilizes our unified human vehicle in the performance range of depth. Depth, meaning the process of going deep within ourselves to upgrade our organismal drives, our levels of self-realization and our general reaction to our environment.

Our organismal drives, what drives us as organisms, can be separated into drives stemming from our biology, from our intellect, and from our spirit. Our levels of self-realization is our awareness of our progression from the consciousness of our human self to the realization of our divine self. The reactions to our environment range from animalistic reactions to human reactions and then to spiritual reactions.

In praying for values and growth and not for things and material gratification, we must go to ever deeper levels within so that we can transcend the external biologic and animal drives to focus on making the inner spiritual drives come to the fore. We pray to expand our consciousness from the human to the divine and we pray that our actions and reactions to our environment are more and more spiritual, filled with love, faith, positive thoughts, selflessness, order and the ability to return good for evil. When people pray to have a problem resolved, it is often answered through our perception becoming more centered in the deepest aspect of ourselves, so that we can bring out the deepest and most spiritual part within. Issues that are a result of a conflict between biological and intellectual drives are resolved by centering on and bringing up our spiritual drives. Issues that stem from animalistic and human reactions are resolved by bringing up our spiritual reactions. So prayer is a very handy and powerful device that enables our unified human vehicle to move into our depths – a dimension in which our personhood is well equipped to traverse.

Prayer as in sending out mental energy to others, such as when we pray for individuals who are ill, has also shown to be efficacious in some circumstances. It is said that it works better when that person knows that they are being prayed for, but some say that it works regardless of their knowledge. But it is not the same as asking God for interceding in your behalf, whether it's for your benefit or others.

Prayer, as in asking God for personal intercession, is an ambitious task. What reasons could you possibly give the Creator of the universe to change his plans just for you? Sometimes prayers work, not because God granted your personal request but because, by praying, you opened up your connection to him so that the blockage which caused the problem in the first place was cleared up. In other words, God's plan had been in line with yours all along, but because of not connecting with him previously, you had caused or imagined the difficulty yourself, which prayer alleviated. So prayer works, even if it is for the purpose of clearing away the rubbish that clogged your line to him. But what if your line to him is clear but you still have some issues in your life with which you need his help? In what circumstances would God personally help you? Death and disease is not an issue with God, after all eternal life and eternal health is available to all, once we are done with this phase of existence. Suffering? Maybe, but since suffering is so much a part of living life as a mortal and since it is often necessary for learning our lessons, there would have to be great extenuating circumstances for the Creator himself or even his delegates to step in. Even in praying for values and growth, such boons would not be easily forthcoming as an unearned gift for they are usually the result of many years of experience, contemplation, soul searching and often suffering. But if one feels that such treasures of the soul need to be granted, how can one proceed? What are the guidelines that would make such prayers effective? Here are some thoughts.

1. Prayer is not a substitute for intelligent effort. You must sincerely and courageously face the problems of daily life.

2. You must have tried everything. You must have given it all you've got.

3. You must have let your ego go and have surrendered your personal desires to the leadings of the spirit. You must have placed your focus on learning true meanings and appreciating genuine spiritual values.

4. You must choose to do the divine will wholeheartedly. Indecision must be obliterated.

5. Your choice to do the divine will must be undivided, unconditional, and a dynamic force that results in action.

6. You must acknowledge that your prayer will be considered by the Creator in relation to your eternal destiny, your entire career in the attainment of divine perfection.

7. Your prayer must be empowered by living faith.

Affirmations

Affirmations can be a form of prayer if God is involved. Many will agree that prayer certainly works when it comes to affirmations. Affirmations are wonderful, and it works best when it comes directly from the soul and is in the presence of the spirit. It is not as effective or long lasting when it is used as a psychological tool using only the power of the mind with no input from the soul. By allowing affirmations to reflect the desires of the soul, we follow the leadings of the spirit so that the affirmative thoughts penetrate deep into even the hardest and most inaccessible parts of our being. When we include God in our use of affirmations, we are entering his field of divine energy by sourcing his divine love and embrace.

By affirming with our souls, in the now, the fact and truth of our perfection in eternity, we displace the transient state of the present with the perfection of our eternal state. Whatever seeming imperfection you see now in yourself, realize that it is not the truth, it is but a shadow of the eternal perfection that is the real you. Affirm this to yourself all the time, regardless of how you feel, what the doctors say, what is in your pocketbook, how bad relationships seem to be. A materialistic atheist might say that it is denial based on idealistic dreams, but that is why he is a materialist. Spirit is a reality, and your faith in the higher truths must cast doubts in his mind, not the other way around. Do your inner work regularly, affirm your eternal status, and your loyalty to spiritual ideals will be majestically upheld.

More on affirmations later.

3. Connecting To Others: Service

Service mobilizes our unified human vehicle in the performance range of breadth which is in the sphere of coordination, association and self-hood organization. Service organizes the self, coordinates people and things in time and space, and service makes for deeper and wider associations with other personalities. Through service, we connect to others.

The word service is used in many ways. There is military service, table service, servicing your car, etc. And of course there is social service. When we use the word service to mean the action of doing good to others, we think of it as an altruistic deed in which there is no thought of reward for ourselves. However, when we do deeds altruistically, there is a reward: we feel good. Service makes us feel wonderful because we are helping others, so service doesn't necessarily mean that there is no thought of benefit for ourselves. We do not have to suffer to be of service to others. The meaning of the word service as it is used here is to do things for the benefit of the whole rather than the part.

When we act in service to the body, we do things that are beneficial for the whole person. When we eat healthy foods, it is for the benefit of body, mind, and soul, and not just for the part of us craving junk food. When we educate the mind, it is for the good of the entire person, and not for the part of us that is lazy and doesn't want to study. When we service our ability to coordinate relationships, we do it for the whole of the community rather than for any one individual. Service is for the whole rather than the part.

Organizing the Self Through Service

In organizing our selves, we must realize that everything is interdependent of each other in the universe. The unified human vehicle can be separated in explanation by saying we are body, mind and soul, but we are more than that. The totality is more than the sum of its parts.

Service begins with the self: organizing matter, consciousness and spirit as they are reflected in the body, mind and soul. We must serve the body and take good care of it, maintaining the material mechanism in which we are housed. When we do not, we become a burden for others and we cannot serve them. We must also serve the mind, educating it and programming it with positive thoughts, for that is the arena in which we make our life decisions. And we must serve our soul, giving it the valuable experiences through which it grows, and we must allow it to contact the spirit from which it draws its strength. Then this service for the body, mind and soul must be organized together so that there is harmony and all conflict is resolved within oneself.

In many people, especially when we are young but not always so, there is great conflict and imbalance between the body, mind and soul. The body may just want to get drunk and fat at the expense of the mind and soul. The mind may want to devote itself to political, social or theological causes without due concern for the welfare of the body and soul. And the soul may lean towards fanatical spiritual ideals with no regard for body and mind. When the self is organized, the three are in harmony and can move as one in power, strength and purpose. When they are out of balance, energy is dissipated, there is no cohesion of purpose, and life is disjointed with no unity of intent.

Before we can organize the body, mind and soul together, each of these components itself must be organized and balanced.

Organizing The Body

A well organized body is a body in which the parts that compose it are in optimum relationship with each other so that it can operate at its peak efficiency. Common examples of bodies in our society that are not well organized are bodies that have too high a fat content, or a body that has too much toxins in it. Unorganized bodies are uncoordinated bodies, imbalanced and not running at close to its fullest potential.

The body is an amazing mechanism. It replicates the cells that makes up its parts, it reproduces itself, heals itself, has mobility, is innately coordinated, and is a wonderful housing for our mind and soul. A normal, healthy body, as long as it is fed the right nutrients, exercises and is not damaged by external means, is a well balanced and dynamic material system. So in most cases, the normal human body does not need to be tweaked in any way to do what it is supposed to do – to be the material matrix for our soul's journey. Unfortunately, many human bodies have problems that are mostly a result of external factors. External factors such as disease, accidents, unhealthy lifestyles, and the like. This is when it becomes necessary to balance it, to take steps to get it back to being a normal, healthy, and well-balanced body, as much as possible.

The body in itself has an innate mechanism to keep it healthy, and believe it or not this is the innate urge to want to do things that feel good. The feeling of wholesome pleasure tells us we're doing the right things, pain is an alarm that tells us to stop. Sadly, many people have those two signals confused. All those things that people do to themselves, things that they think makes them feel good, such as to overeat, eat things that are unhealthy, imbibe harmful but stimulating toxins, and to be sedate are due to the body not being aware of itself. The body wants to feel good, but the reality is that it does not feel good to be overweight, laden with toxins and sluggish. The reason it gets stuck into those behaviors that results in those states is because the mind has made the body think those states are pleasurable. Our minds have been conditioned by society to think it is pleasurable to eat all we want, whatever we want, to get intoxicated regularly and sit around watching TV and we convince the body that this is so. But the body does not think, you might say, that it is has no awareness apart from the mind. Yes and no. To a limited degree, it can think, to a certain degree it is aware. When something gets stuck in the nose, the mind does not need to tell the body to sneeze, it does so of its own accord. When the body feels intense heat close to it, it doesn't need the thinking power of the mind to shrink away immediately. The nervous system of the body imbues it with a certain degree of awareness and power to make decisions. This intelligence comes from a cluster of nerves between the bottom of the spine and a few inches below the navel that is like a second brain. It is the next biggest nerve cluster next to your brain and called the *tan tien* by alternative health practitioners. It is also the center of gravity of the body and is considered the nexus of the body's strength and power by masters of martial arts such as aikido. When the body is in tune with itself and is aware of its own condition it will do what is the healthiest for itself because it knows that that is what feels good, as long as the mind does not interfere by instilling misconceived notions to the body of what constitutes pleasure and what doesn't. Unfortunately, it is not easy to reverse this behavior by the hoodwinked body because the body has been addicted for many years and it needs to keep up this behavior, not anymore to get into a state that it thinks is supposed to feel good, but in order not to feel bad. The withdrawal symptoms of ceasing such habits are too nasty for many people to even want to go there. However, if that person's health declines to the point where the behavior has to be stopped, a decision will usually be made to kick the habit, and to revitalize the body.

Having made the decision to awaken the body, there are some methods that can be used to heighten the awareness and inherent self-healing power of the body. Yoga and tai-chi is effective as is a little known method called katsugen which exercises the autonomic (involuntary) nervous system. There are probably some others of which I am not aware. Select the one that appeals to you and that you are most comfortable with.

To balance the body's energies when it is diseased in order to make it healthy is a problem faced by many. Medical science has made great discoveries and has accomplished much in this regard. It is not the purpose of this book to describe the numerous approaches to medicine. However, in regards to soul and the process of operating the human vehicle, it is wise to take into consideration that although our physical body is a material system, it is a system that is hooked up to other components that are not just material, but also mindal and spiritual. The effect that the mind and spirit has on the body has not been explored sufficiently by western medicine, but looking at the efforts and results of practitioners of alternative medicine, it is obvious that our health is not just a result of fixing or replacing our mechanical components. In attaining health, methods that incorporate the mind and soul as parts of our total being would seem most efficacious and it would be beneficial to look into practices other than just Western medicine, practices that have proven effective such as Chinese and ayurvedic medical techniques as well as others.

The Spirituality of Eating

We eat everyday and we do it so often that we don't really think about it. It's a natural part of our lives that is a basic physical act of survival.

But actually, eating (and breathing) is the material foundation for spirituality in humans.

To eat food is to take substances from the environment and ingest them so that we can create the organs that make up our bodies. We use the energy and the material that we take from plants and other animals so that we can do things with our bodies, so that we can function in the daily activities of our lives. And many of those things that we do are spiritual. The good things that people do for each other: the works of service, of art, of technology, of medicine, of creativity; they are all a result of us converting the matter which we eat into those deeds we do which constitute value. This is a direct path: the plants take the energy of the sun and the materials of the earth and convert them into proteins, fats and carbohydrates. We eat those plants (or other animals eat those plants and we eat them) for our survival and bodily maintenance. We then do things using that matter and energy for various activities, some of which have spiritual value.

So is eating more important than we think? Is there a relationship between eating wholesome, healthy food and doing wholesome, healthy activities? Does our eating habits result in deeds of more spiritual value?

I don't know of any scientific or clinical evidence to prove this, but because of the experiences I have had in my life of eating, I believe that it does. During the times of my life when I was not consciously trying to eat healthier foods and was engaged in drinking and recreational drugs, I was less spiritual and less concerned about others then when I was more health conscious in my eating habits. Now, which behavior caused the other is moot. Did my eating habits make me act less spiritual, or did the growth of my spirituality cause me to eat healthier foods? Which is cause, which is effect? In elliptic philosophy, cause and effect are the same, they are but two sides of the same coin. The truth is that eating is the foundation for our material body and controlling this aspect of our life makes a great difference in optimizing the processes of our mind and therefore our soul.

This is crucial in realizing and recognizing that we *are* the Earth. The material that makes up our bodies are the same material that is around us, the material that makes up this planet. The atoms and molecules that are the building blocks of our bodies are constantly being recycled to make the air, the ocean waters, the microbes, the animals and plants that we see in our environment. And it's been happening since the beginning of life on this planet. Most likely, there is an atom within your body right now that was also in the body of Julius Caesar, of Jesus, of Abraham Lincoln, of Buddha, and many others. Elizabeth Sahtouris' writes in EarthDance: "Every atom that is now, ever was, or ever will be a part of us will live on somewhere in Gaia's ever-evolving dance for billions of Earth years yet to come."

Many people think of themselves as being separate from their environment. In reality, we are one with it. It is only our consciousness that can separate ourselves from the whole, and it is our consciousness that can brings us together. So realize and be conscious that it is the replenishment of our body through eating and breathing that keeps the circulation of matter and energy flowing within the human organism. And eating high quality, nutritious foods result in higher potential in the quality of our behavior. The more energetic and more fresh the life we pass through our bodies, the more life we have. But it is the quality that is important here, not necessarily the quantity. And the quality should be in more than just nutrition. It must be nutritious, but it must also taste good, for good food should feed not only the body but also the soul.

Our minds are starting to become educated on this and yet many are still stuck on quantity. They think that more is better. It was indeed so during the prehistoric days when we were hunters and gatherers on the verge of starvation, when we lived in times when our next meal was uncertain. But now, we have more than we can eat, and many people eat more than is good for them. Food, when consumed to an excess, is like poison, especially if it is of poor quality. It is very important that we are mindful of the benefits of eating quality food that is nutritious and be wary of the dangers of eating foods that are depleted in vitamins, over processed, and mixed with chemicals as well as the temptations of simply overeating.

It's not only true that you are *what* you eat, you are also *how* you eat, and *why* you eat. So be mindful what part of the environment you pass through your body, how you go about it and the reasons why you are eating.

Organizing The Mind

We organize the mind by servicing it. We service it by educating it, stimulating it, and by programming it. (We also need to maintain the hardware that is the material foundation for our human mind, which is the brain, but providing the proper nutrients for the brain would fall under the category of organizing the body, as the brain is just another organ in the material self. Connecting the mind to spirit is also important but that also goes in another category, that of serving the soul. This just emphasizes the fact that the body, mind, and soul cannot be truly separated even in discussion as they are all inter-related and inter-connected as one.)

A well organized mind is a wonder to behold. It is clear thinking, focused, sharp, graceful, intelligent, imaginative, creative, dynamic, flexible and open. One of the ways we can service the mind so that it is well organized is to nurture its ability to recognize and verify reality.

We all have in our minds a quality that, if nurtured and sufficiently developed, can recognize and verify the true nature of reality. It is a universal gift that is a part of our minds which saves us from being fooled by lies, distortions, sophistry, untruths, and other illusions of living. It is called the Reality Response.

This remarkable insight, this ability to see truth or its lack, are innate in the universal mind, which all people connect to, consciously, subconsciously and unconsciously. Life in general tends to develop these three intuitive faculties and they are the foundations of self-awareness and reflective thinking. Unfortunately, these faculties are not well known and even less nurtured and developed. We can service the mind by consciously developing this reality response.

When this ability is developed and unified, it produces an organized mind with a strong character that can correlate and harmonize science, philosophy, and religious experience.

The Reality Response ability recognizes universe reality on three levels. They are:

1. Logic (science, causation, mathematics) -- this is the realm of the physical senses, the scientific method of ascertaining facts, the ability to separate the objective and subjective, results based on concrete evidence, the mathematical proof.

2. Morality (reasoning, duty, meanings) -- the area of morals, whether personal or societal; the ability to recognize relative right and wrong and the meanings attached to action, recognition of duty, being able to judge and evaluate correctness of action through reason.

3. Spirituality (worship, inspiration, destiny) --the domain of spiritual reality based on religious experience, the self-realization of the family of God, the recognition of spiritual values, the consciousness of eternal life, the path from finite existence to infinite existence, from imperfection to perfection, from the now to eternity.

These three ways of looking at any given subject, if developed and sharpened, can be used to intuitively discern the cosmic reality of any given assumption or concept. I believe that it can even be used to determine the cosmic desirability of a relationship, a business proposition, or practically any activity. Of course, it would all be in relation to cosmic reality, to the eternal perspective, rather than to the short term, that is, the need for immediate gratification.

For the purpose of demonstration, we will apply the concept of the Reality Response by evaluating a given assumption. As a visual aid, below is a graphic representation. We will score the assumptions for Logic, Morality, and Spirituality on a 1 to 100 scale, 100 being the highest possible score per category, 300 overall. These scores are totally arbitrary and personal. It will differ for each person.

Just as an example, I have first graded the assumptions of voodoo. Then I did the same for psychotherapy. This is the result:

Logic	Morality	Spirituality	Total
		(Voodoo)	
10	10	35	55
		(Psychotherapy)	
80	90	65	235

The best possible score being 300, my estimation is that most people with a well developed reality response will not wholeheartedly embrace a belief without having a total score of around 250 or over. In this case, given such a score, I will probably never engage in voodoo, but since my score for psychotherapy is much higher, it shows I lend it much more credence, although the score shows that there is some hesitancy to give it my full trust.

Also, I believe the Reality Response is both intuitive and deductive. Deductive reasoning is necessary to pin down the facts in the area of Logic and to understand new meanings of Morality, while intuition is vital to arriving at the insights that lead to those meanings and in appreciating the values of the realm of Spirituality. However, like intuition, I think the reality response is usually quick acting, that when it is well-tuned, it will know immediately if a given assumption is in harmony with cosmic reality. But a chart like the above may be helpful in mapping out our relationship with the universe as we contemplate the decisions we face in our lives. A well developed reality response can be very instrumental in organizing the mind.

We can also service and organize the mind by programming it. Why allow society to program and condition our minds with negativity, when we can program ourselves with positivity? One of the simplest techniques for self-programming ourselves is through affirmations. Affirmations come in many shapes and forms and can also be thought of as a form of prayer as well as service to yourself, because it works best when there is connection to spirit.

Repeating a mantra over and over again is a form of affirmation. A mantra is a phrase that has positive meaning such as, for example, "I reside in harmony with the universe." Many Asian religions use mantras to reinforce their beliefs. Although simple, mantras are very powerful if practiced every day for long durations. I have chanted mantras for hours on end during one period of my life. Through chanting I even kicked a cold that was starting to come on.

Another form of affirmations are written down and repeated often throughout the day. These affirmations are usually more specific than mantras. Some examples are: "I exude confidence in all that I do." "I am a brilliant spiritual being." "I finish what I start."

These affirmations are effective in correcting what you see in yourself as character flaws, vices, or negative tendencies.

It is important to remember when creating your own affirmations that they must come from your soul. You must truly identify with them and work towards that end. They are not magic wish lists that are intoned in hopes of something miraculous happening. Effort in its application is necessary and it must be done with the full cognition of the presence of the Creator and must resound in the deepest parts of your mind. Affirmations that are just surface noise have no effect at all.

They must also be positive. Rather than write "I will not smoke." It is better to write, "I live a healthy lifestyle." Rather than, "I do not overeat." Write, "I eat healthily and in moderation." It is difficult to get excited over something not to do. That is because "to not do" something is to take something away. Affirmations are the most effective when they reinforce positive actions that we add to our lives.

There is also another way of energizing our affirmations that may seem negative but people do it subconsciously without realizing it. Every time a thought of anything unpleasant spurs you on to effort, you are essentially using this method.

This is making use the law of physics which state that to every action, there is a reaction. To jump up, we bend our knees and shift our weight down first. To throw a ball, we first cock our arm back. To send an arrow flying outward, we must first pull the string inward. The initial motion is in reverse to the direction in which we want the object to go.

In using this method for affirmations, think first of the things about yourself that you dislike. Think about why you dislike those aspects of yourself. Don't make any excuses about them or try to analyze yourself, just let them stay in your awareness for a while. Then, allow the natural positiveness inside you to assert what you want to do about it. Let your thoughts spring into where you're going – the desires you have, the dreams you are working towards, your aspirations, let it all come out like fireworks. Fill your thoughts with affirmations of making all those things come true. Stay in that space until you are satisfied. Go into spiritual meditation if you desire.

The two kinds of affirmations are not that dissimilar, it seems like night and day, but even night and day is in reality just two aspects of a full day. It's like when breathing in and out, you ask yourself which you should start first. Some people say when holding your breath for a long time you should breathe out first before getting a lungful of air. But then you have to breathe in before the first breath out, so....?

These affirmations are useful service to yourself in organizing the mind, and they work best if practiced in conjunction with other complementary services to your body and soul.

Mindfulness and Stillness

There have been many books and articles on the importance of mindfulness and they can lead to valuable insights in focusing the mind. Here's an elliptical take on it.

Mindfulness is having a linear focus on a particular thing, whether it is one's breath, eating food, or any activity such as walking, playing music, studying, etc. Mindfulness is important because distraction is what causes a disruption of focus, an obstacle to linear progress. But there is a value to being distracted also.

Recent scientific study has discovered that the ability to be distracted is a survival trait, because if one is too focused on a given task, one is vulnerable to outside threats. We know all to well through our life experiences that being too engrossed in something can keep us from paying attention to the world around us. And if the environment harbors dangerous creatures and circumstances, as it used to and still does, it is good to have a trait that keeps us from being so absorbed that we separate ourselves from the world around us. But that does not mean that we should cultivate mindlessness.

The balance to mindfulness is receptive stillness. This is a state of awareness wherein we are open to everything. This is the state when we are like a flower, open to the warming rays of the sun, or even a satellite dish open to any signals that may arrive; just simply being in a receptive state. It is mindfulness in a different way. The focus is so diffused that one is mindful of the whole universe, rather than on one particular item in the universe. This is the state in which creativity flourishes. It is from such a state of everything and nothing that new thoughts and ideas arise.

In applying ourselves to a given task at hand, we often use focused mindfulness. To become receptive to the All as in worshipful meditation, we use receptive stillness. When we can combine the two in an elliptic way, we have qi, an expression of the soul that is both of the now and eternity, of the linear and circular, of the part and the whole. This is the optimum approach to all endeavors and activities.

Organizing the Soul

We service the soul by allowing it freedom to express itself. The soul is spontaneous and needs to act in order to grow and evolve. An organized soul is one that has the freedom to freely explore, express, love, and follow the leadings of the spirit.

The soul cannot be organized like we organize the body or mind. We can organize the body like we organize things in a box or in an office, arranging things in it in the right proportion and relationship. The mind can be organized like a schedule by doing things in the proper order and through a methodical process. The soul is more fluid and trying to organize it is like trying to organize a container full of water or a balloon filled with gas. It can be done, however, just as water or gas in a container can be "organized" by cooling it or by adding heat; the warmer molecules rise up, and the cooler ones go down. This is a form of organization. Likewise, the soul is organized by the effects we have on it. If we add more spiritual experiences to it, or allow it to explore and even make seeming mistakes, this changes the dynamics within the soul and organizes its attributes. Through servicing the soul by giving it freedom to follow the spirit, it organizes itself.

Conversely, the way to stifle it and disorganize it is to give in to fear, doubt, anxiety, apprehension, mistrust, envy, jealousy and other spirit poisons.

Organizing the Body, Mind, and Soul As One

The mind is the fulcrum of your unified human vehicle. This is where you make your decisions. Your mind coordinates your body and spirit. Your body should be subordinate to your mind, and your spirit has the potential to direct your mind.

Your body is satisfied with being your mind's subordinate as long as it is treated right, receiving enough nutrition, stimuli, shelter, bodily needs and other physical things that keep it relatively comfortable.

Your spirit, the fragment of God that resides within you and leads you, is satisfied in the directive role, directing your human vehicle's upward, inward and sideways movements toward realizing your full potential.

It is in your mind following the spirit's lead that your soul is created and grows in quantity and evolves in quality. The spirit leads best when your mind has faith in it and wants to go where it leads. Often the mind does not, because of fear, misunderstandings, doubt, insecurities, and other circumstances brought about by the environment and its own choices. A mind that does not believe that spirit exists is hampered but not totally bereft of the spirit's direction, as the mind will still receive subconscious suggestions from its mysterious indweller. But a mind fully conscious of the spirit and soul can actively and dynamically work together with them in achieving its Personhood goals.

Your soul is empowered and is at its optimum best when your mind allows it freedom and autonomy, assuming that your soul has evolved sufficiently in quantity and quality to receive that authority from the mind. But even at that point, your mind is not passive, it is still actively participating with the soul's decision making, although careful not to "step on its toes."

The mind itself must be programmed well, whether by itself or through fortunate circumstances. It must have a working knowledge of the body and awareness of its soul as well as being hospitable to the spirit. It organizes the total self the best when it is itself well organized and clear thinking.

A typically disorganized body, mind and soul is a mess: The body wants to go its own way, increasing or decreasing its intake of nutrients to unhealthy levels, imbibing toxins, engaging in destructive practices, unheeding of the mind's will. The mind is filled with fear, doubts, misunderstandings and is only partially conscious of its soul and spirit, if at all. The soul is stunted, not allowed any freedom of expression or contact with the spirit; the spirit is forgotten, left in the dim corners of the mind, the mind ignoring it as much as it can.

Such a human vehicle is sad to behold, especially when it started out as a superb, beautiful, wonderful creation. Looking at it is like seeing a classic automobile, once a sparkling marvel of design and invention, with its body now rusted, the paint peeling, parts missing, the interior dilapidated, the engine not functioning, the wheels falling off, a veritable derelict only suited for the junkyard.

A human vehicle in such a condition may have been due to circumstances beyond the person's control, such as upbringing, economic situations, and medical problems. The good news is that, whatever may have happened in the past, it is within our control to uplift ourselves from such a dire condition

Like an old classic automobile, the human vehicle can be restored. The spirit is the master restorer. By following the direction of the spirit, the body can regain its health, the mind can begin to think clearly, and the soul can continue its inspired evolution. The process of restoration and continued maintenance is worshipful meditation, uplifting prayer and loving service, all powered by faith.

This is service of the self at its highest.

Coordinating Things, People, Time and Space Through Service

Another movement across the breadth of life is manifested in our ability to coordinate people, things, time and space, and the act of loving service lubricates this movement to lessen friction and resistance and to increase momentum and quality of experience.

Coordinating people is best done in service. By serving people, acting not only in their best interest but with the true golden rule in mind, we connect with them, not just with our minds, but with our hearts. Intellectual communication may form bridges, but it is service, the heart to heart interaction of souls that is the substance of true spiritual value that travels across that bridge to create bonding.

Service is selfless, but it is not necessarily self-sacrificing. The best service is done from the perspective of the All, from the eyes of the Creator, so that the benefit gained is for everyone, as much as is possible

Service, for the purpose of self-validation, self-aggrandizement, and for appeasing social and familial pressure, is not true service. True service is for the whole and not the part. True service must come from the soul, by reasoning of mind and through the leadings of the spirit. Intention must be balanced with expertise. One has to be able to implement good intentions with the right techniques, or else service is not accomplished. Good intentions without good implementation can result in disservice, while any action without good intentions is false and deceptive.

Coordinating things, events and systems is also accomplished through service. This service of things can be done through arranging things according to time; by organizing the spatial order of parts in material things and systems; and by modifying the energy flow in systems.

Coordinating time is also service oriented, for we must service our sense of timing. We must be cognizant of the lapse of time, the opportune time, the relationship of our past, the present, and the future and the synchronicity of events in time. A person who is aware of the dynamics and import of time is consistently on time. We service this faculty within us of being conscious of time through effort. We must place a certain amount of importance to it and work towards getting a firm handle on it. A person who is always late and seems to have bad timing usually does not realize its importance and has not made much effort in working with time.

Coordinating space is a concept that may be hard to grasp, as space is usually thought of as nothingness, a vacuum. How do we coordinate nothingness?

Think of it as the space between people, between things, between the moments of time. Space is pivotal to the function of all the above. If there is no space, everything would run into each other and nothing would work.

How much space we place between us and other people are important. Not enough space and we are deprived of privacy. Too much space and we are isolated.

Space between things must be well organized. We cannot cram everything in a room, otherwise there would be no space to live. There must be proper spacing between parts of a machine for the device to function. There must be spacing within a system for an organizational structure to have flow.

Space between moments of time is what makes time. If there was no space between moments, everything would happen simultaneously. Time as we know it would cease to exist. The amount of space we place between events makes for variations in the flow of life, just as the amount of space between notes in music creates patterns in the flow of melody.

We service our awareness of space by giving ourselves space. We give ourselves space by nurturing the stillness, the quietness, and the wholeness of life. This awareness is, again, not a clenching or grasping, but a letting go, a relaxing.

Wider Associations Through Service

As we evolve, our sphere of associations become wider, from the family to city, to the nation, to our planet and to our universe. Our relationships to these ever widening circle of personalities is enhanced, supported and promoted by loving service.

We serve the members of our family and our friends and loved ones, our close and immediate associations, daily. The things we do for them are varied and many. We may cook for them, earn money for them, shelter them, buy clothes for them, support them in their activities, advise them, listen to them, play with them, love them and more.

The amount of service we do for those who are outside of our immediate circle is probably less.

We may serve our employer and fellow employees by doing a good job, being friendly and cheerful, supporting the company functions, and by generally being helpful.

The service we do for the community and/or church may be things such as attending gatherings, helping with social programs such as feeding and clothing the needy, supporting fund drives and other assistance when asked for.

The service that we may do for the city and state may consist of paying taxes, volunteering for social service and participating in elections and other political events.

The service for the nation may be in joining the military, voting, participating in the political process, and contributing money and time to national social programs.

The service we do for the planet may be to help conserve our environmental resources, support movements to end hunger and poverty, to educate, and to work for peace.

The service we do for the universe may simply be to just identify with the All, to be one with the Creator, to achieve cosmic consciousness, for seemingly much of what is outside the Earth is outside of our sphere of influence. But it is not so. What we do here does impact the rest of the universe. Every part of the universe is intrinsically linked and what happens to the part happens to the whole, as what is of the now is of the eternal.

The service that we do enhances, vitalizes and nurtures our existence and our personal relationships in ever widening spheres of dynamic endeavors. Service mobilizes our unified human vehicle in the performance range of breadth.

THE CIRCLE Of CONSCIOUSNESS
From Serving The Self To Serving The Universe
To The Universe Serving You

Serving Yourself and Family

Serving the Community

Serving the Universe

Serving the City/State

Serving the World

Serving the Nation

Chapter Six
Your Next Life Vehicle

Baby you can drive my car
Yes I'm gonna be a star
Baby you can drive my car
And maybe I'll love you

Lennon/McCartney

Trading In Your Body

In most cases, when someone buys a new piece of equipment, such as the latest electronic gizmo, they look at the instruction manual to get an idea of how to operate the device. But if the device is already somewhat familiar, as is the case for a new automobile, and you have been using something similar for a while, you start driving it immediately unless, of course, you are a complete novice, in which case you may first get personal instruction on how to operate the machine. Otherwise, most people will not read the manual until they run into problems that they have no knowledge of resolving themselves based on their pre-existent knowledge or experience.

Will They Take It?

In the case of your human vehicle, you first got basic instruction on its operation from your parents or guardians and then went to school to become further educated. There really was no operating manual, as such, for your unified human vehicle, although there are many books that deal with the various aspects of living a fulfilling life.

Regardless, because of the knowledge you gained from being taught personally and by experience, you would probably not have picked up such a book anyway, until you ran into difficulties in which you needed some additional information. Which means that you, the reader, are probably a mature, experienced individual, possibly even nearing the point when you can see the need for trading in your material body. At the least, with some exceptions, you are cognizant of the limitations of the physical portion of your unified vehicle and have been thinking about when you have to trade it in, if that is at all possible. Is it possible?

There is no scientific evidence that it is possible, but here we are talking about something that is beyond the realm of present day scientific knowledge. Science is very perceptive and thorough when it comes to studying the material vehicle but has no tools for dealing with what the material vehicle contains – the soul and spirit as well as the mind. The study of the mind by science has progressed but is still inexact and not as developed as the study of matter and energy.

Science has no answers as to the continued existence of the soul in another vehicle after the present vehicle has deteriorated. Attempts at answering this question has been left up to philosophy and religion. But even those avenues of inquiry have not given us definite, incontrovertible answers that we can verify with even partial assurance.

What about past history? Has there been any storied cases where someone has come back encased in a new vehicle? Stories are easy to concoct, and stories without credibility come and go, they do not last. Even stories about reincarnation abound, but none has penetrated into the depths of our collective souls, changed entire cultures, has lasted for generations and inspired us. Except for one. There is one case whose story has lasted for millennia, influenced the course of civilization and has resulted in a religion. This is the story of the death and resurrection of Joshua Ben Joseph, otherwise known as Jesus of Nazareth. Unfortunately, much of this story as well as his life and teachings have been distorted, dogmatized and even clichéd, to the point where one is hard put to distinguish between fact and myth. Regardless, it is the one documented story that has lasted the trial of time in which someone had successfully traded in an old vehicle for a new one. This gives us hope, if nothing more.

If the story of the resurrection of Jesus is true, why aren't there other similar cases?

It would make sense that Jesus' resurrection was an exception. The progressive evolution of the unified vehicle, the body, mind and soul, would mean that the new body would not be suited for life on this material sphere. The new body would be composed of material that would be more spiritual and hence not made for groveling around on this ball of mud. Even Jesus did not stick around after he made his few appearances in his new body. It's like the caterpillar metamorphosing into a butterfly. Once the transformation is made the butterfly's new medium is the air, it was not designed for crawling around on tree branches or on the ground. Why crawl, when one can fly?

Does the caterpillar know that it will become a butterfly? Does the chicken know that it will become a chicken while in its embryonic state, existing as an egg? Do they have any idea that they will trade in their vehicle for a new one? Do you? Or, a better question may be, *can* you know?

Previously, I wrote that to survive death and to become eternal, one must identify with eternal values; if you identify with transient values, you will be transient, if you identify with eternal values, you will be eternal. In the same consciousness, if the caterpillar kept on identifying with being a caterpillar and refused to let go of that identity, it could never have turned into a butterfly. If the embryo in an egg kept on identifying with being an egg, it would never have broken out of its shell to become a chicken.

The soul of eternal survival is the self that we need to identify with in order to transform ourselves and continue into the next stage. So nurture the soul, empower the soul and be the soul. And with your soul, return good for evil, convert negativity into positivity. To do otherwise, to return tit for tat, effect for cause is to be a machine, a cog. And a cog is easy to manufacture, it's just a piece of hardware, so what need is there to keep it around? When we need another cog, we'll just pop one out of the woodwork. But a being that can actually turn the negative into the positive? Wow! That is a rarity and someone that the universe would want to keep around forever.

Trade-In Value

For us to become more than human, to be able to trade in our human vehicle for a more spiritual model, we must identify with values that transcend this material body. If we keep on identifying with temporary and transient values based solely on gratification of our material body, we will die with the body.

Look at the way you are living your life. How much of what you do is based on eternal values such as selflessness, unity, reflection, insight, compassion, forethought, altruism, courage, wisdom, honor and goodness? How much is based on transient values such as self-gratification, greed, one-upsmanship, obsession, habit, power and control of others, and ego inflation?

In every endeavor that we do, we can choose between eternal values and transient values. It is when we choose the transient aspect of any behavior that abuse happens. It seems that the activities we do that are the most likely to be abused are those that people consider to be the most sensually pleasurable. Those activities are the ones in which we have to be the most careful for they lead to a life based on transient experiences. That is why society has made taboos and laws regarding sex and drugs.

Eating and drinking is one of the most indulged upon activities that are probably more abused than any others in the United States. Although we do have laws regarding the drinking of alcohol, especially in the case of minors, we do not have laws regarding eating habits because it is such a fundamental necessity to life. It's something that we all must do. So lets take eating as an example of choosing between eternal and transient values.

As Ben Franklin said so well, "Eat to live, not live to eat." Some of the eternal values in eating is temperance, balance, joy, wholesomeness, mindfulness, and goodness and beauty in its preparation and enjoyment. Some of the transient values in eating are gluttony, obsession, excessiveness, lust, mindlessness, and imbalance. Indulging in transient values, whether in eating and/or other activities results in untimely deterioration of the human vehicle. In other words, a human vehicle that has indulged in transient values is not a well maintained vehicle and has less value when the time comes for it to be traded in.

When that time comes, the effort you put into maintaining your unified human vehicle will be considered in the determination of your next vehicle. The effort you made in evolving your soul will be a major factor also, but it is the balanced effort in maintaining and improving the whole matrix of your self that is pivotal in determining the shape of your new form and the spiritual level of your continued existence. The effort you exerted in maintaining and upkeeping your material body is just a portion of all the things to be considered, but it will still be considered.

In regard to your body when it is time to trade it in, what is important is not so much what condition it's in at that time, but rather how much effort you exerted in making the best of it. Some people are born with bodies that are challenged, and some have encountered accidents and diseases that have damaged it to one extent or another. What matters is the effort you put forth to correct, maintain, and improve your health in the most positive way. The same holds true for your mind and soul.

However, giving one's own life, or risking injury and suffering for someone else is a selfless act that has immense universe value. So one should take good care of one's given vehicle but not at the expense of someone else. Keep your organism in top condition so that you can serve others with optimum efficiency.

When the time comes to trade in your human vehicle, the new vehicle must be matched with your soul. In this life, the outward appearance of the body often does not match the quality of the soul. As we progress in our evolution, the external appearance of the vehicle which holds our soul reflects more and more what it contains. Which means that if your soul is so stunted and without substance, if there is hardly any quantity and quality there because you just did not identify with any eternal values, and you did not put out any effort into its nurturance and evolution, there may not be a spiritual vehicle that would be suitable for you, nothing to match your almost non-existent soul. In which case there would be no continuation, Game Over.

What would be the minimum requirement for continuation of life? No matter how maliciously evil a person may have been, it may have been due to the result of environmental circumstances. So after being re-educated, as long as there is remorse and a sincere desire to participate in the eternal plan, to do the Creator's will, to learn from experience and follow the light, a way will be found. A person who has totally negated all urges to follow the light, has made iniquitous decisions consciously and repeatedly and has no remorse or regret may be lost. But in the infinite mercy of the First Source and Center, a second chance should never be counted out.

A person that is dripping with evil, a maliciously wicked person who has committed the most horrible crimes against women, children and people in general may seem undeserving of God's love and mercy. The victims and families of the victims would deem the most severe retribution and punishment as justifiable. They would agree with taking an eye for an eye and even more. But should such final judgments be allowed beings with limited vision and imperfect understanding?

No. Within human society, humans must be the judge in order to keep order within our society, but in the universal family of which God is the father, only he can make the ultimate call. Only he has the infinite wisdom and perfection of understanding to judge a being for all eternity in the grand cosmic courts of the universe of universes.

It would seem to me that if an iniquitous person is beyond redemption, he would be judged as being cosmically insane, and like a rabid dog or a crazed animal, the most reasonable action would be taken to make sure that the evil is ended. The elimination of such a threat by the quickest and most merciful method would be desirable for all concerned.

However, what if a person who has a decent soul had been twisted by upbringing, negative influences, and other forces beyond his control to act in abominable ways? If, in fact, that was the case, retribution would be unjustifiable, an evil deed in itself. Such a person, by being re-educated and awakened to spiritual values could transform himself into a respectable individual, a cosmic citizen who would feel just as much love towards everyone else as much as his own family. No amount of punishment by others would compare to the remorse and self-loathing he would experience because of the extreme amount of horror that he would feel after realizing that, in effect, he had tortured and inflicted excruciating pain to his own family and loved ones. Such a person would voluntarily spend the rest of eternity in atoning for his misdeeds. He would willingly pay for his crimes by becoming a force for good.

For most of us, I have no doubt that life will continue after our material body has been slated for the junk heap. The question is, what can you get in return for your old clunker? What's the trade-in value?

Don't try to talk the "car dealership" into getting more than what you're worth. They know all about you. Just keep your mouth shut and you may be surprised to find that you had underestimated yourself. Whatever it may turn out to be, rest assured, it will be better than the old model. But if you're worried, you're already on the wrong track. Don't be concerned about trading in for something spiffy. After all, we're not really talking about a new automobile. Plus you still have your life and lots of things you need to do. It's the now that matters. And when you identify with eternal values in the now, and the now is realized and actualized on the deepest level, the now becomes the fractal pattern for the eternal.

What Can We Take With Us?

Obviously, we cannot take our material possessions with us. And any baggage attached to our old vehicles will become as dust. Even accomplishments such as works of art, business deals, public service and good deeds, *unless they result in eternal, spiritual values* will be lost. In other words, so-called accomplishments, if done by reason of self-aggrandizement, ego inflation, fear of punishment and desire for material reward would not be part of the universal credit that you will carry with you into eternity.

What you will take with you are all the values of friendships and loving relationships. The fruits of the positive relations that you have chosen and nurtured, including with yourself, your family, friends, strangers and with the Creator, all the sincere service and soulwork that you have done and the progressive movement that you have gained in your personal exploration of the length, breadth and depth of true universe reality will be credited to you in your universal bank account for all eternity.

A Great Deal

There is probably nothing I, or anyone for that matter, can say that will convince everyone that life after death is a reality. Science has no evidence one way or the other. Religion also has no verifiable proof that death of the material body is not the end of personal existence.

Because there is so little evidence, science is skeptical of life after death. Through faith, religion is hopeful of it. Philosophical reasoning cannot prove or disprove it either, but it can give us an incentive for believing in it.

Some believe in life after death and try to be good in this life because they feel that that is the only chance of survival, if survival is possible. Others find this not to their liking because they think they will have to sacrifice their desires and refrain from fulfilling their material passions and cravings, and if they do this and life after death was an illusion they would have led a constrained life for nothing.

The fallacy in this is the belief that we have to sacrifice our desires and passions, that we have to lead a monastic life, forsaking the joys and bounties of life, in order to get to heaven, beliefs that are often espoused by strict religions and rigid philosophies.

The truth is that normal desires, heartfelt passions, and the lure of life's pleasures are a natural part of living life as a human being. What is dangerous and can lead to disaster are obsessions, uncontrolled cravings, fanatic tendencies, extremism, and close-minded intolerance, because they lead to identifying with transient values. But those are merely things that we need to watch out for. We do not need to give up anything. All we need to do is to follow the light. By following the light, all errors in thinking and acting fade away naturally by weight of their own negativity.

Identifying with eternal values is a win-win situation. Even if life after death is not a reality, identifying with eternal values promotes health of body, mind and soul. It produces better relationships, nurtures the best in humanity, furthers goodwill, instills happiness, and develops an environment of peace and harmony. If it also results in eternal life, what more can we ask for? What a heckuva a great deal!

It is a great deal. No matter what we experience in this life, the alternative to it is nothingness: to have never been born, to have never experienced a sunrise and a sunset, the beauty of nature, the warmth and love of our friends and family, the rapture of beautiful feelings and emotions, the sublime enjoyment of the arts, the sensual pleasures of food, sex, and physical stimuli, the heady pleasures of the intellect, and the spiritual experience of being separate and then one with God.

Life is truly a gift. By living life we are getting something for nothing. Try getting a deal like that from a car dealer.

Chapter Seven
The Real World

"Toto, I've a feeling we're not in Kansas anymore."

Judy Garland from
The Wizard of Oz By Noel
Langley

The Power of Self

You literally have the power to change reality for the better and to upgrade to a higher level with a new life vehicle when the time comes. But you have to make the best of the life vehicle you have right now in order to evolve into a new one. The best way for a tadpole to become a frog is live each day loyally as a tadpole. The best way for a human being to become spirit is to live each day loyally as a human being.

This book was not meant for the animal in man. Nor was it meant for the merely human. This book is for those souls that are undergoing a transformation from the physical to the spiritual. For this to happen, there must be a sense of self as well as selflessness. One of the myths we must re-think is the idea that "self" is not desirable on a spiritual path, that ego is bad.

Selflessness is a virtue. But selflessness is a giving of one's self, not a negation of self. One must have a sense of self in order to give it. All of the wonderful things that humans have accomplished in various endeavors happened because the individuals had both a sense of self, ego, plus a desire to be selfless in order to benefit those around them. If one were to be totally without self, without ego, one would be dissolved into the universe and would be as nothing, and therefore useless to the world at large.

The desire to be totally without self is a yearning to go back to the mother's womb, to go back into the comfortable warmth of infinity. This connection to The Source is very important in our daily lives so that we can re-energize our souls, but this is not our goal or purpose. This is where we came from, not where we are going.

We came from Nothing and go into Everything.

We are evolving into becoming separate sovereign entities in our own right; one with the Creator and yet separate. As children of the Cosmic Parent, we are slowly learning to shoulder some of the burdens of maintaining reality.

To choose to live as a separate but connected entity means we are assuming control of tiny bits of the universe; initially starting with our minds, then our bodies, then our immediate environment. We are evolving into becoming able to take responsibility for our reality.

It is not easy. It is much easier to just dissolve into the woodwork forever, but we can always do that by exercising our free will option -- choose to cease to exist.

To be a bonafide spiritual entity, in our own right and in the eyes of the universe, we must be one in body, mind, and soul and have made the wholehearted decision to enter onto the road of self-mastery. This means being totally capable of being held accountable for your actions. If you do not have the minimum level of self-mastery, that is, control of your body, mind and soul, as a whole, then you are not really "real" yet in the elliptical universe. You don't really have a whole "self" until you have attained oneness with yourself.

This path from nothing to something, from imperfection to perfection, from the unqualified to the qualified is a career – a career that spans millions of years and light years, across vast domains of time and space. This career is only possible if we have a sense of self. However, self/ego is double edged.

One must have a sense of self,
and yet one must not be self-absorbed.
One must see oneself in order to see others.
One must like oneself in order to like others.
One must love oneself in order to love others.
One must understand oneself in order to understand others.

And so, one must understand wholeness
in order to understand separateness.
Separateness, to understand wholeness.
To be whole, and yet be separate.
To be separate, yet to be whole.
To have self, yet be selfless.
To be selfless and to find your true self.

Self is the basic unit of conscious volition under your free will. Free will is the ability of spiritually connected beings to break the inertia of cause and effect by making an internal decision. Free will is both a wonderful thing and a curse. With free will we can soar to the heights of attainment, but with free will we can also screw up so badly that we cause immense pain, suffering and hardships to ourselves and others.

But without it, we are like robots, automatons, without volition and hardwired to be slavishly obedient to cause and effect. Purely mechanical.

It's a scary choice. To be godlike or to be an unthinking robot? To be godlike requires a lot of faith and effort, with the possibility of pain and suffering – a tremendous undertaking. To be a robot only requires that you negate your own will and become as nothing.

By regularly connecting with The Source through service, prayer and worshipful meditation we can have the best of both worlds. We can start on the path to universe ascension and yet leave the details to the Creator. After all, we are still spiritual embryos. We are not expected to become brilliantly mature spiritual entities immediately.

So we can lighten up, relax and live loyally each day as a spiritual embryo…and the moment will come when we begin to transform.

When a tadpole has finished growing its legs, it will take to land. The tadpole's tiny brain realizes it's no longer a tadpole, that it is now a frog and makes the leap out of the water.

A fledgling eagle, having grown enough feathers and usable wings must sometime take flight. It may hesitate on the edge of the nest but the time must come when it makes the leap.

A human being, having experienced the vicissitudes of life, makes enough life decisions to empower his soul. The leap happens when he realizes he is no longer human, that there is no longer any attachment to his original medium. It usually happens at the time of mortal death, but sometimes before.

Where Are You?

The light draws us toward perfection. We are led by that divine spark within us to go seek the ideals of existence. All we have to do is to follow those leadings to explore the length, depth and breadth of our journey. With unmitigated faith and unceasing effort, we will surely arrive at our destination.

It sounds easy, and from the viewpoint of eternity, it is. But the minute details in the moments of our temporal existence can sometimes seem daunting.

As we evolve in spirit, we are given more freedom to choose our own paths and routes. A child is given little freedom until she has proven responsible and mature enough to determine her own fate without causing harm to herself or to others. Fractally, it is the same for souls. A soul is given more freedom as it matures and grows in wisdom, as it follows the beacon of divine light within to master the challenges that come its way through the course of life. Then, like a child growing up to become a responsible adult, the soul evolves to become master of the unified vehicle, the Personhood matrix. No longer can the vehicle be derailed by the lusts of the body nor the obsessions of the intellect, for the mind has delegated decision making powers to the soul to allow it to freely follow the directions of spirit. This usually happens gradually, and more and more, the course of life is charted ever increasingly by the evolving soul.

During the infantile years of our soul's evolution, we may pray to God and say, "Not my will but yours be done." This is a negation of our own will, and is in recognition of our inability to determine the best course for ourselves; we defer to the Creator that knows what the best is for us. However, like young children, we are often unable to follow directions and make childlike mistakes. We fall quite often and scrape our knees.

When we evolve a bit more to assume some knowledge of the universe around us, we may then change our prayer to say, "My will is that your will be done." This does not negate our own will but positively asserts our own will to do God's will. Rather than being like infants under the strict command of our parents, we are like respectful adolescents who anticipate the wishes of our parents and proceed to act on them with initiative. We begin to do some good in the world, but our efforts are sometimes lacking in knowledge and wisdom. We may stumble often but hardly fall.

Upon reaching soul maturity, the prayer may change again to say, "My will and yours are as one." This means that effectively, we have become instruments of God. We are his hands, his eyes, his mouth, his ears, and his brains. We act with certainty based on the experiential wisdom of our lives, our education and the existential leadings of our spirit. We become God's representatives on this world, knowing with full assurance that the Creator trusts us to do the right thing. It becomes rare that we stumble, falling happens only in isolated circumstances.

Where you are now determines how you proceed. If your soul is at the infant stage, be humble and defer your will to God. Make efforts to discern his will by sharing your inner life with him regularly. If your soul is at the adolescent level, feel good that you can sometimes distinguish God's will, and proceed to act upon it in the best way you can, with perseverance. If your soul is truly at the adult stage, it means that your faith and effort in soul evolution have reached a degree of fruition and that God trusts you to work on his business without being micromanaged. Have faith that you know what you are doing. Make decisions confidently knowing that you are one with the Creator.

Decisions, Decisions

Trading in the vehicle does not mean the journey has ended. Physical death is not a destination. Rather, it just means that we have need of another vehicle that is more suited to cross the terrain in the next part of the journey. But whatever vehicle we use, whatever terrain we encounter, there is a crucial factor that remains constant in our ability to be progressively mobile in our explorations. That factor in progression is the need to make decisions.

Without decisions, we are lost in limbo, in a gray, nowhereland where nothing happens. It is a state without movement, where you do not go forward, backward, inward, outward, up, down or sideways. It is not even a hell, because at least hell can be a destination. Indecisiveness is halfway to nowhere. It is an incomplete sentence, a joke without a punch line, a story with no conclusion, a song with only one note.

I learned in my early years that making a decision, any decision, right or wrong is better than no decision. I can learn from a wrong decision and backtrack to correct it. If I can't backtrack, I can learn from it and make the right decision next time. Sometimes a seemingly wrong decision will even lead me to paths that will result in something unexpectedly good. To not make a decision is to stall the process. To flounder in confusion, hesitancy and incompleteness.

It is a lesson we learn when we were younger, but like many things it can come back in other forms as we get older. When we put something off, it is the same as an indecision. When we wait for a sign from God, it is an indecision. When we say that we'll let it play itself out, it is an indecision. We do these things more often than we think, especially when it seems we do not have enough information. This is an understandable situation, as we do need information to make the best decisions. But to wait leisurely for the information to set itself down on our laps is not a proactive choice.

Making the right moral decisions are the stepping stones to soul evolution. By making quality decisions many times, over and over, we are creating the building blocks of our souls. A correct moral decision made once or twice can be the result of a temporary state of mind, to make it repeatedly is to prove to the universe that we are firm in our convictions. Often, these loyalties to spiritual convictions are tempered by making errors in judgment, seeming mistakes. We learn what to do right often after we learn what to do wrong, because the painful consequences of the wrong decision points to the correctness of the right decision. But, first, we have to make those decisions. That's where it all starts. We have to abandon fear and indecision and venture out on a limb. It might seem like a risk, but it is an action that is not just necessary, but mandatory, if we are to achieve self-mastery.

Once we have achieved a modicum of self-mastery, we are co-creators with God, partners in creating our lives, and you know that God has made his decisions. You can bet he is doing his part, and magnificently at that! So, if anything is stalling, if something in your life is not going well, you can be sure that it's your end of things that needs shoring up. It's most likely because you have not made your decisions. You haven't completely made up your mind. So waiting for a sign from God won't work because he may be waiting for a sign from you, that you've made *your* decision.

Often, people can't make the decision because they don't have the necessary information, and they don't have the information because they haven't decided. It's a Catch 22. A feedback loop. And the best way to get out of that cycle is to just simply decide. Don't be afraid of making a mistake. There is no such thing. To the soul, a mistake is but a learning experience. The only real mistake is in not trying. So when it comes to relatively simple everyday decisions, try things out, experiment, give it a shot, just do it! Decide.

However, there are decisions that have extreme consequences. Decisions that could take away a person's life or health, even your own. Or a decision which could influence the course of a life. Such momentous decisions should be made with care and with much meditation and reflection. But upon sufficient due deliberation, refrain from agonizing over it. Once you achieve enough clarity, abandon fear, just let go and decide. The decision is yours, the consequence is God's.

It is usually the questions of material loss or gain that require the gathering of data and the sorting out of alternatives in order to chart the best course. When it comes to making moral choices, most likely you already know within what is right. The difficulties that most people face are whether to choose between spiritual gain or material gain – a handful of gold or a heartful of soul? Or even more of a conundrum – a ton of gold or just a smidgen of soul?

These are personal choices. We learn our lessons as we make our decisions.

The more people there are in this world that can make the best decisions, the better our planet will be. These decisions and choices are the ones we make everyday, the little ones that upon repetition become the living flavor of our daily lives. To make good choices are to send ripples of love and good will out from you to the edge of the universe and back. These acts of love generate other acts of love which will eventually make perfect this universe of universes. Acts of evil have a ripple effect also, but as long as there are souls that can convert the negativity into positivity, the total sum effect of love will win out. In the living spiritual universe good makes more good and even evil is turned into good. It is through creatures such as us, high and low, that these conversions are made.

I recently took an online safety course in driving an automobile. I was pleasantly surprised at the similarities of some of the lessons in driving an automobile safely with operating a human vehicle safely. It was so similar that all it took was to paraphrase it a bit and we have this:

What Are You Willing To Do?

Making Decisions

People in the "real" world are faced with making decisions, decisions that could have a positive or negative outcome.

Most people have not read a book such as this one or have explored these concepts and methods. Consequently, their decisions are based largely on how they feel, or what they've been told. Most of them do not know what we know about attaining mastery of their vehicle. Many of them simply do not see that they have choices and the choices they make affect the people around them.

Taking Responsibility

Throughout this book, we have emphasized some important points about self-mastery. Think about each of these each time you make a life decision:

- You are the only person who can control your behavior from within.
- Make your own decisions, your own choices. Do not give up control of your human vehicle to others: individuals or organizations, to random emotions, or to ideas that are not supported by your own internal and/or external experiences.
- Even though there are life conditions which you cannot control (heredity, accidents, diseases, etc.) you can control your own actions and how you deal with those conditions.
- For every life decision you make, there are consequences. The consequences of correct life decisions are that you will have a satisfying and fulfilling journey that will enrich your soul.
- The consequences of poor life decisions can range from a life without meaning to soul death.

The big difference between a mechanical automobile and your human vehicle is that in the material world most of us drive our cars to get to our office where the real work begins. In spiritual reality, the mastery of our human vehicle *is* the work. And a life just being safe is not necessarily the best for us. A person with depth and character is going to experience some things which are going to put a few nicks and dents into his human vehicle. But these are often personal choices. To each his own. Do you want a safe commuter trip or an interesting adventure?

Scales of Perception

Now let's look back to the fractal model, at the bigger picture. We have the brain cells, humans, and then Gaia. How much further does the pattern go? How does it relate to the universe?

Gaia all grown up will be a marvelous and awesome entity! Peace, health and prosperity will reign as all her "cells" will be working together in harmony and oneness. If Gaia can grow up to become an "adult," could there be other "adults" out there?

Recently, due to our latest telescopes, there have been fabulous photos of outer space that show millions of brilliant stars that seem to go on endlessly. Some of those photos, though, are not of individual stars. I saw one photograph and reading the caption realized that each one of those points of light were not stars, but galaxies, each one in turn made up of millions of stars.

The realization hit me that there have been more than ample time and space for the universe to come up with many "adults," even societies of planetary entities, of entire civilizations! Of course! Civilizations that we can barely comprehend. Incredibly wise, with technology and energy systems that would seem Godlike. They would truly be spiritual adults.

Our Earthly civilization is arguably 40,000 years old, give or take. This includes civilizations that have come and gone. It may be a generous figure, but the exact number is not important. The fact is we haven't been around that long compared to the rest of the universe. Our technology has advanced to the point where we are now talking about quantum computers and nanotechnology. Our material quality of living has increased dramatically as a result of science and technology. Many things that were unimagined are now actually being done so that we are able to see glimpses of the possibilities.

Now, if our young civilization could do this in 40,000 years, can you imagine what a million year old civilization could do? A billion year old civilization?

If Gaia is a living thing, could it be that there are other planets out there that are also living? If so, as this is a tremendously huge universe, could there be numerous other living planets out there, maybe a well-organized society of intelligent, spiritual and mature planetary entities? When Gaia becomes fully conscious and somewhat whole, she will realize that the "adults" have been checking up on her all this time, smiling down from their place in the stars nurturing her in the best way. They are there.

However, don't be looking out for starships and flying saucers such as we see in TV, films, and books. I'm talking about "adults" that are far more advanced than we can imagine. It's obvious that their modes of transportation would be so far removed from our present conceptions of space travel that they would be unrecognizable to most humans. The vehicles would be more like living energy fields as opposed to machines, for example; the seraphic transports as mentioned in the codices from outside.

Is there any evidence whatsoever for such a grand (and to modern society, preposterous) idea? If the above is true, why aren't the beings from outside telling us in a overt manner, for instance like parking a space vehicle over the White House and giving us the cure for cancer, a new source of energy and other fabulous technologies?

Logically, it seems obvious that beings from a highly advanced and spiritual civilization will know that if they give us unearned knowledge that we will abuse it. We even know that all too well ourselves. So is it reasonable to think that just because we look out into the universe and try to detect their presence (such as with SETI), that these mature beings will show up at our doorstep and give us information that we can use to propagate our childish agendas? Are you kidding?

If Earth was a person, she would be a toddler or a baby. A baby that rightfully belongs in a nursery, segregated from the "adult" universe society. Which is a more reasonable assumption: That we are alone or that they want us to stay in our crib until we're house trained?

The particular challenge that the "adults" face is that although it is in their hearts and minds to do something to benefit our situation, they do not want to inadvertently do us harm. Like raising a normal child, they don't want to spoil us, but they don't want us doing permanent damage to ourselves or our environment.

So they have been talking to us, but not through primitive channels of communication such as we use, like radio telescopes and such but through the universe intelligence circuits. We are cells, we are humans, we are Earth, and we are the universe, a living organism. And "this material and living organism is penetrated by intelligence circuits, even as the human body is traversed by a network of neural sensation paths."

It appears they have been sending us spiritual information in order to nurture our levels of conscious behavior so that we can function like mature entities within the context of the adult universe society. Before we are invited to mingle with the adults, we must learn how to sit still, to communicate politely, to keep from hurting others, to be tidy and be nice, like adults.

Knowing what you know of the universe, science, spirituality, God and reality, is it so farfetched that our universe is totally organized and planned, that it is filled with intelligent beings, both material and spiritual? That we were born in a friendly universe populated by a family of creatures engaged in a universal, harmonious purpose? That it is only our state of immaturity and under development that keeps us seemingly isolated? That we are, in fact and truth, being watched over, even as we speak?

The universe is family and we can live forever.

If what I say is true, we will not find hard scientific evidence to conclusively prove it to the world. In fact, if what I say is true, such hard scientific evidence is purposely not forthcoming because it would be dangerous and a detriment to mankind. The good thing is that we don't need that kind of information. We are up to our eyebrows in technological gizmos.

We need information that can help us grow up, not physically and materially, but mentally and emotionally. The evidence abounds, however circumstantial and not provable. They have been giving us the information we need to mature. Information as to who we are. Where we're going. What we should be doing here. How to attain self-mastery and to empower the love within our souls.

Health & Eternal Life – The Fractal Perspective

Going even further, let's extend this fractal model all the way to the maximum finite consciousness bordering on the infinite: to the intelligence and consciousness of the universe entity – what some have called the Supreme Being, and relate it to the minimum finite consciousness – our cells. (See graphic on page 21.)

We, humans, are fractal representations of neurons, brain cells, (although some of us act like sperm cells, or muscle cells, or whatever we are patterning ourselves after). Neurons are memory cells. There are short term memory cells and long term memory cells. As you know from your own personal experiences, short term memories are memories that are not really that important, like say, what the color of your toothbrush was five years ago. That data was not important to you so you chose not to keep it. A long term memory may be memory you had of your first kiss or maybe your first child, or how to drive a car. It is memory you find valuable to yourself, to your entire organism.

A short term memory becomes long term memory when the mind decides it is important enough to keep. What happens in the brain is that a short term memory cell gets tweaked so that a gene is expressed. It gets turned on. This is a genetic change so that now it can be copied and replicated. The original cell can die but the stored pattern of connections (memory) will remain in the organism as long term memory.

This is the fractal pattern of eternal life. This is what the religions and philosophies have been trying to tell us all along. It's basically very simple.

If we are of value to the whole organism, to the universe, to God, then we will be kept and we will continue to grow and evolve, participating in the flowering of the universe. If we are not of value, our life will only be retained as static data in the universe hall of records. This also relates to our health. If we are consistently doing things of value, not just to us as individuals, but to the world at large, we have a sense of self-worth and value, are appreciated by other people, and have many friends and loved ones. This results in a happier and healthier life. It is documented that those who commit suicide invariably feel that they are without value, are extremely lonely and feel cut off from others.

It is vital to know how we can be of value to the whole universe as opposed to self interest, or group interest. For instance, we can be loyal and dedicated to our country but if our country is engaged in aggression and war, we are part of a force that is not doing the universe any good. By connecting to the universal consciousness on a regular basis we can know how to best serve the entire whole rather than the part. And by receiving this spiritual understanding from the Source, and by expressing as much of it as we can to those immediately around us, we can spread the universal consciousness, even if one is part of a group that has separated itself from the whole.

The question of whether an individual is of value to the universe is hard to answer. Ultimately, and in the cosmic plan, only God knows for sure. Analytical thinking goes nowhere in this matter. We cannot tally up all the positive things we have done and subtract the negatives and come up with the total value. Our value is just not quantifiable in this way. After all, how can we say that a given good deed is canceled by a bad one? Or a bad action done away with a good one, when each deed is different with different motivations, circumstances and consequences?

But there is an answer to this, which may not be deducible by the intellect but is understandable to the soul. It all comes down to *love*. It is the love within us, and how we manifest that love through action, that determines our value. Not love like in "I love ice cream," or "I love movies," which tends to make the word love trivial, but love that you would give your life for, love that you would suffer pain for, love that would be the most important thing in your life, even over your life. It could be a love for a thing, such as our planet, nature, certain activities; love for a concept or idea, as in freedom, justice and equality; or love of soul and spirit as in loving another person or deity. But this love, truly, as it is manifested in us and through us out to others, is value that the universe would treasure, for it is the essence of God and gives life meaning and makes it worth living.

Awareness

When we decide who we really want to be (for it is our choice, not a box we are forced into by a dictatorial creator) and we find out the range of motions we are capable of, the destination, the landscape that we will be traversing, the personalities involved and the ways of optimizing the means of locomotion, we will be well equipped to enter into the true reality of our soul's new domain. Then, after a while, along the journey we will reach a certain point when we realize that we are driving our unified vehicle well. We are going where we want to go and enjoying the trip.

That may mean that we have achieved self-mastery, the minimum requirement of operating in the real world of trustworthy and responsible entities. Metaphorically, we have been potty trained and become able to eat solid spiritual food without spitting it out. We have control over our animal natures and do not have to be constantly watched over by seraphic babysitters. We do not cry and go into violent temper tantrums: we do not destroy our environment, hurt ourselves or other people. We are mindful of our place in the universe. We can actually control ourselves!

It does not take much awareness of the world to realize that most of the inhabitants of this planet are not yet at this stage. But it does take some level of awareness to see that there is a quickening, a flurry of activity going on that is exciting and promising. Eggs are cracking, caterpillars are weaving cocoons, tadpoles are growing legs.

What we do here at this juncture is extremely important. Our transformation is not just physical, as in the examples above from the world of nature, but it is initiated by our souls, guided by our spirit and implemented by our minds. We must know what we are doing, for it is not by luck, chance or fortune that we enter into this. We are fully responsible and accountable for what we become. That is the meaning of self-mastery. We cannot be credited or blamed for something we have no control over. When we are our own masters, we are co-creators with God of our own destiny. We do not become eternal by accident, only by volition.

So be aware of who you are and the reality you exist in. Be aware of the now and the eternal. Of matter and spirit. Of the internal and the external. They are all one. You do not live in a world of mystical fantasy, nor do you live in a mechanistic world of loveless robots.

Reality as seen by a materialist scientist consists of matter/energy. Reality as seen by the spiritual mystic consists of soul/spirit. The materialist's inner world is filled with spiritual realities, yet he ignores them as being immaterial. The mystic's outer world is composed of matter, yet he ignores them as being not of the spirit. Both of their visions of reality are one-sided and partial.

The idea of spiritual reality is but a mystical haze to most people, even to some who embrace the spirit. To them spiritual reality is a dreamlike, nebulous place of light, brilliance and luminous beings; a dimension not of this time and space, a reality far removed from the atoms and molecules of our material world. They are often told that material reality is an illusion and a shell empty of spiritual values. A place far removed from the realms of God, divinity and spirit.

Such ideas must be abandoned. Ideas that place spiritual reality as being far removed from material reality separates reality into two diametrically opposite ends. God's reality is one, as God is one.

True reality is spirit reality superimposed on material reality, and vice versa. Material reality and spiritual reality exist together, layered over each other, concurrently and simultaneously, converging at any given point. The universe of things, atoms and molecules is the same universe of spirit, God and divinity.

To see true reality, one needs elliptical vision, the vision of the soul. When you look at a magnificent work of art, you see the material that went into the art: the canvas and the paint. But there is something else there that is not visible with the physical eye; the truth, beauty and the inspiration that only the soul can see. To be able to readily discern this invisible part of the world around us requires physical vision plus spiritual vision – elliptical vision. A person's soul is also seen in this way. A soulful singer is more than just the physical body, the vocal chords and the acquired skill, but without those things there would be no performance. Her soul is evident because her physical components are beautifully merged with her spiritual aspects to make a unified and marvelous reality. And so it is with us and the universe. Learn how to discern the mixing of both the material and the spiritual in all things. Practice using your elliptical vision and the wonderful world of true reality will open up more and more in all its awesome majesty.

A material being conscious of spirit sees spiritual reality in the midst of matter. A spiritual being conscious of matter sees material reality in the midst of spirit. The evolving eternal soul sees true reality as a merging of matter and spirit: the universe is elliptical.

The information in this book is also elliptical, a guide for your soul to operate the unified human vehicle. It can be applied directly to your everyday life. The effect it will have on bettering your life condition is the validation of these concepts, concepts based on science, philosophy and religion.

Beyond Meditation

The importance of connecting to the Source on a regular basis cannot be understated. It gives hope to the world's condition that meditation is now achieving more popularity. However, the word meditation as is commonly used is very vague and mystical. It can mean anything from closing one's eyes and relaxing to reflecting on one's day to achieving profound states of spiritual consciousness. That is why meditation is often misunderstood, especially by those who think they are meditating, but may not really be. Even considering the many benefits that can result from its practice, there are some things about it that keep it from becoming a common activity.

1. Subjective experience (mysticism) – People don't know what they're supposed to experience. Are we all in the same state of consciousness when we meditate? How do we know?
2. The mind tends to wander. The untethered mind seeks escape to a dreamlike state and disconnects from reality. People need direction. Unguided meditation is too relaxed and unorganized for many people.
3. Boredom and impatience. Because of the above two factors, there is a tendency to become frustrated and give up.

A Personal Connection To The Source

Meditation is often looked upon as a practice of Eastern religions, although Christianity has a tradition of meditation that has been mostly forgotten or ignored. Worshipful meditation is to combine the refined techniques of Eastern inner work with the Western understanding of a personal deity. Being aware of the personhood of the Universal Father is vital to understanding Love, the founding value of the universe. For Love is a characteristic of a person. A non-person has no Love. A universe Source without personhood is a universe without Love.

I have found that people who see the universe as a mechanism become mechanistic, robotic. People who deny the personhood of the Source negate their own personhood. There is a great value to personhood because all the positive qualities such as love, passion, compassion, creativity, friendship, family, caring, and emotional warmth come from being a person. So it is important to include personhood and all its qualities in our meditations.

In our society, there is a perception that meditation is a passive, mystical and boring non-activity. It can be, unless Love and personhood is added. Those with experience know that it can be a dynamic and an energy filled state of consciousness that happens within out of love and joy. The perception of the general public must be changed. The prospect of meditating must generate love and enthusiasm, not disinterest. It should be thought of as an adventure of seeking, exploring and connecting, rather than as a time of passive sitting and daydreaming. This can be done by linking it with the love of doing great deeds and dynamic personal activities.

For it is indeed this connection to the Supreme, the All, this reaching in and tapping into the Source, that makes champions, geniuses and spiritual masters. To some it happens naturally, but now we know through the latest scientific discoveries that we can all tap into this source, given the effort. By affirming to our youth that it is these moments spent in connecting to the Source that leads to the doing of great things, we can shift the perception of meditation as a passive and boring pastime to that of an enjoyable activity that one looks forward to with eagerness. When kids learn that by training their consciousness they can empower themselves to becoming great at what they love to do; to becoming the most radical skateboarder, or the most athletic basketball player, the most cutting edge musician, the smartest techno wizard, to whatever they love…then they will begin voluntarily to practice going within.

Also, there is genuine pleasure in connecting to the Source that is not well known. Some even look at meditation as a chore and burden, which means that they are not practicing it correctly. It should be looked upon as the greatest pleasure in the universe, the greatest love of all, because it is. When people begin to realize that they can directly experience this pleasure, they will flock to it like "sex, drugs and rock and roll." (Without the negative connotations.)

And this consciousness from regularly practicing worshipful meditation will eventually extend out into other aspects of their lives and activities. This tapping in to the Source and focusing it on a particular activity is elliptical mindfulness – connecting to the Now and Eternity, simultaneously. This is you engaged in your activity with total consciousness, aware of your part and its relationship with the whole. This is total mindfulness of the material surroundings in conjunction with mindfulness of eternal spiritual realities; consciousness that is both immediate and yet goes beyond the immediate. It is the All focused in your material body and your physical actions: penetration of the finite by the infinite.

Scientific research and study is mostly investigation of the part (even the scientific study of the whole material universe is study of the part as it leaves out the spiritual aspect of the larger elliptical whole). Science tends to focus sharply on smaller parts of material reality; your material body focusing on one thing at a time - this is penetration of the finite by the finite.

Conversely, worshipful meditation resulting in cosmic consciousness is a look into the macro world – all of time, space and spirit. It is a diffused oneness of being – your material body focusing on the All - penetration of the infinite by the finite.

Science and spirituality are both necessary, and sometimes it is good to practice them both separately, depending on the occasion. But when we can use them as one: the consciousness of spiritual meditation and the focus of analytic inquiry together, we have something new; a method of relating to reality as a complete whole. This is the qi as embodied in everyday life. To live in the qi at every moment would be the epitome of self mastery.

In order to get to elliptical mindfulness, one must develop the analytical mind through study, but also practice the techniques of spiritual mindfulness, which is what meditation can be. By honing the skill of mindfulness and of seeing the whole during meditation, one can take this same consciousness outside and apply it to the skills and knowledge that we use in our daily activities. That is why the practice of meditation is crucial in achieving this next step, especially the forms of meditation that take into account material reality. Since one of the tendencies of people that meditate is that they are prone to withdraw from the material realities of daily life and lean toward mysticism, there have developed certain techniques that get around this. One is to attach a "tether" to material reality by the use of the spoken sound. Chanting sacred words and phrases out loud, such as *aum* or om (Hindu, Jain, Buddhism), namu-myho-renge-kyo and namu-amida-butsu (Buddhism), as well as in other religions enable the meditator to maintain a connection between the inner world and the outer. Through this process we manifest *being, expression and action,* the three basis for creation. Having one's eyes open while meditating goes hand in hand with that, as well as focusing on breathing and gazing at mandalas as a visual anchor on reality.

Walking meditation, practiced in increasing numbers lately, also keeps one grounded in material reality as we venture into the spiritual realms. It is said that Jesus practiced this form of meditation also. If so, he knew then what science is just now discovering, that voluntary exercise creates new brain cells, as does meditation. So doing them both together is natural. It is good to keep this in mind as you personalize your own way of connecting to the Source. As these meditational techniques become more whole, taking into account not just the inner realities but also the mindal and the physical, they become more elliptical. And so what Jesus did in his walks of communion was an advanced form of meditation, he was connecting to both God and the material universe through elliptical mindfulness.

As you walk in a forest, your mind can be cognizant, through science, of what the trees are made of, how they evolved, how they grow. You can be amazed at the clouds, at how our atmosphere can create such things, at the tiny living insects, the atoms and molecules that make up the glistening dew, the warmth of the air. At the same time, your mind can be at one with the All, connected to the source and origin of the universe, awed by the immense size and scope of time, space and spirit. When this simultaneity is intermeshed with knowledge of yourself and your relationship with it all, there is an immediate understanding that takes place in the wholeness of your being, a love and understanding that goes way beyond mere intellectual comprehension. It is a knowingness and an embodiment of love that is a result of actually being that which you are trying to comprehend. This feeling of universal love is a being-ness, a state of existence, it cannot be expressed in linear form, in so many words, nor can it be proven, or need to be proven to anyone else.

This elliptical mindfulness of universal love is actually more than a feeling, more than a logical thought, it is both and more, a knowingness by being; a love and understanding that comes from the seed of consciousness and lies at the heart of existence. And the more we can live our lives with this elliptical consciousness, the more fulfilling, vibrant and *real* reality is. And this consciousness is accessible to you right now!

The Bottom Line

1. We are in a vehicle that is more than material. We have spiritual and mindal components and qualities that are not visible or quantifiable. But we must operate the vehicle as a whole drawing from the resources and systems of the mind and spirit as well as the physical system.

2. We are traveling in a universe that is also more than material. Our purpose in our journey across the universe is to manifest value in our existences, to do things that make life worth living for us and others around us. We have the ability to exercise relative free will in order to do this. However, this is a powerful tool and can be dangerous if used without intelligence, wisdom and guidance.

3. The universe, because of its sheer size and complexity, is impossible to navigate in without a reference point. The only accurate reference point is the center of the universe: the origin and source of all. Through the regular practice of going within, we can connect to this central source and daily acquire the intelligence, grow the wisdom and heed the guidance so that we can formulate methods and techniques to facilitate our adventures in time, space and spirit. As paradoxical as it may sound we can each become the center of the universe without being egocentric.

The value of connecting to the First Source has been acknowledged by the highest teachings of the sages and philosophers down through the ages and has been confirmed by the latest scientific discoveries in neuroscience. There is overwhelming scientific evidence that the inner mind can actually change the physical wiring of the brain using various meditational techniques. New brain cells and the connections between them can really be created by volition. Free will is an actuality, we can truly make ourselves into who and what we want to be. Whatever you may call it: meditation, worship, centering, sourcing, connecting, etc., there is immense benefit in its practice and when taken to the heights of its potential can change the individual from within by the attainment of cosmic consciousness.

4. Attaining cosmic consciousness is the beginning of planetary consciousness. It becomes more than just about us as individuals in a giant universe. We become one with the natural world around us. We begin to see that, literally, we are all in this together. We are bound together by the air, the water, the microbes, the animals, the clouds, the weather, and by other people. We are truly an intrinsic part of this living planet and what we do affects the course of this planet's life. The healthy growth and development of this beautiful planet rests upon us.

5. By choosing to connect regularly to the Source of All, you choose to become whole. As you become whole with yourself, the planet and the universe, there will be a natural urge within to

share this consciousness with others. Acting on this will create a network of cosmically aware minds interconnected with each other constituting the foundation for planetary wholeness. This will be the beginning of global consciousness and unity which will eventually result in human beings functioning as one mind of the entire living planet.

It starts from each of us. The choice is yours.

Re-Create Yourself

Qualtum Organics

You've heard of quantum mechanics (aka quantum physics) which deals with physical phenomena at microscopic scales, well, *qualtum organics* is a term I coined which deals with spiritual reality on the most basic scale – the root of all value.

Quantum mechanics cannot get a complete grasp of total reality because physics does not deal with things that are not physical: i.e., spiritual reality. Fractal patterns say that small living things make up large living beings; humans are made up of small cells which in turn make up the living planet and on and on. Taking this to the maximum, it appears the universe is a living organism. In other words the universe is organic. It would seem that the universe is not only living but a sentient living being with a mind and soul. The material universe may very well be the body of an evolving supreme being, whose mind and soul is also as yet still not completely formed. If so, spiritual reality is the network of superconscious awareness in higher organic living beings within the maximum universe intelligence.

So *qualtum organics* deals with root spiritual qualities (values) on an organic basis.

Quantum physics says that all phenomena is caused by a singular event that creates a wavefront of all possibilities and potentials. But even before that event, physicists postulate that there must have been a physical law that determined how all creation would be formed. Physicists, though, are only concerned about the material aspect of reality. However, reality is more than physical, it is also spiritual. It is both linear and non-linear. Therefore that initial law cannot be just a linear mathematical formula that defines quantum reality, it must be a non-linear quality, for reality is measured in both quantity and quality. And this primal quality that started everything is Love, used here to mean the highest, widest and deepest of all values. Or as some would call it, God. After all, God is love. Love is God.

Or to put it in another way: Why does God want to exist? What is the purpose of reality? I have stated before that the purpose of life is to choose value. Well, Love is the primal value. And Love is the reason why God exists.

This is how it all starts:

Think of a pebble being thrown in a still pond and the concentric waves that form from that event. God, or Love was that first pebble (or a singularity if you wish.) That initial event created the universe. However, that event, coming from the existential location of the First Source, is all potential. All events at that point is still existential and not actualized or experienced. It is the Second and Third Sources that expresses it and actualizes it. (In Christian theology, this concept is mythologized as the Father, Son and the Holy Ghost.) Potentials become actualized when the wavefront collapses, like an ocean wave breaking over a reef. The mind is like a reef, and each time the wavefronts of potentiality is affected by a mind, it collapses and becomes a reality. So the universe is a result of the existential wavefront created by the First Source being manifested and turned into reality by the succeeding (and decreasing) levels of mind, each one turning the potentials into actuals through the light of consciousness.

Going back to the analogy of the pond, we see that the waves go out until they hit something: the edge of the pond, maybe a rock, a stick or something that cause the initial wave to rebound and create other secondary waves, although much smaller than the original wave. These secondary waves will then create tertiary waves and so on. Some of these wavefronts way, way down the line are the realities that we humans create.

Because our consciousness is derived from the master consciousness (think smaller bubbles on the surface of larger bubbles) we are indeed "Sons of God," we are co-creators in our own right, we have to power to create our own qualtum wavefronts through the use of our free will. We do this whenever we change the negative into the positive, when we abrogate the cause and effect of the universe being put into motion through the use of our free will mind, initiating the leadings of the inner spirit. Whenever we do a creative act, returning good for evil, creating an artistic work, inventing something, doing anything original out of Love, we are throwing our own pebbles in the pond, creating a new reality which spawns even more realities in the future.

Quantum physics has a problem that has stumped a lot of people, it is the question of: If a tree falls in the forest and no one is there, does it make a sound? Does there need to be an observer for reality to be real? The uncertainty principle in quantum physics says yes. It has been clinically demonstrated that on an extremely microscopic scale observation does influence the observed. Science does not have the methods to prove it on the macro scale. But I posit that it does happen on the largest scale, in the realm of the maximum fractal consciousness. If we take as fact that the universe is a conscious living being, then that means there is an observer everywhere. The universe's self awareness would mean that there is nowhere in the universe where there is not an observer.

What happened to create the universe happens to us on the personal scale. Why do we live? Why do we get up to go to work? What motivates us to live and exist? It is because of Love. Love of family, of stimuli, of intelligence, of creativity, of peace, of passion, of doing things we love to do that creates our lives, although on the animal level, people also do things out of fear and inertia. This is the difference between an animal and a spiritually evolving being. Spiritual beings are motivated by love, animals are motivated by the mechanistic biology of the fear and flight syndrome. It is a free will choice. We can choose to make Love the primal inner reality that energizes our life.

Qualtum organics observes this inner reality on the deepest scale. The observation is of this basic core value within ourselves, rather than within matter. The observer must have a connection, conscious or not, with the First Source; God the master observer, Love the primal quality, in order for a new qualtum wavefront to break. In other words, for us to create a new personal reality, we must have a creator based consciousness – God/Love derived. As the first consciousness created the universe, each succeeding consciousness creates its own wavefront – its own reality. Love and consciousness of love, having its origin in the First Source and Center, is at the root of all realities.

This is the conquest of matter by spirit through the mediation of mind. Worshipfully meditate on a level where you become one with the innermost value within your soul. Casually observe it and if you wish, change it by observing a higher God given value, give it a brighter shade of Love! That observation by itself will collapse the potential qualtum wavefront and actualize it in your life. You will be setting off a chain of events that would be the new reality which you initiated. The consciousness pebble is thrown, and concentric waves of your new future are formed. You may have already done this, possibly subconsciously and haphazardly, in the earlier days of your life. And now, knowing how the process works, you can proactively use it to consciously and deliberately chart the course of your life. So whatever you do, whatever decision you make, do it out of love, rather than out of fear, inertia or because you were conditioned to act in a certain way. Even when faced with physical danger, financial ruin, or ego deflation, act out of the love within your life, rather than fear of death, poverty or disgrace. Ultimately, from love comes everything of positive value. So be love, express love and do love. And all is well.

Creative Manifestation

In wanting to manifest a reality of our choosing, we must consider that Universe is looking out for us. Since the manifesting must come from the deepest quality within us, from love, what we want must be beneficial. If we are one with Universe, it will not allow us to manifest something that is detrimental to us or those around us (It's a different story if you are going *against* the universe.) For example, there are things that we might have wanted at a given time and did not get but realized later on that getting it would not have been beneficial to us at all. We see that it worked out for the best. That is the universe looking out for us.

So rather than trying to *project* our wants and try to manifest material things, like say, a billion dollars, it would be better to *inject* values into our life and manifest spiritual qualities such as health, creativity, good relationships, joy and happiness.

To *project* our wants is ego driven; it tries to make happen our individual material desires. To *inject* our values is to draw from the Source everything that we need to be happy, to manifest qualities into our lives that fulfill us.

The most effective way to creatively manifest reality is to reach within and express without. Respiration, breathing in and out, is the key. On the macro scale, the universe respires over trillions of years. On the micro scale your physical body respires every second. Use this pattern to evolve your soul. Train yourself to spiritually inhale and exhale. Inhale inspiration from the Source, then exhale through expression and action. In from the spirit, out through the mind and body.

Using this process during meditation, you can creatively manifest the best things and experiences through envisioning spiritual feelings and qualities. Material things are but means to an end; they are but shadows that cannot appear unless the light is there first. Share and spread the light of love; truth, beauty and goodness and the things you need (*need*, not *want*) will appear. Envisioning the *spiritual quality* of the end result is the optimum way of manifesting reality.

It all starts with the first pebble being thrown into the cosmic pond. That first pebble is Love. The vibration ripples out from that first pebble. It goes out to near and far, to the distant reaches of time, space and spirit.

Love is how it starts, love is how it ends.

More Than Merely

There's more to you than flesh, more to me than blood.
More to life than the physical, more to life than the spiritual.

There's more to life than working, more to success than wealth,
more to substance than glitter, and glitter ain't worth your
health.

There's more to seeing than just looking, more to listening than
sound, more to connecting than just yakking, more to God than
found.

There's more to happiness than mere joy, more to friends than
hugs, more to bonding than mere vows, more to pleasure than
drugs.

There's more to truth than just facts, more to beauty than looks,
more to love than mere sex, more to wisdom than books.

There's more to us than we can judge, more to us than meets the
eye, so smell the flower – smell the weed, you decide what you
need.

You got free will to make the choice, you choose your soul, reject
the mold, 'cause you can feel what is real, the love within, the
spirit bold.

See with your soul, act with your heart, come out of the box and
realize, the world outside your window, can be a living Paradise.

There's more to life than the physical, more to life than the
spiritual, if you're tired of the usual, take a walk into the
elliptical.

Epilogue: The Visitor Goes Home

The Visitor decides to take leave of the Urps one day and he asks if any of them would like to go with him to see the rest of the world. At first, close to a hundred out of the thousand or so inhabitants enthusiastically voice their desire to go see what's out there. But with this or that, family commitments, fear, and other reasons and excuses, only ten out of the hundred actually prepare themselves to make the journey out of their small section of reality.

On the day of departure, the entire population of Urps gather together to see them off. Among much tears and goodbyes, the visitor, along with the ten adventurers bid farewell to their friends and family and begin the trip, which consists initially of a three week hike to the ocean.

The trek is not an easy one, but the Visitor had prepared them for it by having them pack enough food and water to last the entire way. The load is a heavy one and they trudge slowly across the desert and plains headed for the coast.

Being an insular tribe, the Urps had never walked such a distance and some of them begin to question their wisdom as they walk farther and farther from familiar surroundings. Some of them start to lose faith in the Visitor and secretly make alternate plans. One of them even suggests that the visitor is actually a demon leading them to a fiery hell. Thoughts of doing physical harm to him come up but is abandoned quickly. However, three of them decide to turn back. The Visitor wishes them well.

After two weeks of travel, four more decide to go back to their tribe. The Visitor tells them that they only have a week left before reaching the coast, but they are adamant in returning. Sad to see them go, the visitor can only give them his blessings as he watches them leave.

Finally, the long walk ends. Upon cresting a low hill, the visitor and the three Urps see the great ocean. The Urps are stunned, never having seen such an expanse of water. But the ship is nowhere to be seen.

The Visitor tells them they must wait until the ocean liner arrives offshore on its regular schedule which he tells them is soon. They camp out on the beach and relax, getting a much needed rest. Just seeing the ocean has calmed the nerves of the Urps, and they are eager to see what will happen next.

One night, as they are scanning the horizon, a spectacular object of many colored lights appears on the horizon and begins to get larger as it nears. The Urps get to their feet and jump up and down, gesticulating wildly. The Visitor smiles and feeds more wood to the smoldering flames until it is a huge bonfire, a previously agreed upon signal.

The ocean liner closes the distance until it is a few hundred yards offshore. The Urps can't get over how grand and majestic it is. Then, in the moonlight, they see a small boat being launched and make its way to where they are. When the boat is beached, the visitor greets them in a strange language and the Urps are taken aboard, although initially with a bit of trepidation, after which they are rowed to the huge, brightly lit cruise ship.

Their accommodations having been taken care of, the Visitor is at the railing with the three Urps watching the shore recede into the distance. The natives know that they may never see their land again. They are introspective, musing over their fate when one of them turns to the Visitor and asks, "All of this is truly fabulous, but I keep wondering, when are we going to find the great leaf which floats on the water?"

The Urp by his side at the railing grins and putting a hand on the first Urp's shoulder says, "you are *on* the leaf, my friend." Tapping the wooden railing, he explains, "this thing we are on is the leaf."

A puzzling look freezes the first Urp's demeanor. A moment later, realization flashes across his face, "Oh! Of course. It was right in front of my nose all the time." He laughs.

The Visitor smiles and says, "Yes. Many things of which I speak is right in front of you. As your soul evolves, you will become aware of them more and more. Open up the vision of your soul and you will see and do things which are beyond even your imagination. Get ready to be amazed and awed, my friends."

The ship turns away from the shore and heads out to sea. The stars glimmer around the magnificently lit vessel as it leaves a white fluorescent wake streaming behind. The last rays of the sun, now way behind the horizon, tinges the sky over the edge of the world with a hint of dark red as the Visitor returns home with three Urps destined for a new land.

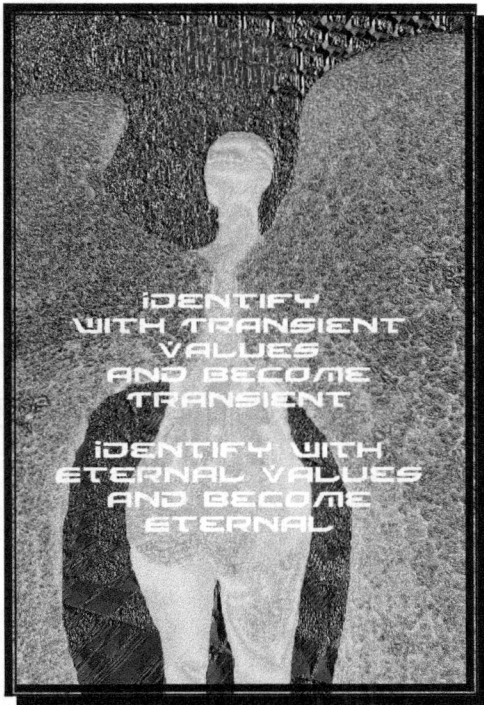

IDENTIFY
WITH TRANSIENT
VALUES
AND BECOME
TRANSIENT

IDENTIFY WITH
ETERNAL VALUES
AND BECOME
ETERNAL

Acknowledgment

First of all, a note of appreciation to those who helped me with this book: Janet Farrington Graham, Robert Burns, Fred Harris and Dave Holt. Also, acknowledgment to Jeff Wattles for his angle on explaining the Seven Adjutants. Of course, I must mention those that help me with my inner vision , those whom I can only perceive with my soul. Thank you.

There may be a little bit of almost everything worthwhile that I have ever felt, thought, experienced and read restated in this book. However, there are some books and teachings from which I have drawn more inspiration than others. The passages that deal with Personality, the range of Personality performance, the Seven Adjutant Mind Spirits, prayer, meditation and the Cosmic Levels are restatements, paraphrases and personal insights derived from *The Urantia Book*. Other sources of inspiration, information, and confirmation are *Science of Mind, The Bible, the Pathway to Roses, Spirits In Rebellion, The Tao Te Ching, Healing Words, The Structure of Scientific Revolution, The Holotropic Mind, The Living Universe, Wisdom of the Body, Train Your Mind- Change Your Brain,* the books of Krishnamurti, Deepak Chopra, David Simon and Thich Nacht Hanh, and my personal experiences with Buddhist philosophy, transcendental meditation and Christian theology.

It was my intention to keep this book from being too detailed in scientific facts as the focus is more on fractal patterns and the whole rather than the parts. Also, the detailing of those facts have already been done by persons more qualified than myself. Further in-depth study of the books I mention here should give the reader enough details to answer any questions that may arise.

All in all, the truths in this book are glimpses of their manifestations in my life. It is through my eyes, my heart and my soul that I have experienced them but they did not originate with me. Where did they come from? Aside from the inner connection, there are books, peoples, music, the arts, events; so many things in life are potential avenues of information from a higher source. Like an invisible Visitor.

Bibliography and Suggested Readings

When it came to using information from other books, because of the personal nature of spiritual insights and perspectives, I did not use many verbatim quotes from the sources that influenced me. In some cases I restated the information to give it my own perspective and to lend it a modern flavor. Also, I felt that the more varied the ways of phrasing concepts are available, the wider the exposure to such concepts would be. In other words, why echo something that is already available on the shelf, when it could be re-expressed in a different way that could be more palatable and/or understandable?

Baker, R. (2006) *Sperm Wars,* Avalon Publishing Group

Begley, S. (2007) *Train Your Mind, Change Your Brain,* Ballantine Books

Braden, C.S. (1987) *Spirits In Rebellion- The Rise and Development of New Thought*, Southern Methodist University Press

Chopra, D (2004) *The Book of Secrets*, Random House

Chopra, D. and Simon, D. (2004) *The Seven Spiritual Laws of Yoga,* John Wiley & Sons, Inc.

Doidge, N. (2007) *The Brain That Changes Itself,* Penguin Books

Doren, C. (1991) *A History of Knowledge*, Ballantine Books

Dossey, L., (1993) *Healing Words – The Power of Prayer and the Practice of Medicine*, Harper Collins

Grof, S. and Bennett, H.Z. (1993) *The Holotropic Mind – The Three Levels of Human Consciousness and How They Shape Our Lives,* Harper Collins

Hanh, T.N. (1999) *The Miracle of Mindfulness*, Beacon

Press

Holmes, E. (1938) *The Science of Mind,* G.P. Putnam's Sons

Kuhn, T.S. (1996) *The Structure of Scientific Revolution 3rd Edition,* The University of Chicago Press

Larson. C. (1994) *The Pathway to Roses,* Newcastle Publishing

Nuland, S. (1997) *Wisdom of the Body,* Alfred A. Knopf

Omura, R. (2000) *Katsugen – The Gentle Art of Well Being,* Writers Club Press

Omura, R. (2000*) The Tao Of God,* Writers Club Press

Praamsma, S. and Block, M. (eds) (2003) *The Sherman Diaries, Vol. 2 – Revelation and Rebellion 1942,* Square Circles Publishing

Schwartz, E.R. and Russeck, L. (1999) *The Living Energy Universe,* Hampton Roads

(1955) *The Urantia Book,* Urantia Foundation

(2003) *The Urantia Book – Indexed Version,* Uversa Press